A STRANGER AMONG SAINTS

STEPHEN HOPKINS
THE MAN WHO SURVIVED JAMESTOWN
AND SAVED PLYMOUTH

JONATHAN MACK

CHICAGO
REVIEW
PRESS

Published by Chicago Review Press Incorporated
814 North Franklin Street
Chicago, Illinois 60610
ISBN 978-1-64160-598-4

The Library of Congress has cataloged the hardcover edition as follows:
Names: Mack, Jonathan D., 1966– author.
Title: A stranger among saints : Stephen Hopkins, the man who survived
  Jamestown and saved Plymouth / Jonathan Mack.
Other titles: Stephen Hopkins, the man who survived Jamestown and saved
  Plymouth
Description: Chicago, Illinois : Chicago Review Press, [2020] | Includes
  bibliographical references and index. | Summary: "The fascinating story
  of Stephen Hopkins, perhaps the most important person on board the
  Mayflower when it sailed from England in 1620. The only member of the
  expedition who had been across the Atlantic before, as a survivor of the
  colony at Jamestown, Hopkins played a vital role in bridging the divide
  of suspicion between the Pilgrims and their Native American neighbors.
  Without him, these settlers would likely not have lasted through their
  brutal first year."— Provided by publisher.
Identifiers: LCCN 2019051058 (print) | LCCN 2019051059 (ebook) | ISBN
  9781641600903 (cloth) | ISBN 9781641600910 (adobe pdf) | ISBN
  9781641600934 (epub) | ISBN 9781641600927 (kindle edition)
Subjects: LCSH: Hopkins, Stephen, 1581–1644. | Massachusetts—History—New
  Plymouth, 1620–1691. | Colonists—Massachusetts—Biography. | Indians of
  North America—First contact with Europeans—Massachusetts. | New
  England—History—Colonial period, ca. 1600–1775.
Classification: LCC F68.H8 M33 2020 (print) | LCC F68.H8 (ebook) | DDC
  974.4/020922 [B]—dc23
LC record available at https://lccn.loc.gov/2019051058
LC ebook record available at https://lccn.loc.gov/2019051059

Cover design: John Yates at Stealworks
Cover image: The Mayflower Compact, 1620, oil on canvas, by Jean Leon
Gerome Ferris (1863–1930)
Typesetting: Nord Compo

Printed in the United States of America

To my mother and father

CONTENTS

AUTHOR'S NOTE

THE DETAILS OF STEPHEN HOPKINS'S LIFE are sometimes sparse. He left no diary or journal. And while several others wrote firsthand accounts of the colonies at Jamestown and Plymouth, they are individual perspectives on events that could be viewed from a thousand different angles.

In order to tell the complete story of what happened four centuries ago, I have sometimes bridged the gaps by providing what I believe to be the most plausible explanations drawn from discrete and fragmentary facts collected from a wide range of sources. These elements are always identified as historically informed inferences, and they are based on my understanding and analysis of the record.

When practical and the meaning uncontroversial, language quoted from primary sources has been rendered into modern English for ease of understanding. Where text was emphasized in the original, it is set in *italics*; where I have added emphasis, it is set in **boldface**.

In Hopkins's time, England and its colonies in America used the Julian calendar's method of tracking dates, known as the Old Style. The Gregorian calendar, which is the most widely used calendar today and known as the New Style, was not embraced by the British Empire until 1752. Adding ten days to a given seventeenth-century date in the Old Style of primary sources will render the date in the New Style of today. Thus, June 6, 1644, on the Julian calendar would correspond to June 16 of the same year on the Gregorian calendar. In addition, the change from Julian to Gregorian shifted the start of the year from March 25 to January 1. Any date noted before March 25 in the Old Style, therefore, would be included in the previous year: e.g., February 1622 in the Old Style would correspond to February 1623 in the modern reckoning. I have chosen to keep the days of the month in the Old Style Julian calendar but to transpose the years into the New Style Gregorian calendar.

Any mistakes are mine and mine alone.

INTRODUCTION

Your tale, sir, would cure deafness.
—*The Tempest* (c. 1611), act 1, scene 2

IN 1609 A MAN NAMED STEPHEN HOPKINS joined a voyage to England's colony at Jamestown—one so ill-fated that it inspired William Shakespeare's play *The Tempest*. After being sentenced to death for mutiny while shipwrecked on Bermuda, Hopkins narrowly escaped and sailed on to the settlement, located in present-day Virginia. He eventually made his way back to England, and in 1620 he signed on to a new colonial venture. This second undertaking was organized by a group of London speculators who hoped to establish another colony in the Americas.

Along with sixty others, he boarded a merchant ship called the *Mayflower* and there met a group of religious radicals, Puritans who so wanted to separate themselves from the Church of England that they decided to sail to the other side of the world. The *Mayflower*'s journey, of course, became one of America's iconic foundational stories, and its passengers, dubbed by subsequent generations the "Pilgrim Fathers," have been examined, feted, and criticized by historians ever since. Despite creating endless volumes of research, scholars have largely overlooked Stephen Hopkins, even though he was a key figure in the Pilgrims' struggles and triumphs in the New World. Certainly, he was the most knowledgeable about the challenges they would ultimately face.

Of the *Mayflower*'s passengers, Hopkins was the only one who'd been across the Atlantic before. He was the only person who'd seen the new continent, tasted its waters, fished its streams, or tilled its soil. He was the only person who'd lived through its frigid winters and sweltering summers. He was the only one who'd seen a working colony firsthand and experienced the catastrophes that could result when it was governed by inept or misguided principles.

He was the only one who'd met with the New World's native peoples and understood the complexities of their societies, which were utterly foreign to his fellow passengers and often dismissed as barbarous.

Because of his unique experience on Bermuda and then in Jamestown, Hopkins might have been the most important person on board the *Mayflower* when it sailed from England. The Pilgrims encountered their own tempest, a furor that started when they anchored off Cape Cod and continued through their first twelve months in North America. Tested by hardships and setbacks, the entire enterprise hung in the balance, and it was during these trials that Hopkins demonstrated his value, both to his fellow Pilgrims and to history. Without him, they would not likely have lasted through that brutal year.

It has been suggested that Shakespeare based *The Tempest*'s rowdy and frequently intoxicated servant Stephano on Stephen Hopkins.[1] Unlike Stephano, whose role is reprised year after year, Hopkins had his hour upon the stage and then disappeared, mostly lost to history, crowded out by figures such as William Bradford, Myles Standish, and Squanto. Now, four hundred years after the landing of the *Mayflower*, it is time to reexamine the facts and make clear the singular role Stephen Hopkins played in establishing Plymouth Colony and setting America on its historic path.

1 | HOPKINS AND THE *SEA VENTURE*

Mercy on us!—
We split, we split!—Farewell, my wife and children!—
Farewell, brother!—We split, we split, we split!
—*The Tempest*, act 1, scene 1

BY MAY 1609 some six hundred prospective English settlers had signed up for an expedition to resupply the struggling colony at Jamestown, which had been established two years earlier.[1] A flotilla of nine ships was assembled, one of the greatest fleets that England had ever seen.[2] The largest was the *Sea Venture*, a vessel built specifically to transport people and supplies across the Atlantic to North America. Construction had been completed only months before. At nearly one hundred feet in length, she could hold three hundred tons and carried 150 passengers. This trip would be her maiden voyage. She was the flagship of the expedition and carried its leaders, along with other dignitaries and high-ranking members of the supply mission, including writer William Strachey and the future husband of Pocahontas, John Rolfe.[3] Also on board was Stephen Hopkins, who was about to change the course of his life forever and ultimately help shape the history of the New World.

An Uncommon Education

Stephen Hopkins was twenty-eight years old when he set sail on the *Sea Venture*. He'd been born in 1581 in Upper Clatford, a small village that was located about seventy miles southwest of London in Hampshire, a county on the southern coast of England.[4]

Social order in England at the time was very rigid. Hierarchy represented the natural order of things, an order put into place by God Himself. Within this hierarchy, there were three general strata in English society: the upper class, consisting of the noble families, such as the king and the aristocracy, dukes, earls, barons, and the like; the middle class, which included a fairly wide variety of affluence, from successful and wealthy merchants, to farmers who owned their own land, to artisans such as blacksmiths or carpenters; and finally, the lower class, which was composed of peasants, laborers, and servants.[5]

Hopkins was not lucky enough to have been born into a privileged family, but he was fortunate not to have been born into abject poverty. He had an older half-brother and half-sister, as well as a younger sister. His father, John, was a farmer. John Hopkins did not own his own fields but rather tilled common fields, sharing the labors and fruit of raising crops with other residents, which would have put the Hopkins family on the top portion of the lower class. The middle class, and greater financial security, lay tantalizingly within reach, yet the Hopkins family's life was filled with small hazards that could interfere with progress and also send them into financial distress.

Perhaps seeing an opportunity to improve his family's position, John Hopkins and his wife, Elizabeth, and children moved from Upper Clatford to Winchester, which lay about ten miles away, when Stephen was five or six years old. In the tenth century, Winchester likely had been the capital of Saxon England, and at the time of the Hopkins family move, it was still a rather bustling trading center. In 1588, when the Spanish threatened to invade, men from all parts of England showed their support by joining the local militia, and John Hopkins served as a volunteer during the family's time in Winchester.[6]

It was in Winchester that Stephen Hopkins likely learned to read and write.[7] His literacy was somewhat unusual for his station in life. In Elizabethan and early Stuart England, literacy was nowhere near universal. While all clergy and the professional classes could read and write, literacy rates dropped in line with social stratification, from 98 percent for the gentry down to 21 percent for farmers of leased or common land, such as John Hopkins, and even lower, to 15 percent, for laborers.[8] Stephen Hopkins may have displayed an early aptitude or interest in learning, or perhaps his parents believed that an education might help their young son advance his interests and status. His education would have begun in what was called a "petty school," which was a class of informal schools that might be run by a man or woman who for a small fee taught children to spell, read, write, and work out the arithmetic necessary for performing basic bookkeeping.[9] Following petty school, a boy who'd shown capability and who had the support of his parents might turn next to a "grammar school" for further education.[10]

Although there is no evidence that John Hopkins was able to advance the family's financial or social position in Winchester, the town was the perfect place for a gifted boy of slender means to gain a good education. At the time, the children of the nobility were often tutored privately, but the children of the middle and even lower classes sometimes had an opportunity to attend grammar schools, institutions intended to provide rigorous education to a large population of poor scholars and prepare them for the possibility of university.[11] Only about a five- or six-minute stroll away from Hopkins's house stood the famous Winchester College, a grammar school that William of Wykeham, then bishop of Winchester, established in 1382.[12] Winchester College was the leading institution of education in the Tudor era, and Henry VIII used the school as a model for a system of schools that he founded using confiscated property, such as monasteries, after he expelled the Catholic Church and created the Church of England in 1534.[13] The school was particularly dedicated to seeking out poor and needy students who demonstrated the character and ability required for the vigorous curriculum.[14]

There is no surviving record that confirms Hopkins's admission to the school, but that is no reason to rule out the possibility; while many of the school rolls exist, "the series is far from complete."[15] And even if he was not formally admitted, Hopkins may have gained access to the school as a supernumerary.[16] Or perhaps he worked on the campus and gleaned what he could. John Harmar, the headmaster of Winchester College during the period (between 1588 and 1593) when Hopkins might have attended, was later quite likely the man responsible for Hopkins's spot aboard the *Sea Venture*.[17] Like Hopkins, Harmar came from humble beginnings.[18] Seeing similarities, he might have taken an interest in young Hopkins and helped him in some informal way, especially as Harmar remained committed throughout his life to aiding the needy in Winchester.[19]

Whatever the case may have been, there is substantial indirect evidence that Hopkins had at least some type of tutelage in a grammar school, for he would later be chosen as clerk to the Anglican chaplain of the Virginia settlement. In that era, a minister's clerk had to be literate, as one of the three primary duties was to read aloud a portion of an epistle for the service, which was likely delivered in both Latin and in English, and to sing from the Psalter.[20] Indeed, it wasn't unusual for a clerk to possess an education on par with the minister himself.[21] William Strachey—the writer who sailed with Hopkins on the *Sea Venture*—specifically described Hopkins as a "fellow who had much knowledge in the Scriptures, and could reason well therein."[22] He also had a working understanding of rhetoric.[23] Scripture and religious dogma were at the heart of education at that time, and boys at grammar school were trained about the moral lessons to be derived from the biblical passages and stories that they studied and learned by heart.[24] The syllabus covered the study of the techniques of rhetoric, which included imparting students with an understanding of social morals and drilling them in the discipline of persuading an audience of the rightness or wrongness of particular actions.[25]

Hopkins All Alone

In 1593, when Stephen was twelve years old and may have already completed a few years of grammar school education, misfortune took a swipe at the Hopkins family. John Hopkins died. His estate was insufficient to support his wife, Elizabeth, and their four children. Elizabeth's options were severely limited. Many widows sought to remarry, thus securing a husband to support the financial needs of her family. If a widow of similar position in England's economic hierarchy didn't marry again, she'd likely be forced to apprentice out her children to relatives, church members, or neighbors, while she herself would rely on the remaining estate of her deceased husband for her own livelihood, perhaps augmented by the charity of family, neighbors, and the church.

There is no record that Elizabeth Hopkins remarried, so it is probable that she found families who would take in her younger children, including Stephen, as apprentices.[26] An apprenticeship would bind the child into service for the new family until the child reached the legal age of majority. In return, the family, at least in theory, would equip the child for employment in adulthood. There is a chance that Hopkins might have stayed on at Winchester College, perhaps with the assistance of John Harmar, until he finished his schooling at age fifteen or sixteen.[27] But it is equally likely that he did not.

If he were unable to remain at Winchester College, Stephen Hopkins would have grown up in an unfamiliar home. At best, it was the home of a relative. At worst, it was the home of a complete stranger. Extended family or not, it would have likely been a shock to the adolescent's morale. As the sixteenth century wound toward a close, life for a fatherless child trapped in the lower class was dark and difficult.

Hopkins in Hursley

After his teenage years, Stephen Hopkins moved to Hursley, a village located about five miles outside Winchester. By 1605, he was married to a woman named Mary and father to a newborn daughter, Elizabeth.[28] He was perhaps farming land owned by a local knight with a history of poor relations with his tenants, or he was helping out in a village alehouse run by his mother-in-law.[29] It was probably a mixture of both, as the sharp inflation of that era was pushing the price of food and other necessaries ever higher, while wages were decreasing. Hopkins probably would have put his hand to anything that would help put food on the table.

The next year, Hopkins and his wife had a second daughter, Constance. In 1608 they had a son named Giles. According to some authorities, four months after Giles's birth, in May 1608, the Hopkins family was forced off the land, which in turn likely led to their leaving Hursley, and perhaps even leaving the county of Hampshire entirely for a place like London, as so many other displaced families of the time were doing.[30] Other authorities have argued that the family remained undisturbed in Hursley, where they stayed until Hopkins left to join the *Sea Venture* expedition to Jamestown.[31]

The Third Supply Mission to Jamestown

In 1609 the colony at Jamestown was on the lips of everyone in London. Yet another supply mission was being organized to support the settlement, which had been established in 1607 about thirty miles up the James River on the Chesapeake Bay in Virginia. Reports released through the London Company— the private entity that founded and administered the colony—were generally positive, invoking, for example, biblical Israel when describing Virginia as a land of milk and honey. The Company, however, was careful in how it released information to the public and censored communications from Virginia so that discouraging news was muted.[32] The reality was much bleaker.

The colony suffered from its very start, partly because of its location on low, swampy ground with brackish drinking water, and partly because most of the colonists were "gentlemen" unaccustomed to manual labor. Four months after erecting the walls of Jamestown, more than 60 of the 105 settlers were dead. Their food production was not self-sustaining, so they traded when they could with the Powhatan Confederacy, the region's dominant nation of Native Americans, sending ships along the coastal waterways to local towns and villages.

Captain John Smith was one of the leaders of the initial expedition. He'd fought on the continent for the Dutch in their long war against Spanish rule and was a true adventurer with years of experience. After fighting the Spanish, he campaigned in Austria against the Ottoman Turks and was captured and sold as a slave. He escaped and spent time traveling in Russia, Europe, North Africa, and Ireland before returning to England and joining the Jamestown expedition. Smith led one of the excursions from Jamestown to trade with the locals for food. The outing ended in a violent confrontation, and he was taken prisoner. The Powhatan wanted to execute him, but the chief's daughter, whose nickname was Pocahontas, purportedly pleaded for Smith's life, a story that eventually turned into legend. Trading, especially with the backdrop of volatile relations, did not fill all the settlement's needs, so Jamestown relied on a fairly constant flow of new men and material from England.

The first supply mission to the colony, composed of two ships with 120 men, arrived in Jamestown only eight months after the first settlers had arrived. The newcomers found less than forty surviving colonists.[33] In the fall of 1608 the Company sent a second supply mission to Jamestown, this time just a single ship with supplies and seventy additional colonists.[34] Neither of these two modest expeditions provided the colony with much-needed stability. It was foundering. In early 1609 the Company restructured itself and determined to act boldly. Unlike the earlier missions, the third such supply mission would include a fleet of nine ships loaded with provisions and about six hundred settlers.[35]

As it did with nearly everything in that era, religion played a critical role in England's colonial endeavors. Certainly, the country desired to maintain its foothold on the American continent in order to keep pace with European rivals like the Spanish, Dutch, and French, but to the English the successful colonization of a new land was the very will of God. The Protestant Reformation, which pitted Protestants against Catholics, was still very active in the early seventeenth century. By claiming more land, the English Protestants would

Portrait of John Smith (1624). *Courtesy of the John Carter Brown Library at Brown University*

be keeping the despised Catholic Church from gobbling up more of the New World. Some historians have anointed as singular genius the marriage of the idea of colonization to not only national pride but also England's national faith.[36] Failure at Jamestown meant failure for the entire country and for the Church of England, which made the third supply mission critically important. The original 1607 undertaking had carried the Reverend Robert Hunt, who played an integral part in the colony and its leadership.[37] Hunt's death in Jamestown in 1608 made finding a replacement to send on the high-profile expedition of 1609 a high priority.[38]

To help, the colony's promoters turned to Thomas Ravis, who was then the bishop of London, the third-highest position in the hierarchy of the Church of England. Ravis had obtained his degree from Oxford, and he chose fellow Oxford alumnus Richard Buck as minister for the third supply mission.[39] With the priest selected, Ravis would likely have considered options for a clerk to serve Buck, since a clerk was indispensable to nearly all parts of the clergyman's responsibilities, a virtual shadow to the minister.[40]

Because of the nationwide interest in the third supply mission and because of the importance of the chaplain's role within the governmental and spiritual life of the colony, Ravis would not have wanted Reverend Buck to travel without the benefit of a clerk. Besides, by his recommendation, Ravis had a personal investment in Buck's success. His failure would reflect poorly on Ravis. And on Oxford. And on the Church. All of which made it likely that Ravis was involved in the selection of a clerk.

Several years before, Ravis had started working on one of the committees that produced the translation of the Bible that King James had commissioned in 1604.[41] Seven other men had served on Ravis's committee. Among them was another Oxford graduate, John Harmar.[42] The translation committees spent three years working very closely together and finished their work in 1609.[43] The closeness of the working relationship within each company meant that Ravis and Harmar would have become well acquainted with each other. The timing of their intensive work coincided perfectly with the vast public effort underway that year on the third supply mission, and it is probable that the two men discussed the selection of Reverend Buck, one of their fellow Oxford alumni.[44] They'd also, therefore, likely have discussed the need to find a suitable clerk to assist the expedition's chaplain. That Stephen Hopkins, a baseborn commoner living some seventy-five miles from London, became the clerk to the single Anglican minister on an expedition unrivaled in scope and celebrated by the entire nation, strongly suggests that he had some connection with Winchester College and that John Harmar proposed his name to Ravis for the job.[45]

Hopkins's Life-Changing Decision

If Hopkins was indeed contacted by John Harmar about the opportunity to join the third supply mission to Jamestown, a question immediately arises: Why would he agree to such an arduous undertaking? He had a young family. His eldest child was only five or six. His youngest was less than two years old. Why would he abandon them? Did he feel a call into divine service? Did he feel a particular obligation to Harmar, who might have helped him as a boy in Winchester? Or was Hopkins motivated by some of the reasons that drew others to the Jamestown cause? The promise of adventure? A chance for gaining worldly prestige for joining such a high profile enterprise? Boredom?

The historical record does not reveal the reasons for Hopkins's momentous decision, but there are hints, and they point to the practical rather than the poetic: Hopkins needed money. In the countryside, as in Hursley, the wages of a husbandman like Hopkins were barely sufficient for subsistence, because wages in that era fell while the prices of staples such as corn, wool, and hides all rose.[46] Income from the small alehouse run by his mother-in-law may have helped, but likely the Hopkins family was situated similarly to most others in the lower classes of England. Times were difficult.

Under the terms of the royal charter then governing the colony in Virginia, every commoner going to the colony promised to serve in Jamestown for a term of seven years. In exchange, the colonist would receive a share of the London Company. After the seven-year term was served, the colonist would be entitled to share in Company dividends.[47] In addition, there might have been the potential for cash compensation. As a representative of the Church of England, the Reverend Richard Buck was entitled to an extra allowance. If, as a clerk to the minister, Hopkins also qualified as a representative of the church, he might have made an additional £20 to £25 per year.[48] It would have seemed an astounding figure to Hopkins, for when his father died, the value of his entire estate—representing a lifetime of savings and accumulation—was only £35.[49] A modestly successful playwright in London might take in £25 a year.[50] Workmen, journeymen, and hired servants made between £4 and £9 per year.[51] For a family just getting by, the lure of £25 per year would probably have been strong. Over the seven-year term of his indenture, if Hopkins was entitled to the extra compensation, he would have been able to earn gross wages of £175—or at least the promise of such wages—a veritable fortune for a commoner.[52]

The fact that by 1620 Hopkins seemed to have turned his family's financial situation from desperate to comfortable, even allowing him to hire and maintain two servants—one of the few aboard the *Mayflower* who was affluent enough to bring hired men—adds weight to the financial draw that might have compelled Hopkins to leave his family in 1609.[53] Whether the money was worth the perils and hardships that Hopkins would soon endure—a hurricane, a shipwreck, and a death sentence, all before even getting to the real work in Jamestown—is another question entirely.

Like Hopkins, his shipmate William Strachey had signed on to the expedition for financial reasons. Strachey was the son of a well-to-do landowner who would become the secretary for the colony. He'd studied law for a while but became more interested in writing and often socialized with London's literary set. The poet and Anglican cleric John Donne counted Strachey among his friends. Strachey wrote a dedicatory verse included in a Ben Jonson play that was performed by Shakespeare's acting company the King's Men in 1603. He held stock in the Blackfriars Theatre, which by 1609 was being used by the Bard's troupe.[54] There were only a handful of shareholders at the time, and Shakespeare was one of them, which likely put the two men on friendly terms.[55] But writing verse and carousing with London's literati was a money-losing lifestyle. By early 1609 Strachey was deep in debt and feared imprisonment. Virginia offered him an opportunity to escape his creditors and perhaps even reverse his fiscal situation.[56]

When the *Sea Venture* left England in early June 1609, Strachey and Stephen Hopkins shared several other things in common. Both men were married and had young families whom they left behind.[57] In an era of patronage where advancement came most often through a person's social network, both men likely landed positions within the expedition because of the people whom they knew.

There was still a significant difference between the two, however. Though burdened with monetary problems, Strachey was a gentleman and still belonged to the upper class. Hopkins was from the lower classes. Strachey became an officer of the colony. Though Hopkins had been chosen for the prominent role as clerk to the colony's priest, he was still only a settler, a man who'd signed away seven years of his life to the colony under a contract of indenture. Nevertheless, the lives of the two men would become intimately intermeshed during the disaster that soon befell the *Sea Venture*.

A Dreadful Tempest

On June 2, 1609, the third supply mission left Plymouth, England, the very place from which the *Mayflower* would depart eleven years later. The timing, the leaders of the expedition knew, was somewhat precarious: the transatlantic crossing would carry them through the height of summer, when the intensity of storms became a grave threat. They couldn't wait for a more favorable time of year, however; Jamestown desperately needed supplies.

The typical sailing route was circuitous and took ships south from England to the tropics off the coast of Africa, where they caught the steady northeast trade winds that pushed them westward across the Atlantic. Once they reached the Caribbean basin, ships would turn north and sail up the east coast of Florida, thus taking advantage of the Gulf Stream current, and so approach the Chesapeake Bay. But there was an alternative, more northerly route to America, one that would shorten the trip, which meant the sailors and passengers would consume fewer provisions, leaving more supplies for the struggling colony. The northerly route offered the added benefit of avoiding hostile Spanish ships that frequently patrolled the Caribbean. These two advantages outweighed the increased risk of taking a less familiar route, and the *Sea Venture* and the rest of the fleet chose the northern option. Instead of sailing all the way to Africa, the convoy turned west at the latitude of Portugal, a path that would take them to the north of Bermuda and directly toward the mouth of the Chesapeake Bay.[58]

The fleet sailed together for a little over seven weeks and were likely within seven or eight days of the American coast when the Atlantic turned ugly. On morning of July 24, the sun never broke through the clouds, which had been gathering thick through the night. The ever-present song of the wind in the ship's rigging turned ominous.[59] Rain started to fall. As the wind and seas picked up and the rain came harder, the ships of the convoy scattered and lost contact. The other vessels somehow found their ways around the worst of the weather, but the *Sea Venture* was drawn deep into the storm's growing maelstrom.[60] The ship had hit a hurricane.

The wind intensified, according to William Strachey, who wrote a detailed account of the voyage:

> a dreadful storm and hideous began to blow from out [of] the northeast, which swelling and roaring as it were by fits, some hours with more violence than others, at length did beat all light from Heaven; which, like an hell of darkness, turned black upon us, so much the more fuller of horror.[61]

The ship lurched and staggered under the onslaught, and the pitch and throw of the waves mounted. The sailors risked their lives and climbed into the rigging to furl the sails, lashing them tightly to the yards, leaving only enough scraps of exposed canvas to maintain steerage.

To keep the ship from capsizing, six and sometimes eight sailors had to man the helm, which under ordinary circumstances was the job of one man. The pelting rain seemed like "whole rivers" flooding the air as the tempest raged on, hour after hour. Fear tightened its grip on everyone, and even the most experienced sailors were shaken.

> The storm in a restless tumult had blown so exceedingly as we could not apprehend in our imaginations any possibility of greater violence; yet did we still find it not only more terrible, but more constant, fury added to fury, and one storm urging a second more outrageous than the former, whether it so wrought upon our fears or indeed met with new forces. Sometimes strikes in our ship amongst women and passengers not used to such hurly and discomforts made us look one upon the other with troubled hearts and panting bosoms, our clamors drowned in the winds, and the winds in thunder. Prayers might well be in the heart and lips, but drowned in the outcries of the officers. Nothing heard that could give comfort, nothing seen that might encourage hope.[62]

The storm's frenzy so drove and tossed and battered the *Sea Venture* that it opened a mortal leak. The sea flooded into the hold, and before anyone even realized the magnitude of the problem, the water level was five feet above the ballast of stone piled in the lowermost part of the ship. The *Sea Venture* sagged. Sailors swarmed below on their hands and knees with candles, creeping along the ribs of the ship, pausing to listen for running water, desperately checking everywhere to find the source of the catastrophic leak.

While some sailors searched, others jumped to the ship's bilge pumps, which by manual power—usually by several men working large levers or cranks in unison—drew water from the hold and discharged it overboard. But because the rising water in the hold was upending cargo and supplies, the pumps became choked with loose debris. For every moment the pumps were dormant while men scrambled to clear the blockage, the water gained and the *Sea Venture* settled deeper into the ocean.[63]

By the next morning, the crew still had not been able to find the leak. All that could be done now was to try to keep the rising water from taking the ship under. The entire company of men—sailor and passenger alike, some 140 out of the 150 total number of people on the *Sea Venture*—were organized into three groups. Each of the three was responsible for part of the ship: one group for the forecastle, one for the middle of the ship, and one for the stern.

Within each group, men were divided into two alternating shifts, with one shift working for an hour at the pumps or hoisting buckets of water to be dumped overboard while the other rested. Everyone lent a hand, from the aristocrats to the lowly settlers, like Stephen Hopkins.[64]

They labored from Tuesday until Friday morning without food or sleep, and the *Sea Venture* ran on and on through towering waves, driven by a veering wind that whipped white froth from the sea into the blasting rain. Despite heroic efforts to gain on the leak, the ship continued to take on more than the combined company could pump out. She settled lower and lower into the water. Strachey reckoned that over the course of their struggles, they removed about two thousand tons of water from the *Sea Venture*. And still, she floundered. By that Friday, July 28, they were ready to give in. Every last person on board was spent. The end seemed to be upon them. They discussed closing the hatches, "commending our sinful souls to God, [and] committing the ship to the mercy of the sea."[65]

It was at that moment that one of the leaders of the expedition spied land and cried out to the others. Hope surged and animated weary bodies. The broken ship was urged toward an island, toward salvation. They came into shallow water and staggered violently to a stop. With the beach still three-quarters of a mile away, the *Sea Venture* was grounded on a reef. They jumped to the ship's longboats, and by nightfall every man, woman, and child was safely on the island.[66]

Bermuda

After being battered by the tempest for days, the exhausted survivors of the shipwreck assembled on the shore of the northernmost point of Bermuda, a small archipelago of islands that lay a little over seven hundred miles from Cape Henry and the Chesapeake Bay. Given their approximate location when the hurricane hit the convoy, the experienced sailors knew immediately that their island had a sinister reputation: according to an English sailor who in 1593 had survived a shipwreck off its coast, it was known as "the Isle of Devils, [a place] that all men did shun as Hell and perdition."[67] A place "to all seamen no less terrible than an enchanted den of Furies and Devils."[68] A place, William Strachey lamented, "so terrible to all that ever touched them, and such tempests, thunders, and other fearful objects are seen and heard about them, that they . . . are feared and avoided [by] all sea travelers alive above any other place in the world."[69]

London's theatergoers would soon learn about the island's notoriety. Sometime between 1610 and 1611 William Shakespeare wrote what many believe to be his last play, *The Tempest*. In it, an aging sorcerer imprisoned on a remote island conjures a powerful storm to sink a passing ship carrying the men responsible for his exile. The survivors reach the shore, where the sorcerer takes his revenge. The idea for Shakespeare's play came from Strachey's account of the *Sea Venture*'s shipwreck.[70]

Shakespeare echoed Strachey's sentiments about Bermuda when the sprite Ariel describes the ship that the sorcerer Prospero doomed in his magical storm:

> Safely in harbor
> Is the Kings' ship; in the deep nook, where once
> Thou call'dst me up at midnight to fetch dew
> From **the still-vex'd Bermoothes**, there she's hid.[71]
> —*The Tempest*, act 1, scene 2

As the storm slowly blew itself out, the sailors' tales of devils and witches raced through their ranks, and they began to gather themselves for what they believed would be a dangerous time. They were utterly exhausted, not only from their endless physical toil at the ship's pumps but also from the emotional exertions of dealing with the terrors of emergency and catastrophe and of the imminent prospect of death. Their backs ached. Their hands were raw. Their clothes were soaked through. The day had ended, and the dark of the night was deepening on the Isle of Devils.

Three aristocrats were in charge of the group. Sir Thomas Gates had been appointed to serve as governor of Jamestown. He would oversee the colony if the castaways were able to find their way to Virginia. Sir George Somers had been named as admiral of the convoy. Somers had overall responsibility for the expedition while at sea; as governor, Gates's responsibility would start where the sea met the shore. Captain Christopher Newport, who'd sailed back and forth on the previous supply missions to Jamestown, served as vice admiral and as such commanded the *Sea Venture*.

Reverend Buck led everyone in prayers.[72] They gathered around the flickering light of campfires, the surf pulsing in a distant rumble on the offshore reefs, a reminder of how near death they'd come. Gratitude mixed with apprehension likely dominated everyone's thoughts. When the service was over, Governor Gates organized watch parties to take shifts and keep guard through the night. Although aboard the *Sea Venture* Gates had deferred to Somers and Newport—both of whom were sailors—he asserted his authority now that they were on land.[73]

Dawn on Saturday, July 29, brought the passengers and crew the sight of their ship wedged on the reef off the coast. The Atlantic sent wave after wave crashing against the *Sea Venture*, which overnight had become a fractured wooden hulk that would never sail again. They were trapped on a spot of land in the middle of the Atlantic with no way off. They were alone, for this place was empty of inhabitants, and their needs were immediate. They lacked food and shelter, but most of all they lacked water. Urgency now spurred their stiff and aching limbs. They wiped the sand and caked salt from their faces and got to work. They immediately dug a provisional well. It wouldn't be a stable supply for the long term, but it was sufficient for the time being.

After slaking their thirst, they split into groups. One started fishing for food, and another started putting together temporary housing, the men felling trees while the women gathered palm fronds to be used for roofing.[74] They worked together, but the utter unity of desperation that had compelled their efforts during the hurricane soon started to reveal fissures. Human nature began to reassert itself, and while some stepped to the fore and wholly applied themselves, others slunk to the back and shirked as best they could.

Wary of losing control to the chaos of individual whim, Governor Gates worked quickly to impose a structure around their lives while on the island. They'd all come from a very regimented society, with every person knowing his or her place in the social order, from the king to the lowliest laborer, a fact which Gates exploited. His power derived from a set of written instructions that the London Company, which administered the colony, had provided him before they had sailed from England. The instructions specifically declared him as the governor of Virginia, a position of absolute power. King James had delegated his authority via a royal charter to the Company, and the Company commissioned Gates, thus making Gates, in a very real sense, a direct agent of the king.[75]

The instructions in Gates's commission were intended, of course, for Jamestown, not Bermuda, and they covered various topics, from governance to dealing with the Powhatan. Few could be applied directly to their current situation, for a shipwreck before reaching Virginia had not been anticipated. But that didn't stop Gates from assuming the authority of the king. Only God stood higher still in rank than King James, so Gates began to establish order on the island by observing religious ceremony, instructing Reverend Buck to perform traditional services on their second day on Bermuda, which was Sunday, June 30. Stephen Hopkins helped the priest, reciting the Psalms and other liturgical readings.[76] It would have been a makeshift affair, but Gates was determined to try to establish a sense of normalcy as the group's leader.

Gates had reason to assert himself. Tension was already rising among the castaways, and there developed an early split between the *Sea Venture*'s sailors, who allied themselves with Admiral Somers, and the colonists, who gravitated toward Gates. Each man had been given primacy over their charges, but Bermuda presented a difficulty, since it fell neatly into neither category. It was land, and so Gates claimed control, but there was a critical weakness in his position. While Gates was a soldier and veteran of the Low Countries' war against Spain and was used to taking command, he was also a highly trained lawyer. As such, he would have known that his only source of power rose out of his commission, which was flawed because no one had predicted anything but a successful voyage from England to Virginia.[77]

Indeed, the 1609 supply mission was different from the previous missions to Jamestown because it sailed under a new royal charter. Gates carried with him the direction and authority to institute an entirely new regime in Virginia. The London Company had been reconstituted, and the new charter transferred all the rights and obligations of the former Company to its new incarnation. A formal change-of-control ceremony was even specifically outlined in Gates's instructions to mark the succession of power passing from the current colonial government to the new administration.[78] The current administration in Jamestown was to continue until the moment at which the Company, via its new designate Gates, ceremonially installed the new administration. The ceremony itself was not unlike that used in the Royal Navy, where a captain assigned to a new ship would gather the crew on the ship's deck and publicly read his commission, which triggered the formal change of command from the old captain to the new.[79] It was only after this public presentation to the colony that Gates would be "settled in [his] government" and thereby have the power to formally appoint a council of advisers. Underscoring the prospective nature of Gates's commission of authority, the instructions following those concerning the installation of his government were specifically written in the future tense.[80]

An early incident highlighted growing distrust between the mariners and the colonists. A sailor named Robert Waters had a dispute with another sailor and struck the man dead with a shovel. William Strachey provided no details of what might have caused the confrontation. Under Gates's authority, Waters was seized and ordered to be hanged the next day. Waters was bound to a tree and guarded by five or six of Gates's men. The guards fell asleep, and a few of Waters's fellow sailors crept up and cut his bonds. They hid him in the woods, bringing food to him daily, until Somers intervened on his behalf. He spoke with Gates, after which Gates changed his mind and concluded that the homicide was justified. He reversed the death sentence and let Waters off. In exchange for Waters's freedom, Somers apparently agreed to "many conditions" to keep the sailors from challenging Gates's authority on Bermuda.[81] Despite this particular resolution, the atmosphere between the two men—and between their respective groups of followers—remained tense.[82]

Early in their stay, Gates turned his attention to the *Sea Venture*'s longboats and ordered that the largest be modified for ocean travel. They would send it to the mainland and seek help from Jamestown. Several sailors volunteered to pilot the craft for a trip that would take a little over a week. It was agreed that if all went well the volunteers should be able to return with a rescue party within a month.

The *Sea Venture* survivors waited a full two months, each day scanning the western horizon for a sail, before giving up.[83] The mission had failed, the small boat lost or sunk, the men dead. The castaways were alone and would remain alone. No help was coming. Whether they lived the rest of their lives on this remote chain of islands would depend on their own ingenuity and resolve.

Slowly, the disappointment faded, and they found that the sailors' stories about the Isle of Devils were just that. Reality was quite different. Coral reefs, not evil enchanters or devils, lay at the bottom of seafarer dread. On the north-ern side of the island chain, the reefs extended as far as ten miles from the shoreline. Unsuspecting mariners not keeping an eye on the depth of the water over which they sailed might run afoul of these sharp, rocky formations, which could rip into soft wooden hulls, just as had happened to the *Sea Venture*.[84]

This island was no hell. It was paradise, a tropical wonderland bursting with life. Bermuda was teeming with feral hogs descended from the few sows and boars left by the Spanish navigator Juan de Bermúdez, who'd given the island archipelago its name more than a century before, and by a few subsequent shipwrecks.[85] Its bays and lagoons—protected by the encircling reef—were filled with fish. Thousands of birds called the islands home, and huge sea turtles came in from the open ocean during their mating season.

Among the interests on the island were two of their fellow castaways, for along with English settlers the *Sea Venture* had carried two members the Powhatan Confederacy. They were Namontack and Machumps, and they'd traveled to England on Captain Newport's most recent trip back from North America. Now on their journey home, they were stranded on Bermuda with the rest of the shipwreck survivors.[86] The two Powhatan men established a camp away from the main settlement, and for the most part kept to themselves.

Though there was a level of distrust, Englishmen such as William Strachey sometimes visited the pair and used the interactions to learn about their language and culture. During such visits, hand signals and a mix of English and Algonquian[87] allowed the two groups to cover a broad range of topics.[88] Given the understanding of Algonquian that Hopkins later showed in New England,[89] Hopkins likely joined Strachey or others who called on the two Indians over the ensuing months, thus acquiring exposure to their language and way of life. The interactions would have created a firm foundation for the experience and knowledge he later gained in Virginia.

Despite the island's bounty, Gates was anxious to get to Jamestown, where his authority would be unquestionable. He'd been retained by the Company to restore order to the struggling colony. That was his duty, and his personal and professional honor depended upon the fulfillment of that duty. Failure was unacceptable.

With Bermuda providing them easy sustenance, the ocean between the island and the mainland was the immediate obstacle for Gates. With the largest longboat lost, he ordered a new ship to be built. Instead of sending for help, they'd help themselves. The new vessel would be large enough to accommodate most of their company. Among them were able carpenters and even a few ship designers. From pieces they salvaged from the ribs of the broken *Sea Venture* and from wood hewn from Bermuda's native cedar trees, the castaways slowly started building their deliverance. While teams cut down the great cedar trees, others helped the carpenters turn the raw timber into planking and worked on the assembly. Somers and Gates next decided to build a second ship to carry the rest of their group, and Somers took some of the carpenters and many of his sailors and retired to a smaller island in the archipelago, where they started to build their own vessel.[90]

Everyone settled into a new rhythm of life on Bermuda, where they would remain for nine months. They worked on the boats. They gathered food and wood and fresh water. They maintained their shelters. Religion lay at the heart of their routine and, by design, was a critical part of Gates's exertion of authority on the island. On Sundays, with Stephen Hopkins at his side, Reverend Buck delivered two sermons, focusing in particular on two themes: the importance of unity and the gratitude that everyone should still feel for their deliverance from the tempest as well as for the easy bounty that the island provided. On every other day, Buck and Hopkins led the people through morning and evening prayer services, at which time the ship's bell was rung and roll called. Any people absent were punished.[91]

Hopkins helped Buck perform other duties of his office during their nine-month stay on the island. Perhaps using bread and wine salvaged from the *Sea Venture*'s wreckage, Communion was celebrated in October 1609 and again on Christmas Eve. Despite their exotic location and circumstances, the joys and heartbreaks of normal life still visited them. In November, Buck officiated a wedding between one of the sailors and a maidservant. In February 1610 Buck christened the daughter of John Rolfe and his wife. The child was named Bermuda. In March another baby was born, a boy named Bermudas.

Buck and Hopkins also buried several people before they left, among them Rolfe's infant daughter and his wife, as well as Thomas Gates's wife.[92] Counted among those who never left Bermuda was Namontack, one of the two Powhatan travelers, who apparently died at the hands of his companion, Machumps.[93]

Mutiny

Somers and most of his sailors kept to one isle, Gates and the rest to another. The narrow stretch of crystal blue water that separated them was a physical representation of the tensions between the sailors and landsmen. Sailors held a traditional disdain for the landlubbers, whom they considered to be more a hindrance aboard a ship than the inert cargo they might carry deep in the hold.

This unease was visible in the personal relationship between Gates and Somers as well. Both were proud men who'd found success in their respective fields. Both had attained the exalted position of knighthood as recognition for their accomplishments. Both had been given command of a particular function of the 1609 expedition, and each considered his authority as a grant directly from the Crown. While the admiral never overtly contested Gates's authority, he did not overtly submit to his command, either.[94] A rift developed between the two men that might have included open hostility.[95] According to some of the passengers on the island (who later related their story to John Smith), "such a great difference fell among their commanders, that they lived asunder in this distress, rather as mere strangers than distressed friends."[96]

The clash between Gates and Sommers—and more generally between sailor and landsman—was not the only source of discord. Another was a rumor about the miserable conditions that awaited them in Jamestown. Most of the colonists of the 1609 supply mission had left London knowing very little about Virginia.[97] What little they knew—or thought they knew—came primarily from the London Company's propaganda machine. That changed for the men and women stranded on Bermuda. Many of the *Sea Venture*'s crew had already been to America. They'd been on the ground in Jamestown, if for no longer than it took to ferry passengers and supplies to the colony's fortified enclosure. These sailors knew the truth, and they shared it with the settlers.

Slowly, whispers circulated. The New World was not a land of milk and honey. It was a land of destitution and despair. Food was in short supply. The Native Americans were not embracing Christianity or the English. There had been ambushes, with small groups of settlers caught outside the walls of the fort vanishing or being found dead. Disease and famine threatened the rest. Ironically, the Isle of Devils was proving to be a garden of bounty, and the promised land of Virginia now seemed like a barren purgatory where only "wretchedness and labor" and the threat of punishment awaited the colonists.[98]

Work on the ships continued, but progress was slow, and the months slipped past while the castaways continued to be charmed by the allure of their temporary home. Despite the occasional tropical storm, the climate was nicer than that in England. And it was nicer, according to the sailors who'd been there, than that which awaited them in Virginia, with its swampy lowlands, hot summers, and bitter winters. Hunger was unknown on Bermuda. The amount of food and the ease of gathering it astonished those of the lower classes, who were used to striving and scraping for a miserable diet of bread and boiled meat.[99] Many started to lose the desire to leave this wonderful place.[100] According to William Strachey, "dangerous and secret discontents" began among the seamen, who then tried to lure the would-be settlers to the cause of abandoning the effort to reach Jamestown.[101]

In September 1609 a band of sailors working with Gates's group were the first to revolt. They refused to work on the shipbuilding project.[102] The sailors were determined to create a new life on Bermuda and decided to leave their fellow castaways and establish themselves on one of the dozens of smaller islets of the archipelago.[103] Their plot was discovered before they were able to steal away, however, and the men were apprehended. For punishment, Gates gave them what they desired: he had them deposited on a remote islet without any provisions. The punishment proved effective, for not long after their banishment, the men repented and begged to return to the company and its stores of food and supplies. Gates acquiesced.[104]

The episode provides some insight into the mind of the governor. He was quick to mete out punishment because of his uneasy grasp of command. He needed to condemn any act of disobedience or chaos that might erupt. Under the martial law that regulated the colonial enterprise, mutiny was a capital offense punishable by death, and Gates's instructions from the Company specifically spelled out this particular crime and its punishment.[105] That Gates didn't impose the death sentence and that he quickly acceded to pleas of mercy might be taken as examples of a softer side of the old soldier. Perhaps Gates was a man of compassion.

More likely, however, is that Gates was simply being pragmatic. The mutineers were sailors, and Somers was in a unique position to challenge Gates, which was something that he feared. Somers had been given charge of the expedition while traveling to Jamestown. Bermuda was arguably a simple, albeit dramatic, detour during that journey—akin to a stop at some island cove in order bring on fresh water—and thus still within the scope of Somers's authority. Such an argument—if raised—would likely have been seen as more persuasive than Gates's position, which in theory and in legal effect did not commence until such time as the formal change-of-control ceremony anticipated by both Gates's commission and the royal charter. Somers was untouchable, and Gates knew it.[106] This is most likely why Gates had backed off when Somers had approached him about the murder committed by the sailor Robert Waters, and this is most likely why Gates now dealt gingerly with the band of sailors involved in the September mutiny. They were all Somers's men, and because of it, they were too untouchable.

Regardless of his intentions, however, Gates's handling of the September incident didn't entirely calm the waters of dissent. In January 1610 another ripple swirled, and Stephen Hopkins was at its center. By this time, Hopkins was about twenty-nine years old. He'd labored feverishly at the pumps with the others during the tempest to save the *Sea Venture*. He'd helped find food, build shelter, and cut down timber for the boats being constructed. He'd faithfully been discharging the duties of his office of clerk to Reverend Buck.[107] By all measures, Hopkins seemed to have adapted well to the castaways' predicament. He seemed to have been content.

Nevertheless, on January 24, he spoke to two men at some length about Gates's authority. Strachey recorded the substance of the conversation:

> [Hopkins] alleged substantial arguments, both **civil and divine** (the scriptures being falsely quoted) that it was no breach of honesty, conscience or religion to decline from the obedience of the governor or [to] refuse to go any further led by [Gates's] authority (except as it so pleased themselves) since the authority ceased when the wreck [of the *Sea Venture*] was committed, and with it, they were all then freed from the government of any man. And for a matter of conscience, it was not unknown to the meanest [that] we were [only] bound . . . each one to provide for himself and his own family.[108]

Echoing some of the arguments raised by the September mutineers, Hopkins said that there were two reasons to stay on Bermuda. First, there was "abundance by God's providence of all manner of good food." They could therefore stay as long as need be. Let Gates go on to Jamestown. They'd stay behind. Second, when they did decide to leave, they could simply build their own boat and sail back to England.[109] If forced to go to Virginia, Hopkins warned, food would be in short supply, and they would lose their chance at freedom, since, according to Strachey,

> they might well fear to be detained in that country by the authority of the Commander thereof, and their whole life to serve the turns of the adventurers [i.e., the London Company] with their travails and labors.[110]

In other words, Gates's authority would be unassailable once they reached Jamestown. They'd be subject to his absolute and arbitrary exercise of power. There is no record of the context in which Hopkins made these statements. Who were the two men? Did Hopkins seek them out? Was he actively fomenting mutiny? Or did the two men seek him out, perhaps in his capacity as the minister's clerk, with honest questions about authority and their futures? Hopkins was a commoner and thus approachable, but he was also someone with learning like the gentlemen and aristocrats, which made him an attractive source for advice. More questions arise: Was Hopkins earnest and serious and willing to commit acts in furtherance of the lofty objectives he advocated? Was he ready to defy Gates? Or had he spoken at some distance to the subject, like a soliloquy that might be delivered during a sweaty pause in hard labor? Perhaps the three men had been resting after felling one of the towering cedars, and Hopkins uttered a momentary gripe while rubbing his aching hands.

Though the exact setting for the exchange remains unknown, the results are not. The two men reported Hopkins to Governor Gates, who reacted decisively. He immediately ordered a trial. Gathering the entire company together with the ominous tolling of the ship's bell, Gates paraded Stephen Hopkins before the assembly under guard and bound in iron manacles. The two witnesses recounted their conversation with Hopkins, and Gates forced Hopkins to respond to the charge of mutiny. Hopkins's response was emotional. "Full of sorrow and tears," he pleaded "simplicity and denial." Gates was unmoved. The punishment would be death.[111]

Where Gates had previously decided temporary banishment for the rebellion of the preceding September, he now was willing to condemn a man to die. Why? Given the fact that Hopkins was found, somewhat humorously, to be "both the captain and the follower of this mutiny"—that is, that he was the only person involved—it would seem that in terms of seriousness, Hopkins's one-man insurrection was not too far advanced. Gates's punishment would seem to have been rather extraordinary, given that there had been only one person involved and that no affirmative steps had been taken to oppose authority. Hopkins wasn't accused of shirking any of his duties or responsibilities. He wasn't accused of shrinking off into the woods like the September mutineers. He didn't murder anyone. He didn't strike anyone. He merely raised a few— albeit substantial—arguments that if one *were* to decline an order from the governor, such an act would be "no breach of honesty, conscience or religion."

Hopkins seemed more to be speaking in the realm of hypotheticals than to be planning concrete actions.[112] Why, then, did Gates mete out a dramatically more severe punishment than that given to the September group, which without a doubt took more affirmative steps to further their mutiny?

The most plausible answer lies in the "civil" arguments that Hopkins raised against Gates's authority. What Hopkins said probably pricked Gates's ear, for it went to the heart of his uncertain command. Hopkins claimed that Gates had no authority because they were on Bermuda. In so doing, he not only challenged Gates, he also challenged the London Company's authority. King James had given the Company a charter for Virginia. The *Sea Venture* survivors were now outside the bounds of that royal prerogative. Because it was essentially true, Gates likely knew that if others took up Hopkins's argument, everything on the island would fall apart. Neither he nor any of the other leaders of the expedition would be able to impose control. Each castaway would be, as Hopkins put it, obligated to provide only for himself and his family. In such a state, order could only arise by mutual agreement, a concept that was likely anathema to an aristocrat and soldier like Thomas Gates. This, then, was most probably the reason why Gates instituted such a harsh response to an otherwise almost preposterous conspiracy of only one.

When he heard that he was sentenced to die, Hopkins broke down. He fell to his knees in penitence. He moaned in anguish. With tears streaming down his face, he pleaded for his life. He begged Gates to consider his wife and children in England. They depended upon him. They'd be destitute. Ruined.

Gates was unmoved. The decision stood. But, according to Strachey, Hopkins's pleas moved "the hearts of all the better sort of the Company." Here was this poor commoner, they probably reasoned, who wasn't one of the ignorant ruffians that likely stood in the assembled group, a squalid tough from the rough streets of London. He was an intelligent and knowledgeable man who'd won praise for his role in their religious services, helping the group establish order and routine from the chaos of being shipwrecked. A man with a young family. His tears and moans seemed genuine. His one-man mutiny seemed more conjectural than anything else. No concrete steps had been taken. No harm had been done. Was death the proper outcome? A group of the aristocrats, including Strachey and even Vice Admiral Christopher Newport, went to Gates to ask for leniency. "With humble entreaties and earnest supplications . . . [we] never left him until we had got [Hopkins's] pardon."[113]

What ultimately changed the old campaigner's mind? Did compassion somehow percolate into his thoughts? Did he realize that it was unfair to treat Hopkins so differently than he had the September mutineers? Did he realize that it was unfair to condemn Hopkins to die for mere whispers when he'd earlier pardoned Robert Waters for murder? Did the aristocrat somehow come to see the lowborn Hopkins as a human being—a man much like himself—rather than one of the faceless unwashed? Probably not, for only two months later, he had another man executed for refusing guard duty and striking one of Gates's soldiers.[114] In Hopkins's case, the more likely explanation is that Gates bowed to the uproar of his peers. When leaders like Christopher Newport wouldn't leave his side and wouldn't accept any answer short of capitulation, Gates was presented with a dilemma. It was one thing for a lowly clerk to discontentedly murmur about authority. It was quite another if Gates let the episode taint his relationship with men of position and rank—men who could possibly supplant him. Gates needed those men to support his assertion of command. They are the likely reason, not remorse or sympathy, that led Gates to change his mind and let Hopkins live.

Unless he truly had been only tossing out theoretical grumbles, what possibly could have motivated Hopkins to take any steps toward sedition? Hopkins must not have liked Gates, disapproving of either his personality or his governing style or both. But there must have been more, and Hopkins's relationship with Reverend Buck might provide some clues. The two men hadn't known one another before boarding the *Sea Venture*. As clerk and priest, Hopkins and Buck would have quartered closely together on the cramped sailing ship. Some of the language Strachey recorded that Hopkins used during his mutinous speech suggests that Buck considered Hopkins as much a domestic servant as a religious adjunct.[115] For example, Hopkins insisted that when the *Sea Venture* wrecked not only did it free them all from the authority of Gates, it freed them "from the government of **any** man." The only man outside of Gates under whose command Hopkins might have been was Richard Buck.

Further, Hopkins's statement about being bound only "to provide for himself and his **own** family" suggests that he likely was spending at least part of his time attending to the needs of Buck's wife and children, who'd accompanied him on the voyage.[116]

And finally, while Strachey named himself and Vice Admiral Newport as two of the gentlemen who pleaded for Hopkins's life, he did not identify Reverend Buck, a noticeable omission that hints at possible enmity between minister and his clerk. Hopkins had committed himself to seven years at Jamestown. If Buck was mistreating him, the relationship might have been a motivation for Hopkins to voice his displeasure with the continued voyage.

A final question arises about Hopkins's mutiny: If, as it appears, Gates issued the death sentence because of Hopkins's argument about Gates's civil authority on Bermuda, how did Hopkins become aware of this specific issue? Was it a coincidence that Hopkins stumbled upon the one great weakness in Gates's assertion of control? Perhaps. Certainly, a knight and aristocrat such as Gates would not have shared the sensitive details of his commission with a commoner. At least not willingly. But Hopkins may have learned about the precariousness of Gates's authority through Richard Buck. As it appears that he was serving Buck both in a domestic capacity and as his religious clerk, Hopkins likely would have waited upon him during any dinner hosted by the leader of the expedition.[117] Talk would have probably included the topic of Jamestown, and Gates's instructions from the Company would have likely arisen as well, for he openly referred to them in the communications he drafted that were sent in the failed mission by the longboat to Virginia. Perhaps Gates even spoke directly with Reverend Buck about the importance of implementing religious order, as it would help secure a general order.[118] Without such a proper command structure, there would be chaos. They needed discipline, for without a coordinated effort from everyone, their ships would not get built and they would not be able to continue to Jamestown to fulfill their mission.

Regardless of how Hopkins's one-man mutiny unfolded, the episode must have shaken Hopkins to his very core. He probably kept his own counsel after that and maintained a dutiful and low profile. By late spring, construction of the new vessels finally neared completion. Gates's team had combined native cedar with timber and parts from the wreckage of the *Sea Venture*, while Somers's boat was made only of the wood from local cedar trees, without the use of any metal, except a single bolt in her keel. After nine months on Bermuda, the castaways sailed for Virginia on May 10, 1610. They reached Jamestown fourteen days later.[119]

2 | HOPKINS AT JAMESTOWN

Oh, I have suffered
With those that I saw suffer.

—*The Tempest*, act 1, scene 2

AFTER SURVIVING A HORRIFIC HURRICANE and some nine months on a deserted island, the settlers bound for the New World finally arrived at their destination. While the sailors had been wrong about the Isle of Devils, they'd been right about the condition of the colony. In fact, it was even worse than the worst rumors.

The spring and summer of 1609, when the *Sea Venture* had set sail from England, had been relatively dry in Virginia. The inclement weather had stifled the settlement's meager agricultural production. Though the reefs of Bermuda had ended the *Sea Venture*'s part in the third supply mission, the rest of the convoy had straggled into Jamestown. Those ships had brought over three hundred settlers but few provisions, which only increased the demand for food. John Smith, then governor of the colony, had been severely injured months earlier. Whether by accident or an intentional act, someone had dropped a lighted match into his lap while he slept during an excursion on the James River. His musket's powder bag exploded, and the fire burned through his clothes and peeled the skin from his thighs. Political rivals had sidelined him in his weakened state, and in October 1609 he had left for England, missing the arrivals from Bermuda.[1]

After Smith left, relations between the English colonists and the Powhatan had quickly soured. Confrontations turned hostile, and the settlers were forced to keep within the fortified walls of the settlement as the Powhatan kidnapped or killed those who attempted to tend the fields. Jamestown was basically on an island, with only a narrow stretch of land connecting it to the mainland, which limited the land available for farming and hunting game and made it extremely vulnerable to the Powhatan blockade. Expeditions by ship to trade for food with more distant native villages had been unsuccessful. Food had quickly run out.

The winter of 1609–1610 in Virginia was harsh, and hundreds of Jamestown residents died in what became known as the Starving Time. Trapped in their stockade, even basics became scarce. Hunger drove people to eat horses and cats and dogs. They had eaten rats next. And then snakes. They chewed leather. Some may have even resorted to cannibalism. George Percy, who'd become acting governor at Jamestown in the wake of John Smith's departure, provided a firsthand account:

> Nothing was spared to maintain life and to do those things which seem incredible, as to dig up dead corpses out of graves and to eat them. And some have licked up the blood which has fallen from their weak fellows. And amongst the rest this was most lamentable: One of our colony murdered his wife, ripped the child out of her womb, and threw it into the river. After this he chopped the mother into pieces and salted her for his food, which wasn't discovered until he'd eaten part of her. For this cruel and inhumane act, I adjudged him to be executed.[2]

By the time Stephen Hopkins reached Virginia, Jamestown had been decimated. Of the five hundred men, women, and children living at the settlement the prior year, only sixty remained. The town itself was in ruins.[3] Very little now remained. Its protective palisade was torn down, the gates hung askew from their hinges, and most of the houses had been stripped and torn apart for firewood in a desperate attempt to stave off the cold.

For Hopkins and the other *Sea Venture* castaways, it must have been a very emotional arrival. They'd spent ten months in paradise on Bermuda and now had arrived on the doorstep of hell. The worst of their fears had been realized.

Hopkins would be trapped here for the rest of his seven-year contract. With about one year done, that meant six more years, the beginning of which was marked by a somber ceremony. Thomas Gates, having finally reached the place where he could legitimately claim authority, immediately initiated the formal change of control. He ordered that the church bell be rung. As Reverend Buck's clerk, Hopkins was likely the man who rang the deep-sounding signal that called for the assembly of everyone in the settlement. Buck stepped to the fore and delivered a heartfelt prayer lamenting the misery of the colony's condition. When Buck finished, Gates caused his commission to be read aloud to the group, which was the critical step in investing his power to form a new colonial government. Acting governor Percy was so weak from hunger that he was scarcely able to stand through the ceremony. After the reading of Gates's commission was completed, Percy surrendered to Gates the former charter from the London Company and his own commission, thus completing the ceremonial protocol that formally established Gates as governor.[4]

The next order of business was survival. Though the two ships built on Bermuda carried some of that island's bounty for provisions, they didn't have enough to support themselves and the emaciated settlers. After only two weeks, Thomas Gates made his first and only major decision as governor of the colony: the settlement would be abandoned and they would return home. His great project was a failure before he could even begin. But as dejected as Gates must have been, people like Stephen Hopkins were likely elated. It would have been a great relief to quit this awful place after only a number of days rather than after years of toil and danger.

The Jamestown survivors and the *Sea Venture* survivors boarded ships for a trip home. The mood of the departing colonists who'd lived through the Starving Time was captured in an incident on their last day. A group of them tried to set aflame the last bits of the settlement's wooden wreckage. Gates and his soldiers had to physically restrain the emotional settlers and herd them onto the waiting vessels.[5] Finally loaded, the ships started down the thirty miles of James River toward the Atlantic.

Any jubilation Hopkins had was dashed before they even reached the open ocean. A longboat raced up the river to meet them, bringing news of the arrival of a new convoy from England. Colonial overseers in London had assumed that when the *Sea Venture* hadn't reached Jamestown, all its passengers and crew were dead, which meant that the settlement needed a new governor. Another expedition was organized, headed by Thomas West, who in 1602 had become Baron De La Warr.[6] De La Warr and his three ships and 150 additional colonists—and significantly, provisions ample enough to feed four hundred people for a year—had just arrived after a three-month voyage from England.[7]

Picking Through the Ruins

De La Warr's arrival meant the colony would not be abandoned, a decision which was met by considerable grief. Most of the Starving Time survivors and settlers from the *Sea Venture*, like Hopkins, were looking to put North America far behind them.[8] By June 10, 1610, they were back at the ruins of Jamestown.

As Gates had done only a few weeks before, De La Warr's first priority was a church service and the formal investment of his administration. Everyone gathered and listened to another sermon delivered by Richard Buck, with Stephen Hopkins no doubt playing his role as clerk for any liturgical readings.[9] Hopkins likely would have struggled to keep his composure, trying to mask the bitter disappointment he must have felt. De La Warr promptly had his commission read, the ceremony by which his legal authority was established. The ritual included Gates surrendering to De La Warr his own commission and the royal charters from King James—both the original and that created in 1609 specifically for Gates's third supply mission.[10]

Once the formal transfer of power was completed, De La Warr immediately put the colonists to work in rebuilding the settlement. Between the survivors of the Starving Time, the *Sea Venture* castaways, and the colonists that De La Warr brought, the colony had about 350 people.[11] The days began at six o'clock in the morning, and repairing the damaged church was a top priority. Once that work was completed, Hopkins helped the others rebuild the rest of the fortified town. Work was interrupted only for meals and for religious services.[12] Buck delivered two sermons every Sunday. On Thursdays he also preached. Hopkins would have helped with every service.[13] Consistent with the rigid hierarchy of English society, the upper class took positions of special prominence during worship services.[14]

As a ministerial clerk of that era, Hopkins probably had other obligations to Reverend Buck, many of them of a type akin to a domestic servant, which is likely why Buck apparently treated Hopkins as one. Wherever the priest went, so too did the clerk. Indeed, in some parishes a clerk could not leave town without special permission from the priest. A clerk would help in ministering the sacraments, such as baptism, the Eucharist, and marriage ceremonies. He would accompany the parson when visiting the sick. He might light the ritual lamps and candles, fetch coal, keep a fire lit in the chancel, near the altar. He might be required to fold up the priest's vestments and other items used during the worship service, such as books or the chalice, as well as be responsible for arraying the appropriate cloths to adorn the altar before services and for removing them afterward. He likely was responsible for looking after the church and its grounds, which meant daily sweeping, and cleaning windows, pillars, walls, stalls, and seats, and even cleaning the roof if necessary. He might have been required to sprinkle water in church every week to keep it from dust and to clear cobwebs from high corners. And finally, he probably also was required to keep the church registers, where weddings, christenings, and burials were recorded.[15] And like a servant, Hopkins was specifically charged by Buck to begin to make improvements on a one-hundred-acre tract of land that the Company had granted the priest.[16] In addition, Hopkins and Buck both probably would have taken on active roles during moments of need, such as defending against any attacks and responding to any alarm, as did all the men of the colony.[17] Circumstances demanded it.

Within a few months of De La Warr's arrival, more than 150 of the 350 total population were dead from disease.[18] The adaptation of Englishmen to the diseases and climate of Virginia became known as "seasoning," a process which took a heavy toll for decades, much like the way European diseases like smallpox and measles devastated native populations. Most of those who immigrated to the colony died within the first two years, with 50 to 75 percent of every shipload of settlers dying during the seasoning period. The settlement's location contributed to the staggering loss of life, and it has been criticized for centuries by scholars as a gastrointestinal death trap.[19] Hopkins's shipmate, William Strachey, recorded what most newcomers quickly came to see for themselves:

[Jamestown is] seated in somewhat an unwholesome and sickly air, by reason it is in a marish [i.e., swampy] ground, low, flat to the [James] River, and it has no fresh water springs serving the town, but what we draw from a well six or seven fathom [thirty-six to forty-two feet] deep, fed by the brackish river oozing into it [and is therefore] the chief cause . . . of many diseases and sicknesses which have happened to our people, who are indeed strangely afflicted with fluxes and agues [dysentery and fever].[20]

Although hundreds of new colonists arrived during the years of Hopkins's stay at Jamestown, the high mortality rate kept the maximum number of colonists fairly constant during that period. There were about 350 people in the summer of 1610 when Hopkins arrived. Six years later there were 351.[21]

Hopkins in Virginia: 1610–1616

Hopkins remained in Virginia until 1616, which fulfilled his seven-year indenture to the London Company. Among the main colonial objectives during this period were to establish some sense of stability and discipline among the settlers, to remove the immediate native threat to Jamestown, and to create an adequate supply of food.

The chief antagonists of the Jamestown colonists were the Powhatan, a confederacy of thirty tribes that included up to twenty-one thousand people, who were led by a man generally known by the name of his people. The Powhatan Confederacy peopled the entire Chesapeake Bay region. They spoke a dialect of Algonquian and were related to the native nations that stretched north into Canada, nations that included the Wampanoag in modern-day Massachusetts, as well as the Abenaki of modern-day Maine, both of whom Hopkins would later encounter when he returned to America in 1620 with the Pilgrims. The Powhatan were also unique in at least two critical ways: they were the only one of the Native American nations of the eastern seaboard that proved capable of forcing the English off their lands, and they were the only nation to launch a comprehensive war to exterminate the foreign settlers.[22]

The relationship between the English and the Powhatan fluctuated over the span of years from Jamestown's founding in 1607. There had been hostility—scattered attacks and ambushes of foragers or scouting parties—as well as hospitality—gifts exchanged and trade for food and supplies and generally friendly relations. As would be the case with the Pilgrims, without the initial help of the local native people, the English settlers at Jamestown would likely have succumbed during the first years, especially over the first fall and winter in 1607 to 1608. By 1609, however, the relationship had become so strained that it gave way to steady conflict that lasted for years.[23]

Skirmishes with the Powhatan continued after De La Warr's arrival, and he responded using tactics he'd learned and practiced in English campaigns in Ireland, burning, for example, entire villages to the ground if he suspected that the local chieftain had lied to him. The Powhatan retaliated whenever the opportunity arose, killing dozens of the English, for instance, as the settlers mounted exploratory excursions up the James River, primarily in the hope of finding gold mines. For De La Warr the seasoning period proved a greater foe than the Powhatan, however, and by April 1611 he was so weak from disease that he gave up his post as governor and left Virginia.[24]

An aristocrat named Thomas Dale replaced him. Like Thomas Gates, Dale had served in the Dutch wars against Spain. One of the first things Dale did as governor was recognize the life-threatening disadvantages of the location of the settlement. After surveying the immediate vicinity, Dale set about establishing a few satellite settlements in new spots. One was called Henrico in honor of King James's eldest son, Prince Henry. It was situated on a piece of high land about fifty miles farther up the James River, beyond the reach of the brackish tidal flows from the ocean, which ensured a clean water supply. In sojourns away from Jamestown to create the new outposts, Dale took as many as one hundred men in order to ward against any Powhatan attacks. Because of sickness afflicting the newcomers who'd arrived with Dale, much of the work of the colony fell to the shoulders of the men who'd already survived the acclimatization period, men such as Stephen Hopkins.[25] Thus, it is probable that he took part in the fortification of Henrico. High, dry ground, rather than low, isolated swampland, gave a settlement an advantage. This would prove a valuable lesson, and may have influenced the Pilgrims' decision in 1620 to locate their colony on the hillside above the legendary Plymouth Rock.[26]

It was during excursions outside Jamestown that Hopkins likely learned a great deal more about Native Americans, for some local natives on friendlier terms than the general Powhatan populace accompanied the English work crews and taught them about the land and its people and climate.[27] For nine months on Bermuda, he'd had the opportunity to learn from the two Powhatan who'd sailed with him on the *Sea Venture*. Although one of the men had been killed on the island, the other had come with the English castaways to Virginia and apparently had maintained contact with them even after rejoining his own people.[28] These additional interactions with the native populace would have helped solidify Hopkins's understanding of the Algonquian language, giving him some command of the native tongue, a skill he would later employ when he returned to America on the *Mayflower*.

In building Henrico, Dale worked the men so hard that some started deserting, running into the wilderness and seeking refuge in local native villages. Many were caught and brutally executed to serve as a stark warning to the rest of the settlers. The conflict with the Powhatan, meanwhile, kept simmering. Numerous Powhatan visited Jamestown with gifts of food but in reality had been sent as spies by their leader to gather intelligence about his enemy's numbers and condition. Several of the spies were seized and executed.[29]

By 1613, John Rolfe was experimenting in planting tobacco, a crop that in later years would have a profound impact on Virginia's economy and the growth of slavery in America. In March of that year, an English ship was exploring the Rappahannock River, which enters the Chesapeake Bay about forty miles to the north of the James River. While ranging up the Rappahannock, the English learned that Pocahontas was in the area. She was the daughter of Powhatan who was reported to have saved John Smith during the first years of the colony.

As a girl in her early teens, Pocahontas had often visited Jamestown before relations between the English and Powhatan deteriorated into outright war. During that time, she became an ally of sorts to the English, helping them understand how to relate to the people of the Powhatan Confederacy. She was also a favorite of her father, which made her a valuable asset in the eyes of the Englishmen sailing the Rappahannock, for if she became a prisoner, they might be able to exchange her for several recently captured Englishmen and perhaps even strike a peace deal. They exploited Pocahontas's familiarity and friendliness with the English to kidnap her. After taking her to Jamestown, they opened negotiations with Powhatan. After an initial exchange of terms, diplomacy fell apart for nearly a year. During her long captivity, Pocahontas developed a relationship with Rolfe.[30]

Their relationship was provocative to all concerned. Such was the condescension that the typical Englishman felt toward the native population that Rolfe felt compelled to write a very long and formal letter to Governor Dale requesting permission to pursue a romantic relationship with Powhatan's daughter.[31] For her part, Pocahontas sought approval from her father and family. Despite the ingrained differences between the two peoples, despite the years of open warfare that had taken the lives of hundreds from either side, and despite the English kidnapping of Pocahontas, both Dale and Powhatan saw an opportunity in their romance.

In April 1614 Rolfe and Pocahontas were married in an Anglican ceremony presided over by Reverend Buck and assisted by Stephen Hopkins. Pocahontas's uncle gave the bride away, and two of her brothers sat in attendance. The marriage helped facilitate peace, which held for nearly eight years, allowing the English to plant corn and other crops, breed their cattle, and hunt and fish without danger of violence.[32] For the first time since Hopkins and the other *Sea Venture* survivors had landed at the ruins of Jamestown in 1610, the settlement finally had a chance to get itself onto stable footing.

The relationship between Rolfe and Pocahontas likely had a lasting impact on Stephen Hopkins. By April 1614, Hopkins and Rolfe had spent nearly five years together, often in harrowing circumstances. They'd bailed and pumped for days when the *Sea Venture* floundered in the hurricane. They'd both staggered ashore on Bermuda after the hapless vessel wrecked. On the island, Hopkins had helped welcome Rolfe's daughter into the world, only to bury her a short time later along with Rolfe's first wife. When they finally arrived they'd witnessed the devastation of the Starving Time. Together, they'd worked to rebuild the settlement. The two men were certainly acquaintances, but more likely, they'd become friends of at least a casual nature. Given that likelihood and his participation in Rolfe's wedding in Jamestown, Hopkins would have been brought into contact with Pocahontas.

By all accounts, Pocahontas was a remarkable woman. She was well liked among her people, as well as the English. John Smith counted her as exceptional even as a child when she'd come visiting the English encampment. In her youth she was precocious, curious, charismatic, and as an adult, courageous, dignified, and articulate. As Smith remembered, "for wit and spirit, [she was] the only *nonpareil* of this Country." She was integral to the early survival of the entire colony, and, of course, in helping to bring to a close the violent and bloody war between the English and Powhatan.[33] When she visited England after marrying Rolfe, she impressed the most dominant dignitaries of English society, and even King James himself.[34] Some scholars have asserted that Pocahontas was one of the most important figures in the history of Jamestown and even America.[35] Such a person would probably have made a singular impact upon Stephen Hopkins.

If he came to know Pocahontas on a personal level and witnessed the bond that developed between her and Rolfe, it might have helped Hopkins to be able to see past the historical bigotry that encumbered the typical

Englishman's view of the world outside his country. The native people of Virginia were vastly different from the English in so many respects—in appearance, in language, in culture, in religion, in economy. But they were not so different once the barrier of unfamiliarity was overcome. As Pocahontas and Rolfe proved, a woman and a man could still love one another, no matter how different their appearances and cultures. They could start a life together and, in so doing, end a bloody war stoked by suspicion and ignorance.

Hopkins had experienced life in the New World both during and after the war with the Powhatan. He'd struggled in hunger and deprivation and fear, clinging to the protection of high palisades and large groups when any shadow in the woods could launch a volley of arrows. And he'd seen the difference that peace brought, when he and his fellow colonists had more time and energy to spend not on campaigns against their native neighbors but on husbanding the natural resources of the land. For Hopkins and the other Jamestown settlers, Rolfe's marriage to Pocahontas was an enormous tipping point, marking a transition between despair and hope. The experience probably had lasting implications for Hopkins, and through him, for the Pilgrims and Plymouth Colony and America.[36]

Despite the peace that Pocahontas helped establish, Hopkins likely observed the Powhatan were not the only impediments to stability for the colony in Virginia. The very political and social structure of the colony itself also contributed to volatility. Patricians ruled in Jamestown. They made the law and imposed it upon everyone else. The rigid social hierarchy and aristocratic dominance of the governance structure caused lasting friction. When colonists didn't comply, the aristocrats wielded the hammer of martial law and enforced military discipline through punishment and executions. According to official records, it was so bad that the London Company itself later condemned the administration of this period as being based on "a book of the most tyrannical laws written in blood."[37]

The colony's leadership was also dysfunctional.[38] From the very beginning the ambitious noblemen fought among each other for prominence, for prominence was necessary for personal glory and for professional advancement, which were the twin goals of every aristocrat associated with the colonial effort. Upon any loss or setback, each leader would blame his rivals, one in 1607 even accusing a peer of treason, for which the man was tried and executed.

Portrait of Pocahontas, also known as Matoaka and baptized as Rebecca (1616).
Courtesy of the John Carter Brown Library at Brown University

The governmental turnover that happened during Hopkins's residency in Jamestown added to innate competition. Thomas Gates, Lord De La Warr, Thomas Dale, and George Percy all traded the governorship between each other from 1610 to 1616, sometimes serving terms as short as three months. Each man wanted to bend the will of the settlement to his own priorities, which sent the settlers into paroxysms of work toward different goals. Seeing how a rigid, top-down style of governance could negatively affect the struggles of a colony was another valuable lesson that Hopkins probably carried with him when he sailed with the Pilgrims on the *Mayflower* and likely influenced the creation of the Mayflower Compact.[39]

Some of the other experiences that Stephen Hopkins probably had in Virginia may not have been as significant as his exposure to the relationship between John Rolfe and Pocahontas, but they nonetheless likely made an imprint upon him and upon history. For example, shortly after the peace accord struck in 1614 between the Powhatan and the English, Governor Dale and a group of fifty Jamestown colonists visited another tribe in the region, the Chickahominy, who lived in the neighboring watershed of the Chickahominy River. Though the Chickahominy lived within the domain of the Powhatan, they'd successfully remained more independent than the other tributary tribes of the Powhatan Confederacy. As such, the Chickahominy were not necessarily bound by the English's treaty with the Powhatan. Hence, Dale decided to visit them to negotiate directly, trying to leverage the peace with the Powhatan into an even broader, regional peace.

The visit was a success. To commemorate the accord, Dale promised an annual gift of a small tomahawk to each of the Chickahominy warriors, and to each of the eight men on the tribe's council of leaders, he promised a red military horseman's coat.[40] The English uniforms were a trivial detail of the peace settlement, but that detail would make its way into Pilgrim lore when years later Stephen Hopkins and another Pilgrim delivered a red horseman's coat to the leader of the Wampanoag Confederacy to substantiate a nascent peace treaty.[41]

Hopkins likely was the link between the gift presented to the Chickahominy leaders and the gift presented by the Pilgrims. There is a distinct possibility that Hopkins was one of the fifty men who accompanied Governor Dale's delegation. But if he did not, he certainly would have heard of it, as the news of the peace deal was significant to the colony at Jamestown. Also, Hopkins had a close connection to at least one of those who did participate in the meeting. A man named Ralph Hamor, who served for a while as secretary to the colony, was with Dale when he met with the Chickahominy. Hamor and Hopkins were long acquainted, as Hamor traveled to Virginia on the *Sea Venture*.[42] Hamor and Rolfe were good friends, which means it was likely that Hopkins was also an acquaintance.[43] Hamor would have naturally shared some of the details of this important mission to his friends and associates.[44]

Hopkins probably learned from Hamor one other minor diplomatic technique that later was adopted by the Pilgrims. At some point after the English at Jamestown and their Indian neighbors had become reconciled, Governor Dale sent Hamor as an emissary to visit Powhatan. Hamor took with him as an interpreter a young Englishman who'd lived for three years with the native leader. Powhatan greeted the boy warmly and then turned to Hamor and grabbed him by the neck, looking for a particular chain made of pearls. When Hamor professed ignorance about such a chain, Powhatan explained that he'd given the chain to Dale to use as a token, instructing the English governor that if he sent anyone to speak with Powhatan, that person should wear the necklace so that Powhatan could be assured that the messenger came from Dale.[45] The Pilgrims would later employ a similar method with the leader of the New England natives, giving him not a pearl chain but one made of copper, so that if he wanted to send a messenger to the English colony, they might know the emissary by the copper chain he carried.[46]

Hopkins Returns Home

In the spring of 1616, Stephen Hopkins likely sailed back to England on the same ship that carried John Rolfe and Pocahontas. He'd served the full seven-year period of his indenture to the London Company,[47] and he was traveling with a heavy heart, for during his absence his wife, Mary, had passed away.[48] The ship arrived in June 1616. Whether it touched first at one of the ports on the southern coast, such as Plymouth, or continued straight to London, Hopkins would have taken his leave at the most convenient point to get home to the Winchester area and Hursley, where his three children were living under the care of two of the village's families.[49]

Hopkins's six years in Virginia had entered him into a very select group of people. Only a small percentage of those who traveled to the New World stayed—or survived—as long as he did. Hopkins spent three times as long in Jamestown as did the famous John Smith, whom the Pilgrims in 1620 would try to hire as their adviser.

After arriving in London, Pocahontas was treated like royalty. She was feted by the bishop of London and met King James at a magnificent reception where a play by Ben Jonson, William Strachey's acquaintance and literary rival to William Shakespeare, was performed.[50] Pocahontas never returned to America. In March 1617 she and Rolfe boarded a ship in London to return to her homeland, but she fell ill and died and was buried at Gravesend, a town a few miles from the mouth of the River Thames.[51]

After Hopkins was reunited with his children, he soon started looking for a new spouse. Childrearing required a wife and a husband, one to look after the kids and keep the home, the other to find employment, whether in the fields or in a trade. It took Hopkins a little over a year and a half to attend to his affairs in Hursley and to find a woman who'd take him as a husband. He did so in London, in the parish of Whitechapel located just outside the eastern side of the ancient London Wall. In February 1618 Hopkins married Elizabeth Fisher in the Anglican church St. Mary's, Whitechapel.[52]

Shakespeare's *The Tempest* was performed, perhaps for the first time, in November 1611, while Hopkins was struggling to make it through each day in Jamestown.[53] The performance was one of several plays presented during the winter of 1612–1613 to celebrate the marriage of King James's daughter, Elizabeth.[54] Many scholars believe Shakespeare used William Strachey's account of the *Sea Venture*'s voyage to America when he wrote *The Tempest*.[55] It is unknown whether the play was performed during the period that Hopkins lived in London, which started sometime before his Whitechapel marriage in February 1618 and ended in July 1620 when he left on the *Mayflower*. Thus, it is unknown whether Hopkins might have had an opportunity to see the comedic character, Stephano, a gullible and often drunk servant who railed against authority, whom Shakespeare may have based on Hopkins. One thing is clear, however. Shakespeare's character did not resemble the man that Stephen Hopkins had become.

"Ariel, Caliban, Trinculo, and Stephano," by H. C. Selous (1868). *Courtesy of Dr. Michael John Goodman, Victorian Illustrated Shakespeare Archive*

3 | THE PILGRIM EXPEDITION

> Their manners are more gentle-kind than of
> Our human generation you shall find
> Many—nay, almost any.
> —*The Tempest*, act 3, scene 3

THE GENESIS FOR THE VOYAGE OF THE *MAYFLOWER* began nearly a century before the famous ship left England's coast in 1620. Religion was the single most significant element in the decision by the Separatists to immigrate to North America. Indeed, religion played a singular role in that age, which experienced constant, violent turmoil between the Catholic Church and insurgent Protestants first animated in 1517 by Martin Luther and his Ninety-Five Theses.

Through the Protestant Reformation, Protestants sought to cast off the traditions and hierarchy developed through the centuries by the Catholic Church. They wanted to return to the basics contained within the Bible, for they believed that the intercession of priests and saints was not necessary to have a relationship with God. The pope reacted by branding Protestants as heretics. Church institutions expanded to counter the movement. The Spanish Inquisition, for example, opened a branch in the Low Countries of the Netherlands tasked with searching for and punishing anyone suspected of heresy. Acting at the behest of the Church, civil governments rounded up Protestants and burned them at the stake. Protestants responded by trying to win over their national rulers, arguing that because their monarchs ruled by divine providence, they could control the religious aspects of their citizens' lives without interference from the pope and his bishops.

41

England was not immune, and trouble embroiled the island during the century after Henry VIII broke with the pope and created a new state-affiliated Protestant faith, the Church of England. Subsequent English monarchs either embraced or rejected the national church according to their own predilections, creating titanic swings that profoundly affected the nation and its constituents. When a Protestant ruled, churches, hospitals, schools, and almshouses associated with the Catholic Church were turned inside out, with brethren and sisters kicked to the curb and sick people sent home. Saintly shrines and pictures were destroyed. When the next monarch practiced Catholicism, everything was overturned again, this time with Protestant institutions being torn down or shuttered. With each cycle, dissident views were suppressed, and hundreds of English men and women were brutally executed. Rebellions broke out and were mercilessly suppressed. The Protestant Reformation was an age filled with atrocities without equal until the world wars of the twentieth century.[1]

Henry's Protestant daughter, Elizabeth, became queen in 1558 and would reign over England for nearly forty-five years. The country flourished under her rule. After her coronation, she immediately turned to the boiling religious divisions that had been exacerbated by her two immediate predecessors and now threatened stability. During his brief time as king, her half-brother Edward had ambitiously pushed Protestant reforms. During a short reign, her half-sister Mary had bitterly prosecuted Protestants.

Queen Elizabeth sought a middle ground between the two extremes. Protestantism resumed its place as the national religion, but early in her reign, she allowed Catholics to worship in private. Despite what she considered to be a balanced approach, several Catholic conspiracies to topple her gained traction. In 1570 the pope issued a decree that Elizabeth was not the lawful queen. In response, Elizabeth started actively persecuting Catholics. Being Catholic meant turning one's back on the national church, which was tantamount to treason.[2] Treason led to execution, and hundreds of Catholic priests over the following years were put to death.[3]

In 1586 a Catholic plot was launched to assassinate Elizabeth. The conspiracy was discovered and the collaborators sentenced to death. Spain's involvement in the coup attempt only heightened already strained relations between the two countries, which were also at odds over a revolt in the Netherlands, which at the time was under Spanish control. Though their Spanish ruler was Catholic, many of the Dutch people embraced the Protestant Reformation. A clash of religious cultures fomented between the Protestant provinces and Catholic Spain and eventually erupted into violent clashes, which in turn morphed into open rebellion. Spain's King Philip sent an army of ten thousand men to put down the uprising. The fighting continued for decades. Queen Elizabeth intervened by sending English troops to help the Dutch Protestants.[4] Though the English support was modest, the combination with the growing economic strength of the Dutch, whose entrepreneurial, trade-based society was creating a very wealthy region, gave the Dutch an advantage over Philip, whose own finances were under immense pressure.

Elizabeth's slap against Philip in the Low Countries, plus England's ongoing attacks against Spanish silver galleons in the Americas, deepened the rift. In July 1587, Spain obtained papal support for an invasion of England, which culminated in one of the most legendary confrontations in history when the country sent its invincible Armada.[5] Philip assembled 130 ships, which carried twenty-five hundred guns and more than thirty thousand men, two-thirds of them soldiers, most of whom had fought against the Protestants in the Netherlands. The plan was to sail up the English Channel, land the soldiers on the south coast of England, and invade the island nation. England was united as it prepared for the coming onslaught. Catholic Englishmen joined their Protestant compatriots and rallied for their country against the threat of foreign invasion.[6]

The Royal Navy had only thirty-four ships at hand. Nevertheless, they attacked the huge Spanish convoy as it crept up the English Channel. The English ships raked the decks of the Spanish vessels, killing the sailors and demoralizing the soldiers they transported. The English suffered only minor losses. The surviving Spanish ships sailed northward, intending to circle around Scotland and Ireland instead of chancing another run down the channel.

Autumn storms turned their retreat into disaster. Many ships were wrecked on the shores of Ireland, killing thousands of men. Only sixty-five ships, about half the fleet that had put to sea, eventually reached the safety of Spanish ports. The English didn't lose a single ship and lost only a hundred sailors.

A swell of religious emotion swept across the country. Medals commemorating the victory were inscribed, "God blew and they were scattered."[7] Pride in their faith and in their country surged in the hearts of Queen Elizabeth's subjects. With Spain's fleet shattered, England stepped onto the European stage as a first-class national force.

While the Church of England battled Catholic insurgency, a new group had emerged within the Anglican faith: the Puritans.[8] Though they agreed that there should be a single national church, they believed that earlier reforms had not gone far enough to separate the English church from its Catholic roots. The Puritans asserted that the Christian faith had been corrupted over time by human intervention. The time had come to restore the faith back to its purity.[9]

Internal tensions grew. A fissure was opening in English society, one that would widen into a gulf. Even Parliament split into two camps, those who thought that religious reforms had gone far enough, and those who wanted to push even further.[10] The Separatist movement grew out of Puritanism. Rather than fight to reform the Church of England from within, they wanted to leave it altogether, much as Henry had left the Catholic Church. They wanted to separate themselves from the national institution and form independent local churches, with each becoming a sovereign ecclesiastical organization that democratically chose its own ministers and principles of worship.[11]

Queen Elizabeth died in March 1603 at the age of sixty-nine.[12] She left no heirs but saw to it that her cousin, James VI, the king of Scotland, would become her lawful successor. He became James I of England and ruler of both kingdoms.[13] Like his cousin, King James was raised a Protestant, but the Catholics in England were hopeful, as James's mother, Mary, Queen of Scots, had been an advocate for their cause and an inspiration for several Catholic rebellions in England.[14] The Puritans were also hopeful, given James's education in the Calvinism of their own religious views.[15]

Both sides were soon disappointed. James checked the Puritans at a religious conference in January 1604 at Hampton Court, condemning them and their Separatist allies: "I will *make* them conform . . . or I will harry them out of the land!"[16] And in a blow to Catholics, he also looked to enforce laws penalizing those who did not attend services of the national Church of England. Even missing a single Anglican service might bring large fines.[17] For those who could not pay, land and personal property would be confiscated.[18] More than six thousand Catholics suffered in one year alone.[19]

The persecution fueled insurrection. A small group of Catholic gentry nearly blew up James and his whole Parliament by packing gunpowder in the cellars under the Palace of Westminster.[20] The Gunpowder Plot, as it became known, was uncovered before any match could be struck. In November 1605, one of the conspirators, Guy Fawkes, was caught near midnight in the cellars underneath the Houses of Parliament with over thirty barrels of gunpowder. Several of his coconspirators ran and were shot dead by pursuing officials. The rest, including Fawkes, were arrested, tried, and executed.[21]

In the wake of the foiled plot, Parliament added seventy new articles to the penal code that specifically targeted Catholics.[22] Prisons soon became crowded with Catholics who wouldn't swear an oath of allegiance to King James over the pope. Some Protestants took matters into their own hands, and even the elderly and infirm were subjected to violence. The Crown executed eighteen Catholic priests and seven church laymen solely for their profession of the faith.[23]

Continental Religious Wars

While it wracked England in its throes, the Protestant Reformation raged even more violently on the European continent. The centuries-old framework of power was crumbling. Now, and for many generations to come, all of Europe was divided upon the issue of being for or against the Protestant Reformation.

The magnitude of the conflict is difficult to understand by today's measures.[24] For example, the Dutch Revolt against Spanish rule was in large part a war for Protestant freedom from the Catholic Church. Started in 1568, it would continue—with a twelve-year pause in hostilities from 1609 to 1621—until 1648. It would be known for the outright length of conflict as the Eighty Years' War. In France, as many as three million people died between 1562 and 1598 in religious conflict between the Catholics and Huguenot Protestants. Mobs roamed the cities, killing at will. Civilians were massacred. Entire villages were razed to the ground. Nobles were assassinated, and so too was the king.

By 1606, violence between Protestants and Catholics was erupting in German provinces. By 1618, the bloodshed spread into what has become known as the Thirty Years' War, one of the most destructive conflicts in world history.[25] For the people who fought and lived through it, the conflict was a world-ending war between good and evil. Such were the stakes that the ends justified any means. While the saying is a cliché, the reality was anything but: any means truly meant any means. Catholic and Protestant militants did not see their foe as human beings, but rather as incarnations of wickedness. Entire regions on the continent lost up to half their populations. Some areas took nearly two hundred years to recover to their pre-conflict populations.[26] Overall, eighty million people died.

The Separatists in the Netherlands

In England, the Separatists became an early target of James's displeasure. Accused of treason against the state, they were aggressively hunted and persecuted. Some were seized and sent to prison. Others were forced into a form of house arrest and watched both day and night.[27] In 1607 and 1608, a group of over a hundred Separatists fled to the Netherlands, where they were able to follow the tenets of their beliefs and bound themselves together into a fellowship to practice their faith.[28] In so doing, they formed an exclusive body of believers—of "Saints"—who sought to keep themselves from the taint of all the corrupted forms of Christianity.[29]

One of those was a man named William Bradford, who'd joined the radical group at an early age and was only eighteen years old when he left England for the Netherlands. He became one of their leaders and ultimately helped plan their exodus. He was also a gifted writer and produced what would become *Of Plymouth Plantation*,[30] the most authoritative history of the group's time in the Netherlands, their eventual departure for the New World, and the establishment of Plymouth Colony. According to Bradford, the Separatists found the Netherlands to be an orderly place. Though the Dutch Revolt against the Spanish had been ongoing for some thirty years, the northern provinces where the English settled were still vibrant with trade, and in late 1608 the Dutch and Spanish were on the verge of a truce that would last for another twelve years. This part of the Netherlands had working governments, courts, and laws that were enforced by armed officers. The countryside was filled with, as Bradford wrote, "fair, and beautiful cities, flowing with abundance of all sorts of wealth and riches." Fleets of ships laden with goods coming from and going to points that spanned the entire world sailed in and out of ports such as Amsterdam. There were few households of extraordinary wealth, but there were also few households that struggled in poverty. Everyone was seemingly well off.[31]

The Saints settled in Leiden, a flourishing town of forty thousand just off the Dutch coast between The Hague and Amsterdam. In Leiden there were homes to rent, markets that provided fresh food, and healthy local commerce where furniture makers, printers, and weavers sold and traded goods. There were schools and the prestigious Leiden University, the oldest university in the country. The city presented the immigrants, in Bradford's words, "a sweet situation."

The Saints, of course, did have to adapt to their new country. They were forced to learn a new language, and most had to embrace new ways to earn a living. Their greatest struggle was against poverty. But with the help of Dutch neighbors willing to extend them credit, the Saints were able to find at least some level of contentment, learning "such trades and employments as best they could, valuing peace, and their spiritual comfort above any other riches whatsoever," according to Bradford. At length, they established themselves and were able to enjoy "many years in a comfortable condition, enjoying much sweet and delightful society and comfort together."[32] For the remainder of their stay in the Netherlands, their chief worries were of ecclesiastical and spiritual matters, dealing with occasional dogmatic and interpersonal strife within the body of their growing congregation.

The Saints ultimately decided to leave Leiden for the New World for several reasons. Ironically, the foremost reason was the fear that fellow Separatists still in England would not join them in the Netherlands.[33] Another of their primary reasons was a growing concern over the spiritual future of their children who, naturally, were being influenced by Dutch society and its culture. They were growing up with Dutch children and were beginning to acclimate, which was distressing to the adult Saints, who sought to inculcate the next generation with the strongly held and exacting religious tenets that drove them from England. As Bradford would write,

[Of] all sorrows most heavy to be born, was that many of their children, by these occasions, and the great licentiousness of the youth in that country, and the manifold temptations of the place, were drawn away by evil examples into extravagant and dangerous courses, getting the reins off their necks, and departing from their parents. Some became soldiers, others took upon them far voyages by sea, and others some worse courses, tending to dissoluteness, and the danger of their souls, to the great grief of their parents and dishonor of God. So that they saw their posterity would be in danger to degenerate and be corrupted.[34]

Another of their chief reasons was a fear that if they stayed in the Netherlands, they'd eventually disband and scatter as age and infirmity began to take hold of the congregation's members. And finally, they hoped to spread the Gospel to the "remote parts of the world."[35]

Some in their Dutch congregation were alert to the perils and argued that the plan to leave the Netherlands for America was too ambitious. Besides the well-known danger of a transatlantic voyage, there were any number of unknown dangers and hardships once they reached their destination. It was too much and likely to destroy them all. The New World would have none of the infrastructure of European social institutions and "famine, nakedness and want" would haunt those who would live on that faraway shore.[36] And there was a near-hysterical panic about the native population, who were believed to be, in Bradford's words,

> cruel, barbarous, and most treacherous, being most furious in their rage, and merciless where they overcome, not being content only to kill and take away life, but delight to torment men in the most bloody manner that may be: flaying some alive with shells of fishes, cutting of the members and joints of others by piecemeal, and broiling [them] on the coals, and eating collops of their flesh in their sight while they live.[37]

Despite these alarming objections, the group decided to leave the hospitality of the Netherlands, which was similar in so many ways to England. It was a civil and rich commonwealth that was separated only by the narrow channel, as opposed to the breadth of the great Atlantic Ocean. Though the dangers were great, the Saints naively believed them to be "not desperate," and though the difficulties were many, they deemed them to be "not invincible."[38] Subsequent events showed that the Saints miscalculated the risks.

Turning an idea into reality, however, required more than mere desire. The Separatists lacked the financial resources to fund what would be an expensive expedition. They needed ships and sailors to pilot them. They needed supplies and equipment, not only the baggage and effects of the would-be colonists, but also food to subsist upon during the long voyage, and to sustain them once they reached the distant shore. And they needed tools—the axes and shovels and saws to carve out a spot in the forestland and build a settlement from scratch.

In the autumn of 1617 the Separatists sent two men, Robert Cushman and John Carver, to England to try to organize their venture to America. While in the Netherlands, Cushman had practiced the trade of wool carding, one of the early steps in wool processing necessary to create wool thread out of the raw material. Carver was a deacon in the Separatist congregation. Their qualifications didn't necessarily lend themselves to the unusual task of organizing a colonial expedition to North America. Cushman himself lamented that they had much "to learn and none to teach."[39] Nevertheless, the Separatists forged ahead.

Thomas Weston and the Merchant Adventurers

They were ultimately introduced to Thomas Weston, a London ironmonger who offered to finance the expedition. Weston was a type of Englishman not uncommon then: part adventurer, part trader, part explorer—an amalgamation closer to freebooter than anything else. His mind was set upon schemes of accumulating vast and sudden wealth from North America, and he was prepared to put his plans in motion.

Weston was affiliated with a company calling itself the Merchant Adventurers of London, a group of about seventy London merchants who were seeking opportunities to "adventure"—that is, risk—their capital in speculative commercial ventures, particularly in America.[40] Economic motives drove them, for they hoped to exploit natural resources by obtaining and selling animal furs, fishing the rich coastal waters, and harvesting timber and other plant-based commodities such as sassafras.[41] The Separatists and Weston's group formed a partnership that was to last for seven years, with the financial backers to supply the money necessary to equip, transport, and maintain the colony, and the colonists to work and produce income from the New World for the partnership in addition to sustaining themselves. At the end of the seven years, the assets of the venture were to be divided into two parts, with the "adventurers" taking one half and the colonists taking the other.[42]

The Separatists' choice of and reliance on Weston as a partner in the expedition to America would make a difficult enterprise even more so. Preparations were marked with stops and starts and peppered with tumult. One of the many important tasks was obtaining permission from King James to settle in America. In May 1619 they obtained, at great cost of time and money, a formal grant from the Crown allowing them to proceed, but they wound up not making any use of it.

Perhaps one of the reasons that this particular grant wasn't used was that it was lost in the chaos surrounding William Brewster, a ruling elder in the

Separatist congregation, who at about that time was wanted by the English government for allegedly printing seditious religious pamphlets in Leiden.[43] Agents were searching for him in the Netherlands. Had he been caught, he'd likely have been hanged. Brewster, who was one of the Separatist leaders involved in organizing their move to North America, likely fled to England to evade his pursuers and there remained out of sight for almost a year and a half when he joined the company on the *Mayflower* just before its departure.[44] It wasn't until February 1620 that a second grant was obtained from the king through the London Company, which controlled the settlement rights for an area on the North American coast that stretched from the south, starting near the border between modern North and South Carolina, to the north, ending at the Long Island Sound.[45]

Because Thomas Weston did not organize a formal corporation, instead relying on a group that was, in Bradford's words, "knit together by a voluntary combination in a society without constraint or penalty," the funding for the colonial venture was not ironclad, a weakness that would later create confusion when the expedition was preparing to depart.[46] To entice his colleagues to provide front money, Weston had been relying on the hope of obtaining a monopoly to exploit American fisheries.[47] That effort failed, and during the spring of 1620 many of Weston's merchants withdrew their financial promises.[48]

In order to raise new funds, Weston demanded that the colonists promise to dedicate nearly all their time working to generate income for the venture. Under their prior agreement, the Separatists were to have two days each week for themselves. Now, Weston wanted them to spend even more time laboring for the financial backers.[49] The Separatists in Leiden objected, calling the new terms "fitter for thieves and bond-slaves than honest men."[50] The problem was, however, that by the time they learned of the new terms, their agent in London, Robert Cushman, had already agreed to them out of fear that the entire enterprise would otherwise have to be aborted.[51] In correspondence to John Carver, their other agent in London, the Separatists criticized the new terms and criticized their own coreligionist and friend, Cushman, calling him "most unfit to deal with other men."[52] The conflict over how many days labor each week the colonists would devote to the partnership would continue to simmer and remain unresolved until the very moment they were to leave England for America.

A Group of Strangers

Throughout the back and forth between Leiden and London, Thomas Weston had started to assemble a second group of voyagers to help ensure the success of the commercial aspects of the venture. The Saints would call them Strangers. Not only were these Strangers apparently not Separatists; some of them were not even Puritans. In fact, some of them were members in good standing of the Church of England, the supposedly corrupt institution from which the Separatists had fled.[53]

Some historians have casually lumped Hopkins in with the Separatists, arguing that he'd somehow become sympathetic to their views.[54] This would supply a straightforward rationale for Hopkins's voyage, if it were true. But not only is there no evidence that Hopkins migrated into the Separatist camp, all the extant evidence argues against such a proposition. Hopkins lived and worked for seven years as an Anglican clerk, singing and reading the Psalms according to the liturgy of the Church of England. By all contemporaneous accounts, he performed well in his role, winning praise from his fellow congregants. Not long before stepping onto the *Mayflower*, he'd been married in an Anglican ceremony. If Hopkins had any sympathies for nonconformists, it might have been toward the more generic strains of Puritanism, but certainly there is no evidence that he'd drifted into the kind of militant Separatism that drove the Saints first to the Netherlands and then, ultimately, to America. During his life in America, he was never associated with the Saints, but rather remained among those whom William Bradford labeled as Strangers.[55]

The only background the Strangers shared with the Saints, and one which would play a pivotal role in the colony's success, was that none of them were true English aristocrats. Coming from a highly stratified society where rank alone bestowed privileges beyond the reach of the majority, a loathing of the social stagnancy that an aristocracy encouraged likely drove many of the Strangers to sign on to the colonial mission. Driven by the hope of economic freedom as much as the Saints were driven by the hope of religious freedom, the Strangers risked all for the chance of a fresh start in North America.

The Lure of the New World

Given his past experience traveling to and settling in America, why did Stephen Hopkins decide to return to the wilderness that he'd fled only a few years before? He'd encountered grievous danger, hardship, and misery during his first foray. Why would he undertake such risks again, this time with his entire family? He'd married Elizabeth only two years earlier, and together they'd recently welcomed their first child into the world. Their daughter, Damaris, would have been less than two years old. His eldest child, Elizabeth, would have been only sixteen, although she might have died by this point, for it is not believed that she sailed on the *Mayflower*. Constance was fourteen; Giles was thirteen. And on top of that, Hopkins's wife was pregnant.[56]

Stephen Hopkins had left England in 1609 as a poor man struggling in the lower class, a servant. When he'd returned to England in 1616, his fortunes were changing, and by 1620 he'd joined the class of men known as masters, one of only a handful of the *Mayflower* passengers affluent enough to bring along servants of their own.[57] Thus, it would seem that the hope of financial windfall would not have been a determinative factor when he and Elizabeth considered joining the venture.

Whatever the reason, it must have been fairly substantial, considering the unsavory obstacles before them. The sea itself was a dangerous place, as Hopkins could himself have attested. Indeed, less than a year before the *Mayflower*'s voyage, catastrophe had fallen upon a separate attempt to start a new colony in Virginia, when disease ravaged a ship carrying 180 English settlers, leaving only 50 survivors.[58]

And the peril didn't end with the journey. America, too, was a dangerous place, occupied by a strong people who might not willingly share its resources. Death was no stranger to the men and women of seventeenth-century London, but surely its likelihood was greater for a Londoner living in North America. Hopkins's back and his hands would have reminded him of the pain of working unfamiliar soil, of all the effort needed to even clear a field for tilling: felling trees, digging out roots by hand, clearing out rocks and stones. Only then could come the equally hard work of hoeing straight lines in the dirt, of planting, fertilizing, keeping the vermin and birds away, clearing the weeds, and praying for rain. All with no village marketplace to replenish supplies if a harvest failed. Lack of opportunities or resources might have persuaded many of the nonreligionists to join the expedition to Plymouth, but why would someone like Hopkins, who was financially well off?

A couple possible explanations present themselves. First, despite the hardships he'd endured, perhaps Hopkins was hungry to return. His New World adventure had been life changing. Though he'd have remembered the dangers, pains, and discomforts, the intervening years might have softened the memories and encased them in a veneer of nostalgia. The crowds and bustle of London might have stirred a longing to return to the endless forests of North American coastal plains where a simpler, if more demanding, life awaited. To such wistful thoughts might also have been added the singular memories of his contact with Indians. Whether because of his prolonged interactions with such a figure as Pocahontas or because of his time traveling the countryside during colonial excursions, Hopkins had learned a great deal about the land's native people. His exposure seemed to have influenced him deeply.

Alternatively, perhaps Hopkins was convinced to return by Thomas Weston or other members of the Merchant Adventurers, who specifically sought him for his knowledge and experience. After all, he'd spent more time in Virginia than even the acclaimed John Smith, who left Jamestown in 1609 after little more than two years. Though Smith never returned to Jamestown, he did return to the continent in 1614, this time cruising the northern seaboard, where he charted and mapped what is now Massachusetts and Maine, an area he called "New England." His map was the most detailed of that region yet produced, and the names he gave to many geographical features, such as the Charles River and Cape Ann, survive to this day. There was little doubt that, at the time, he was considered a leading English authority on North America. Indeed, many credit Smith as the primary reason that Jamestown survived its early trials and did not quickly disappear from history like the lost colony of Roanoke.

When the Saints began planning to move to America, they'd sought to convince the seasoned adventurer to accompany them. Ultimately, the Separatists and Smith could not agree on financial terms, and it appears that wariness played a role in the Saints' frugal negotiation stance, for they worried that Smith might take advantage of the imbalance of experience. Because of Smith's knowledge, they would be captive to his decisions. He had a firm personality and could therefore become a dominant force amongst them. His worldliness might therefore threaten the integrity of what they planned as a religious enclave.

When the Saints passed on Smith, the expedition was without any real New World experience among the would-be settlers. Although a few of the sailors who ultimately piloted the Pilgrims had previously visited America, none of those who intended to stay had been before.[59] Perhaps this critical

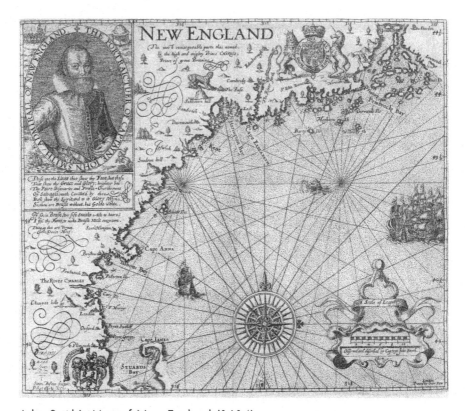

John Smith's Map of New England (1614).
Courtesy of the John Carter Brown Library at Brown University

knowledge deficit prompted the Merchant Adventurers to seek out veterans from the country's colonizing efforts in Jamestown.

Those who'd risked their lives, their capital, or their reputation on England's ventures in the New World moved in overlapping social circles in London. For example, minister and poet John Donne had been interested in Virginia since 1607, when the first Jamestown expedition set sail. Indeed, Donne may have even considered joining the 1609 resupply expedition that included the *Sea Venture*, and he remained a colonial enthusiast for many years. Donne counted among his close friends many principals in the London Company and later himself became an honorary member.[60]

Another friend, of course, was William Strachey, Hopkins's *Sea Venture* shipmate.[61] Together with other mutual friends, Donne was a member of an informal London club that patronized the Mermaid Tavern in Cheapside off

Bread Street, meeting once a month or so to drink and share stories and debate.[62] William Shakespeare is reported to have frequented the Mermaid.[63] Strachey's friend, Ben Jonson, was a member.

So, too, was Samuel Purchas, an Anglican minister like Donne and also a fervent supporter of England's colonial endeavors who assembled and published a massive volume that collected hundreds of descriptions from those who'd explored all corners of the world. Purchas met with Pocahontas and John Rolfe when they returned from Jamestown and obtained a monograph from Rolfe about Virginia for his extensive book.[64] Purchas also obtained Strachey's report about the *Sea Venture*'s shipwreck on Bermuda that contained Hopkins's harrowing deliverance from execution.[65]

Yet another Anglican priest supporting England's American colonies was William Crashaw, who in 1610 preached a sermon to Lord De La Warr before he sailed to Jamestown on a special relief mission after the *Sea Venture* had gone missing. In 1618 Crashaw became vicar at St. Mary's, Whitechapel, the London church where Hopkins married Elizabeth Fisher only a few months before, and which they were presumably still attending.[66] In Crashaw Hopkins might have seen an agreeable acquaintance, for Crashaw had become very familiar with the *Sea Venture*'s wreck on Bermuda and the eventual experiences of its passengers at Jamestown, even writing extensively about them in a dedication that was published in 1613 alongside an account of a Virginia colonist.[67] And though in his preaching Crashaw called the Native Americans "savages" and pressed for their conversion to Christianity, he also recognized their humanity, admonishing would-be colonists against mistreating the native populace:

> We will take nothing . . . by power nor pillage, by craft nor violence, neither goods, lands nor liberty, much less life (as some of other Christian nations have done to the dishonor of religion). We will offer them no wrong, but rather defend them from it.[68]

He saw the natives of Virginia as brothers to the English, "for the same God made them as well as us, of as good matter as he made us, gave them as perfect and good souls and bodies as to us," a view that would have likely resonated deeply with Hopkins.[69]

If Thomas Weston and his association of Merchant Adventurers were looking for someone with New World experience to join the Separatists' expedition, they would have turned to this network of Virginia colonists and supporters. Through contacts like William Strachey and the Whitechapel minister Crashaw, they might have easily heard of Stephen Hopkins. Whether prompted by nostalgia or by the urging of the financial backers of the Separatists' venture to North America, Hopkins ultimately yielded to a second call for adventure. Virginia and its inhabitants seemed to have left a great impression upon him. Only a powerful attraction could have moved Stephen Hopkins to make the momentous decision to give up his life in London and convince his wife and children to join him on another dangerous journey across the sea. His interest in the New World and its inhabitants would guide him throughout the remainder of his life.

A Lack of Experience

Hopkins probably realized fairly quickly after signing on that this expedition was not well organized. On his previous journey he'd traveled as part of an armada, a large convoy of ships each filled with supplies and craftsmen and soldiers and aristocrats who'd had a plan. The present venture was coming together in a more piecemeal fashion.

Though the Saints had experienced the rigors of immigration, moving to the Netherlands from England was of a different nature than moving to America. Up to this point, the difficulties were more inconvenience than peril, as when William Bradford upon his first landing in Amsterdam was brought before a magistrate to explain why he'd come from England before being welcomed and directed toward his fellow Saints.[70] The enterprise did not even have a proper physician, although one Separatist taught himself the rudiments of seventeenth-century medicine.[71] They did bring someone with military experience: Captain Myles Standish, who'd served with the English forces sent to fight for the Dutch Republic against Spain.[72] Though possibly not a Separatist himself, he'd become acquainted with the group during his time in the Netherlands, which paved the way to his inclusion in the expedition to America.[73] But while soldiering gave Standish a background in certain important aspects of colonization, such as setting defenses and mobilizing a militia, the experience was limited to northwestern Europe, a relative hive of urban centers located in a low and flat country of grasslands full of dikes and canals and windmills—a place quite unlike the eastern seaboard of America.

Fishing the coastal waters was to be one of the primary financial objectives of the colony, as well as an essential source for sustenance, yet apparently none of the colonists had any saltwater fishing experience.[74] Rather, they were laborers, merchants, farmers, and tradesmen. Among the Saints were two tailors, three weavers, two printers, a businessman, a blacksmith, a hat maker, two merchants, a yeoman farmer, and a woodcutter. Most of the artisans had learned their crafts during their years in the Netherlands. Before that, according to Bradford, they'd been simple people used to a "plain country life, and the innocent trade of husbandry," working fields that had been under plow for centuries.[75]

Less is known about the backgrounds of the Strangers, but numbered among them were at least a weaver, a shoemaker, a carpenter, and three merchants. A few of the more affluent among both the Saints and the Strangers— like Hopkins—brought servants. There was also a third group of people: five hired men, who had contracted to remain with the colony for a year before being released either to return to England or to stay on.

As a group, the Pilgrims did possess some critical characteristics that helped them succeed. First and foremost, they each had that particular form of courage that it takes to begin a dangerous journey into the unknown. Fear of death was real, and it started the moment the ship left the dock. Even a brisk trip westward from England to America took nearly two months. A trip starting in the late summer or early fall, as the *Mayflower*'s voyage had, meant sailing across the kind of warm waters that nursed tropical depressions and strong winds, systems that sometimes would deepen and grow into tempests like the hurricane that overwhelmed the *Sea Venture*. Even mild storms could challenge a seventeenth-century sailing ship, pushing her off course, delaying the transit while passengers and crew consumed dwindling supplies of food and fresh water. All the while, the wind would work on the ship, pulling at its seams while the ocean fought to gain entry, battering the hull. Calm winds, which might be prayed for during a storm, could equally delay the voyage. Becalmed ships could twist without direction for days on end, ringed by the accumulated waste from the hundred or so passengers. Delays, either from storms or calms, only increased the perils of shipborne diseases such as scurvy and dysentery.

Most who would eventually depart on the *Mayflower* probably would have heard about the disasters that'd beset the colony at Jamestown. They'd have known about the whispered accounts of the Starving Time during the winter of 1609–1610, when hundreds of the settlement's colonists starved to death. America did not promise paradise, and the would-be settlers likely knew it. The Saints and Strangers nevertheless overcame their own anxieties, or ignored them altogether, and pressed ahead.

Disarray and Delay Before Departure

Because the Strangers recruited by Thomas Weston were in London and the Saints were across the English Channel in Leiden, it was agreed that the two groups would meet in July 1620 at the port of Southampton on the southern coast of England. As the date for departure from Leiden approached, the Separatists decided who among them should attempt the arduous voyage, with the understanding that the rest might try to join them once a colony was established.

At the time, the congregation included about three hundred people. A little less than half of them agreed to the trip. By May, they'd pooled their money and bought and outfitted a small ship called the *Speedwell*. By June, Weston procured the services of the *Mayflower*, a vessel of 180 tons—about three times as large as the *Speedwell*. Both were merchant ships designed to carry a wide variety of trade goods, such as wool or broadcloth or even barrels of salted fish. For this particular voyage, however, the cargo would be passengers, who during the transatlantic voyage would occupy the space where freight was typically stored, with little or no modification. While the *Mayflower* was to be used only for transportation, depositing the colonists and their supplies and then returning to England, the smaller *Speedwell* was to stay with the settlers, who intended to use it for fishing and coastal trading excursions.[76] Toward that purpose, the *Speedwell*'s captain and crew had contracted with the colonists to stay on for a year.

In mid-July 1620, Stephen Hopkins and his family and two servants boarded the *Mayflower* in London with the other Strangers. They sailed down the Thames into the English Channel and followed the coast toward Southampton, where they would take on their final supplies for the transatlantic voyage. The Saints gathered in the Netherlands aboard the *Speedwell* and made tearful good-byes to loved ones who were to remain behind. On July 22 the *Speedwell* left the Netherlands for its rendezvous with the *Mayflower*. At Southampton, the two groups met for the first time.[77]

The final days were chaotic. Weston had hired a man named Christopher Martin to work with Carver and Cushman to purchase the equipment and supplies necessary to outfit the expedition.[78] Martin was haughty and willful and refused to coordinate with the two agents of the Separatists, leading to bickering and confusion.[79] Anxiety deepened among both the colonists and their financial backers at the approach of the departure date, which would be the point of no return. Bradford wrote, "Some of those who should have gone in England, fell off and would not go; other merchants and friends that had offered to adventure their money withdrew, and pretended many excuses."[80] Apprehension even infected the crew of the *Speedwell*, who started having second thoughts about their agreement to stay on for a year after the voyage to the New World.

Thomas Weston traveled from London to Southampton to meet with the Separatists about the unresolved financial terms. Though Cushman, as their agent, had earlier acquiesced to Weston's demand that the colonists devote all their time to fishing or trading or other income-producing activity for the partnership, the Saints decisively rejected it. They insisted that they be allowed some time for themselves in order to farm the land and to maintain their settlement. Weston flew into a rage and immediately deserted them, telling the colonists that "they must then look to stand on their own legs." This left them without sufficient funds to pay the suppliers who were loading the ships for the voyage, forcing the Pilgrims to sell some of their invaluable provisions in order to leave the English port.[81] As Bradford wrote at the time,

> We are in such a strait at present, as we are forced to sell away £60 worth of our provisions to clear the Haven, and withal put ourselves upon great extremities, scarce having any butter, no oil, not a sole to mend a shoe, nor every man a sword to his side, wanting many muskets, much armor, etc.[82]

The two ships left Southampton on August 5, 1620. Once at sea, the *Speedwell* began leaking. The condition was so severe that both ships turned back, landing at Dartmouth, which lay on the English coast about a hundred miles southwest of Southampton. After repairs, and a delay because of unfavorable winds during which more of their supply of provisions were consumed, the ships set sail once again. They sailed about three hundred miles before

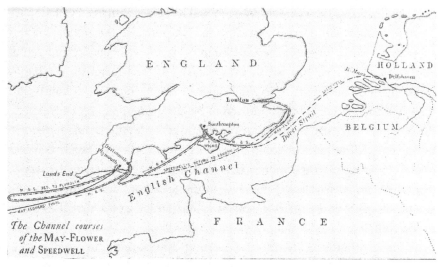

"The Channel Courses of the May-Flower and Speedwell," from Azel Ames, *The May-Flower and Her Log* (Boston and New York: Houghton, Mifflin and Company, 1907); image digitally adapted. *Courtesy of the University of Toronto*

the *Speedwell* once more started leaking. Again, they returned to England, this time touching at the port of Plymouth, which was located about thirty miles west of Dartmouth. In Plymouth, they decided to abandon the *Speedwell*. At the time, the Pilgrims wrote the leaking vessel off to misfortune, but they later realized that the damage had been intentional, the ship compromised because the sailors were afraid of starving to death on the foreboding shores of America.[83]

The loss of the *Speedwell* meant leaving behind many of the Separatists, for not all her passengers could fit into the *Mayflower*.[84] William Bradford recorded how they decided who would remain in England:

> Those that went back were for the most part such as were willing so to do, either out of some discontent or fear they conceived of the ill success of the voyage, seeing so many crosses befall and the year['s] time so far spent; but others [were left behind because] of their own weakness and charge of many young children, [or] were thought least useful and most unfit to bear the brunt of this hard adventure.[85]

Perhaps because of the fallout over the bungled negotiations with Weston, Robert Cushman was one of those left behind.[86] The loss of the *Speedwell* exacted a significant toll on the project. Twenty of the Saints, over 35 percent of the total number of parishioners who'd agreed to the venture, were forced to quit before they'd even escaped the coastal waters of England.[87] On September 6, 1620, two months after they'd intended to depart, the *Mayflower*, crammed with people and provisions, finally began its voyage to America. Looking back on the turmoil years later, William Bradford would lament over their early difficulties and give thanks that "God brought them along notwithstanding all of their weaknesses and infirmities."[88]

The *Mayflower*'s final company was composed of families with children, married couples, and single men and women. Together, not including the crew, there were fifty men, nineteen women, nineteen children, and fourteen juveniles who'd not yet reached the age of majority. Only 41 of the 102 passengers aboard were Separatists.[89] Eighteen of the settlers were servants, who were split between five of the Saints' families and four of the families of the Strangers, including the two young men who traveled with the family of Stephen Hopkins. The delays because of the *Speedwell* caused about four weeks of food supplies to be consumed before the journey began, leading to speculation by some on board that they wouldn't have a month's worth of food when they finally got to America.[90]

Before the *Speedwell* had been left behind in Plymouth, a "governor" had been chosen for each ship, primarily to organize the passengers and see to it that provisions such as food and fresh water were equitably distributed during the voyage. Perhaps because of his role as purchasing agent, Christopher Martin had been selected to be governor on the *Mayflower* and remained in that position after the ship finally left for America.

Martin's relationship with the Separatists was strained from the start. They'd suspected some irregularities from his handling of supply purchases in Southampton and confronted him. Martin deflected, refusing to give them an accounting of the money he spent on behalf of the expedition. When pressed, he cried out, accusing the Separatists, as reported in William Bradford's account, of "unthankfulness for his pains and care" and scorning them for their suspicions. Martin didn't limit his abrasiveness to financial matters. He insulted everyone, as if they weren't "good enough to wipe his shoes." Any complaints were considered mutinous. Even the sailors were so "offended at his ignorant boldness" that they threatened to harm him when they weren't mocking him.[91]

In addition to the abuse from Martin, the colonists also had to contend with the contempt with which the *Mayflower*'s fifty crewmen held them.[92] Shortly after leaving Plymouth, many of the settlers began suffering from seasickness. One of the sailors, a young and boastful man, openly ridiculed the passengers, "cursing them daily" and telling them that he hoped to toss half of them overboard before the ship reached America.[93] Hopkins had seen this type of antipathy between sailor and landsman again and again during his previous excursion to North America, where, as William Strachey observed, the sailors' "villainy and mischief" had been so severe that it was responsible for "the death and starving of many a worthy spirit."[94] Some kind of justice ultimately revealed itself on the *Mayflower*, however, when the "profane" sailor became ill with a "grievous disease" and died. He was the first casualty of the voyage, and the Separatists might have taken it as a sign of divine providence when, according to William Bradford, he "was himself the first that was thrown overboard."[95]

For many days, the *Mayflower* enjoyed fair winds, and the company tried to endure the trials of seventeenth-century ocean travel as best they could.[96] The ship was a typical merchant vessel of her day.[97] Three masts, each hung with spars and sails and knitted to the ship by a spider's web of rigging, towered above her main deck.[98] She was about a hundred feet in length and was rated at 180 tons, which meant that she could accommodate 180 casks of cargo. The deepest portion of her hull was called the hold and in it were stored the ship's ballast and stores and supplies.[99] The level immediately above the hold was an area called the 'tween decks, which usually accommodated cargo and crew. This is where the *Mayflower*'s passengers lived and slept during their journey, sharing the space with the crew and the ship's magazine, where gunpowder was stored, as well as its armory.[100] With 150 people on board and the necessary stores for a voyage that usually took months, there was little comfort.[101] The ship's size allowed for about a four foot by four foot area for each passenger.

Sheets were likely suspended in the 'tween decks area to create little niches of privacy for families. The passengers and crew probably ate where they slept, sitting either on the deck or on a chest. Food was closely rationed, especially given the already-depleted state of food supplies on the *Mayflower*. Within a week or so at sea, the practice of basic cleanliness would have become difficult for most people. Fresh water was precious and used only for drinking. None was available for washing. In fair weather, ports lining the sides of the 'tween decks area and hatches leading to the main deck allowed in some fresh air, but still the lower decks were close and stuffy. Soon the atmosphere stank of filthy travelers and garlic, which many chewed to help mask the stench of close quarters. Over time, food inevitably started turning bad and added to the smell, some provisions becoming so corrupt and rotten that they were fit for only rats, which thrived in the hold.[102]

As food turned rancid, it often became the source of epidemics of dysentery, which not only added to the overall squalor of living conditions but also, of course, could claim lives. The supplies of water, too, could become contaminated over time as it sat in stale wooden casks, so tainted, in fact, that people couldn't endure the scent of it, let alone drink it. Ships, therefore, also carried beer, which better resisted the microbes that turned water sour. Trapped together in the crowded, stinking conditions, the lower decks often also became ripe for propagating contagious diseases such as yellow fever, smallpox, and the bubonic plague, which could bring a mortality rate of more than 90 percent.[103]

Telling Stories

Even when all went well—when disease was kept at bay and favorable winds kept the ship moving toward its goal—passengers of that era had to deal with the slow pace of travel. A sailing ship of that era might travel two and half miles per hour, turning the three-thousand-mile Atlantic crossing into an affair that lasted several months. The sailors, of course, would be occupied with the maintenance of the ship and its progress. For the passengers, however, each long day was filled with ceaseless monotony. Parents like Stephen and Elizabeth Hopkins had to deal not only with their own weariness, but also manage their young children, who without room to roam might become unbearable to their neighbors. Frustration, boredom, and seasickness remained tireless companions of the passengers during the slow passage.[104]

Gossip and games and storytelling would likely have been the most common diversions available to passengers. On the *Mayflower*, Stranger and Saint alike would probably have started to share information about themselves as they started the adventure of their lives together. Of course, word probably spread quickly that this was not Stephen Hopkins's first time to North America.

He likely would have been encouraged by his shipmates to share the tales of some of his prior experiences.[105]

William Brewster of the Separatists carried with him the most extensive library of those aboard the *Mayflower*. Among his books was a copy of Captain John Smith's *A Description of New England*, which had been published in 1616 and offered a glimpse of the northern part of America's coastline, describing wildlife and plants and geographic features such as rivers and bays.[106] Aside from this source, however, the would-be colonists possessed an alarming lack of information about the place where they planned to live for the foreseeable future. The only certainty they understood was that if they somehow survived the dangerous voyage, the only people there to greet them would be potentially hostile natives.[107] Hopkins and his stories about Bermuda and Jamestown and how a lowly villager came to be part of a national expedition to the New World would likely have been a chief form of diversion during the voyage, both educational as well as entertaining.

Storms and the Giant Screw

After a time, the fair weather yielded to a more typical pattern for September in the North Atlantic, when westerly gales begin to howl.[108] The ship was trying to sail *to* the west, but now the seasonal winds were blowing *from* the west. This forced the *Mayflower* to beat to windward, which required a series of long diagonal legs that took her slowly westward. With stronger winds, the seas ran higher, putting more stress on the ship as it shouldered its way through the swells. The taut rigging hummed, and the wooden ship groaned and creaked. With seas coming over the ship's sides, the ports were closed. The living area turned dark, and the smells of 150 unwashed people and rotting food intensified.

The forces of wind and sea were strong enough to bend the *Mayflower*'s stout planks, and her upper works started leaking. Water also came up and over the side as waves buffeted the ship and sloshed around on the main deck, which was the roof over the heads of the passengers in the 'tween decks living area. As the ship heaved and banged, the seams in the deck opened, and water poured onto the heads of the colonists. At one point, a strong gust of wind or an odd wave shook the *Mayflower* so fiercely that one of the huge beams supporting the main deck bowed and split under the pressure. Between leaking water and the broken beam, the passengers rightfully became alarmed that the vessel might not be able to continue. Even the sailors started muttering that the *Mayflower* might no longer be seaworthy.[109] The problem was that no one knew exactly what to do. They were in the middle of the ocean. England was weeks behind them. America was weeks ahead of them. Which way was the best course?

The opinion of the mariners was split. They'd lose their wages if they didn't complete the journey. "On the other hand," recorded William Bradford, "they were loath to hazard their lives too desperately."[110] The captain of the *Mayflower*—a position known at the time as a ship's master—was Christopher Jones. He was also a part owner of the vessel. In 1620 he was about fifty years old and had been at sea much of his life. He'd been master of the *Mayflower* for over a decade, sailing her on various trading voyages.[111] He'd handled her in rough weather before and knew what she could take. Jones inspected the damaged beam with his carpenter and comforted the passengers and doubting sailors by declaring that the *Mayflower* was strong and sound under the waterline.[112] She was still seaworthy. She wouldn't fail them. As for the cracked beam, an ingenious solution was at hand.

The Separatists had brought what Bradford described as a "great iron screw" with them from Leiden. Using the screw and extra posts that the ship carried, the ship's carpenter forced the broken beam back into its correct position and knocked a more permanent support post into place directly under the spot where the beam had failed. Once the timber was back into place, the sailors recaulked the seams between the planking of the main deck and the upper works in an effort to minimize leakage into the passenger compartment. With the continuous working of the ship, however, the seams eventually opened back up, allowing water into the living area, but according to Bradford, Master Jones assured everyone that "there would otherwise be no great danger if they didn't overpress [the ship] with sails. So they committed themselves to the will of God and resolved to proceed."[113]

Storms continued to batter the *Mayflower*. Increasing winds transferred more stress to the ship through its sails, risking the very "overpress" of sail that worried Jones. One by one, he ordered the sails to be taken down to decrease the strain. As the canvas came down, however, a new dilemma presented itself. The force of the wind on the sails is what gave the *Mayflower* the ability to steer. Without steerage, the ship risked becoming a victim of random turns, listing and rolling to the movement of the seas, just like when a ship became becalmed. The difference between a calm and a storm, though, was significant, for the higher, more powerful waves in a gale could easily swamp a ship without steerage or, worse, could roll the ship over.[114]

The winds grew so fierce and the seas so high that if the crew unfurled even one knot of sail, the forces at play might rip out the ship's masts or yards and severely compromise the *Mayflower*'s seaworthiness. Faced with this increased danger, Jones decided upon an extraordinary measure. He ordered that all the sails be furled and lashed tightly to the yards. Everything on deck was secured, and the hatches were covered. Jones then turned the ship *into* the wind, a maneuver known as lying ahull. Rising some twelve or so feet above the main deck in the aft-most part of the ship was the master's cabin and the poop deck.[115] With the ship facing into the wind, the superstructure at the back of the ship would act as a kind of wooden sail, helping maintain some modest amount of steerage that allowed the helmsman to keep the ship's beam from being hit broadside by the piling waves.[116]

Hunkered down, the *Mayflower* and its passengers rode out several storms over the course of many days.[117] During these intense periods, Hopkins might have tried to reassure his fellow travelers, whose faces were likely etched with stress. He might have told them not to despair. While the winds outside might seem severe, they were nothing compared to the tempest that had tossed and smashed the *Sea Venture* for days on end. The water leaking now from the deck above their heads was but a trickle compared to the floods that had swallowed the ship he'd taken to North America eleven years before. They'd make it through.

Land Ho

During one of these storms, an indentured servant of one of the Separatists ventured onto the deck of the lurching ship. A steep wave violently pitched the vessel, and John Howland, who was about eighteen years old at the time, was thrown overboard. As he fell, he spotted a rope dangling over the side. He grabbed hold of it as he plunged into the cold Atlantic. The scudding ship swept past him. The rope played out and when it tightened, Howland was dragged deep under the ocean's surface. He was strong, and surging adrenaline would likely have made him stronger. He clung to his lifeline. While he was being towed underwater, time doubtlessly seemed to stand still. He eventually popped up, likely gasping for breath. Struggling to keep air in his lungs, he skimmed and skipped behind the ship in the whitewater that churned on the turbulent sea. One of the sailors happened to spot him. He and his mates hauled in the rope. Using a long boat hook, they were able to lift him back onto the vessel, where he coughed and threw up salt water. But he was alive and, in fact, would go on to outlive all but two of the other male passengers of the *Mayflower*.[118]

As the leaky ship approached the end of its voyage, Elizabeth Hopkins, one of three pregnant women who'd boarded the *Mayflower*, gave birth to a son. Perhaps in honor of his friend John Rolfe, who'd given the name of the island on which they'd been castaways to his daughter born there, Stephen and his wife named their child Oceanus.[119]

The joy of the birth was soon tempered, however, by the death of a Separatist servant. On November 6, William Button, who'd recently fallen ill, died, likely from scurvy.[120] The disease, which results from a lack of vitamin C, could surface after only a month of a diet without sufficient vegetables or fruit. The Pilgrims had then been at sea for over two months.

When Button died, the passengers and crew didn't realize how close they were to shore. Three days later, on the morning of November 9, 1620, after sixty-five days at sea, the lookout hailed the deck.[121] He'd spotted land.

4 | THE MAYFLOWER COMPACT

> No more dams I'll make for fish,
> Nor fetch in firing
> At requiring,
> Nor scrape trencher, nor wash dish.
> 'Ban, 'Ban, Ca-caliban
> Has a new master. Get a new man.
> Freedom, high-day, high-day, freedom,
> freedom, high-day, freedom!
>
> —*The Tempest*, act 2, scene 2

BECAUSE OF THE ADVERSE WINDS AND STORMS, the *Mayflower* had managed an average speed of just two miles an hour during its crossing of the Atlantic Ocean. The ship's master, Christopher Jones, couldn't yet identify their landfall, but he knew that they were far to the north of his passengers' destination, which was the mouth of the Hudson River, a place that lay within the scope of the grant they'd obtained from the London Company but not too close to the Anglican influence of the other English settlements in the area of the Chesapeake Bay.[1] Jones ordered the crew to close with the land, so he could reconnoiter.

Everyone who was able likely climbed to the main deck and watched in the chill November air as the *Mayflower* approached the foreign continent. At first the details were imperceptible, but slowly the cap of green above brown dunes of the coastline resolved into pine trees and shrubby undergrowth. The head of the dunes were tangled with tufts of beach grass. At their foot, a beach swept down into the Atlantic, where it met a line of white breakers.

Master Jones's suspicions based upon his latest latitude reading were confirmed. What they were nearing was Cape Cod, a thin headland of high dunes of sand topped with rolling green hills.[2] Illuminated by the rising sun, the sand probably glistened like gold. The peninsula jutted over sixty miles into the sea from the mainland, and its "back side," which faced the ocean, stretched some thirty miles north and south.[3] Writer and naturalist Henry David Thoreau spent time on the barrier beach in the mid-nineteenth century, describing it using the familiar imagery of an arm:

> Cape Cod is the bared and bended arm of Massachusetts: the shoulder is at Buzzard's Bay; the elbow, or crazy-bone, at Cape Mallebarre [i.e., Monomoy Island south of Chatham]; the wrist at Truro; and the sandy fist at Provincetown,—behind which the State stands on her guard, with her back to the Green Mountains, and her feet planted on the floor of the ocean, like an athlete protecting her Bay,—boxing with northeast storms, and, ever and anon, heaving up her Atlantic adversary from the lap of earth,—ready to thrust forward her other fist, which keeps guard the while upon her breast at Cape Ann.[4]

Passengers and sailors alike probably murmured their thanks to unseen benefactors. The dangers of the North Atlantic were at last behind them. The perpetual damp of the hold, with its close and noxious air, likely seemed already a little less oppressive. It was morning. And there was land.

In 1602 English explorer Bartholomew Gosnold gave the headland the name it retains today, and his journey eighteen years before, as well subsequent European visits, affected the area's inhabitants so deeply that the Pilgrims would feel the effects shortly after they anchored.[5] But the ship didn't immediately stop, for its passengers and Christopher Jones first needed to contend with opposing demands. On the one hand, there was pressure to land immediately. Disease was starting to appear on board the *Mayflower*. William Button had been the only passenger to die, but others were also showing signs of scurvy. Many were too weak to leave their beds. Furthermore, food supplies and drinking water were getting perilously low, the combined effects of the twice-interrupted start from England as well as the delays brought on by the contrary Atlantic gales. They'd run out of firewood and were eating cold provisions. Supplies of beer, which was then considered essential to a healthy diet because of the poor quality of drinking water, were also dangerously depleted. They needed to get off the *Mayflower* soon, or more people would die.[6]

On the other hand, Cape Cod, now so tantalizingly close that they could probably smell its sandy loam, was outside the bounds of their grant from King James. The grant—or patent—that the Separatists had acquired from the London Company gave them permission to settle at the mouth of the Hudson River, a location some two hundred nautical miles from Cape Cod. The Cape was outside the very bounds of the London Company's authority, for the king had divided the American coast between the London Company and a second entity called the Plymouth Company. The northernmost part of the London Company's charter ended at the western end of Long Island Sound. Everything farther north, including Cape Cod, fell under the terms of the royal grant to the Plymouth Company. Setting aside—as nearly all Europeans did at the time—the claim that the New World belonged to the Native Americans who'd lived there for hundreds of generations, the Pilgrims didn't have authority to land here at Cape Cod.

The Pilgrims consulted Jones. The weather was fair. The day promised to be clear, and the wind was coming out of the north, coming from a direction that would propel them southward, toward the Hudson River, and the jurisdiction of their patent. They chose to turn that way.[7] Master Jones probably had no maps or charts of the waters between Cape Cod and the Hudson River, but he likely figured it would be an easy cruise as all they had to do was follow the coastline.[8]

Heading South, Turning Back

The sun climbed higher in the sky, and the back side of Cape Cod slipped by on their right side as the *Mayflower* coasted southwards. After the deep blue of the open Atlantic, the water along the coast was pale green. The tide was with them, for the time being, and the following wind pushed the *Mayflower* along, its prow cutting through the water, sending a curling bow wave trimmed in white beneath the passengers lining the rails. The day was crisp. The trees covering Cape Cod stood out in sharp relief. Unfortunately, the idyllic conditions didn't last long. The tide turned, and the water's surface developed a chop as wind and tide worked at cross purposes.[9] And then it got worse, according to William Bradford:

> After they had sailed that course about half the day, they fell amongst
> dangerous shoals and roaring breakers, and they were so far entangled
> therewith as they conceived themselves in great danger.[10]

The sandbars and shoals off the Atlantic side of Cape Cod were—and still
are—notorious dangers for shipping, a stretch of seashore that has been littered
with so many thousands of wrecks that it has been called a ship's graveyard.[11]

The "dangerous shoals" that Bradford described were likely a particular
perilous section in that area now called the Pollock Rip, which is an ever-
changing maze of sandbars and underwater banks stretching southward fifteen
miles from the elbow of Cape Cod to the tip of the island of Nantucket.[12]
An enormous volume of water constantly shifts back and forth through this
channel from the open Atlantic to the east and Nantucket Sound to the west.
With currents running from the west and deep-ocean swells coming from the
east colliding over a shallow shelf of uneven ocean floor, the Pollock Rip can
produce crashing mountains of water and is one of the most dangerous points
along the New England coastline, accounting for half the shipwrecks along the
North American coast.[13]

The piling, tumbling seas of the Pollock Rip started buffeting the *Mayflower*, heaving it one way and then another. The bucking motion no doubt sent
some of the bystanders below. Even with their two months of seasoning, the
abrupt kicking and tossing would have dampened even the heartiest souls. As
the wind was inevitably forcing the *Mayflower* deeper into the frothing danger,
Master Jones likely had his sailors ready the anchor, trusting the heavy iron
to catch on the ocean's floor and arrest their movement. The sailors would
have known that they hovered on the brink of crisis. Someone like Stephen
Hopkins, a veteran of hurricanes and sinking ships, might have read the fear
in the voices and furtive glances between Jones and his men. If so, he'd probably have sensed the gravity of the situation and would have helped usher the
rest of the passengers off the main deck, where the sailors needed space to
respond to Jones's commands.

As the day turned to dusk, the northerly wind forcing the ship into the
threat began to die and gave way to a breeze from the south. Christopher Jones
quickly considered his options. The *Mayflower*'s current course to the Hudson
River appeared to be blocked by the deadly shoals. It would take much more
time to look for an alternative route, time that they did not have because of

escalating health concerns and low provisions. With the wind now blowing against that purpose, Jones made a decision, one that would carry historic consequences, both for the Pilgrims and perhaps even for western civilization. He ordered the ship about. Their path took them back up the forearm of Cape Cod.

The next morning, November 11, they rounded its northern tip and dropped anchor in present-day Provincetown Harbor, which William Bradford described as "a good harbor and pleasant bay circled round . . . about four miles over from land to land."[14]

A Dispute About Authority

Cape Cod remained a dilemma for the Pilgrims, as it fell outside the scope of their patent. If they established a settlement here, it would be unlawful in the eyes of the Crown, and that fact threatened the entire enterprise. The patent was critical not only to the settlement's legitimacy, but also to the Pilgrims' administration of daily affairs. Before they'd departed from England, the colonists had installed a provisional governance structure for the voyage. The Separatists' pastor of their Leiden congregation, John Robinson, who remained behind in the Netherlands, described the situation in a letter that had been read to the assembled company shortly before the *Mayflower* and *Speedwell* first left Southampton:

> Lastly, whereas **you are become a body politic, using amongst yourselves civil governments**, and are not furnished with any persons of special eminence above the rest to be chosen by you into office of government, let your wisdom and godliness appear, not only in choosing such persons as do entirely love and will promote the common good, but also in yielding unto them all due honor and obedience in their lawful administrations, not beholding in them the ordinariness of their persons, but God's ordinance for your good, not being like the foolish multitude who more honor the gay coat, than either the virtuous mind of the man, or glorious ordinance of the Lord. . . . And this duty you both may the more willingly and out the more conscionably to perform, **because you are at least for the present to have only them for your ordinary governors, which yourselves shall make the choice for that work.**[15]

By virtue of their patent from the London Company, the colonists had become a "body politic," which term at the time was used to describe a corporation.[16] Significantly, only the king could create such a legal entity,[17] and did so directly, for example, when he issued the charter that created the London Company[18] and did so indirectly to patentees authorized by the London Company to settle Virginia.[19]

Under its charter from King James, the London Company retained the power to establish a permanent governance structure for any colony established under its authority but did delegate to its patentees the ability to establish a temporary framework—"at least for the present," in the words of Robinson—through which to regulate themselves.[20] Such an approach conformed to the London Company's longtime practice of selecting the governor and his assistants for colonies, as they had done over the years with Jamestown, installing a succession of governors from afar. Because the Pilgrims' goal, in Bradford's words, was "to live as a distinct body by themselves under the general government of Virginia,"[21] their original plan, either before or immediately after touching at Hudson's River, was to contact the colonial governor of Jamestown Colony,[22] someone who presumably would have then helped organize a more permanent local structure of governance for them.

Before they left England, the Pilgrims had needed to institute some interim management system for the passage across the Atlantic, which is what they did after reading Robinson's letter aloud. According to Bradford,

> Then they ordered and distributed their company for either ship [i.e., the *Mayflower* and the *Speedwell*], as they conceived for the best. And chose a governor and two or three assistants for each ship to order the people by the way, and see to the disposing of provisions, and such like affairs. . . . Which being done, they set sail.[23]

As earlier noted, Christopher Martin was named as governor of the *Mayflower*. Likewise, it appears as though John Carver, one of the two agents the Saints sent from Leiden to London to help organize the expedition, was likely selected to be governor of the *Speedwell*.[24] Bradford's explanation of the ships' governors' rather mundane responsibilities—such as distributing provisions—suggests that those administrations were truly of an interim nature, just as Robinson had related in his letter.

But, of course, the *Speedwell* never made the voyage, the *Mayflower* never called on the administration at Jamestown, and the temporary government established under the now-unusable patent was therefore without effect. Without the imprimatur of the king, their body politic was no more. Some of the Strangers on the *Mayflower* seized upon this fact to claim that the leaders of the expedition—and perhaps Christopher Martin in particular—therefore lacked legitimate authority. Without legitimate authority, the passengers were free to do what they pleased. A controversy broke out, which Bradford described as being marked by "discontented and mutinous speeches."[25] These unnamed Strangers argued

> that when they came ashore, they would use their own liberty, for **none had power to command them** [because] the patent they had being for Virginia, and not for New England, which belonged to another Government [i.e., under the auspices of the Plymouth Company], with which the Virginia Company [i.e., the London Company] had nothing to do.[26]

Tension simmered and threatened to come to a boil unless a solution was found. Before anyone was allowed to go ashore, they needed to settle the matter. They'd invested three years of time and great expense to launch the expedition. They'd just completed a risky transatlantic journey and even more recently escaped the perils of dangerous shoals. Now they had to confront a different type of exigency, albeit one that also threatened the future of the enterprise, for if each were allowed to go his own way, the very purpose of the venture would fall apart.

Any defections would necessarily weaken the group. Their numbers had already been depleted when the *Speedwell* had been forced to abandon the voyage. In all, the colonists at this point numbered 102, but as many were showing signs of sickness, they might lose more during the approaching winter.[27] The 1607 convoy that had created Jamestown had an almost identical number of settlers, and within a few months over half of them had died.[28] Would a similar fate befall the colonists on the *Mayflower*?

Jamestown would have failed in its first year if subsequent supply missions had not quickly been sent. There were no plans to immediately supply the Pilgrims with more settlers and stores. They were on their own, which meant unity was critical. Their meager numbers combined with the threat of disease at the onset of winter meant that their situation allowed for few, if any, mistakes. They would need everyone to lend a hand to tackle the difficult first steps of colonization.

They were starting utterly from scratch. They needed to locate a source of fresh water. They needed to gather food before their supplies ran out. They needed to find a suitable site for settlement. They needed shelter, which meant that they needed to fell hundreds of trees and then shape that raw timber into posts and planking. They needed to frame and enclose homes. They needed to collect thatch for roofing. They needed to build a palisade for protection. They needed to clear fields for planting, which meant that more trees must be cut down. Roots pulled up. Rocks removed. All of this effort would require every able person to contribute. Their very lives depended upon cooperation. Mutiny threatened all of that.

The Solution: A Voluntary Compact

In the end, the potential mutiny was averted by an agreement that later became known as the Mayflower Compact. The two primary sources do not provide much detail of the historic incident.

Mourt's Relation is a firsthand account of the Pilgrims' first year in New England. Written between November 1620 and November 1621, it was published in London in 1622. Although the name of the author or authors did not appear in the publication, scholars believe most of the text was written by William Bradford and Edward Winslow—a Separatist who would later become the colony's primary diplomat and who also would serve several terms as governor—and was based on journals the men kept at the time the events unfolded.[29] For the creation of the Mayflower Compact, *Mourt's Relation* simply summarized how the Saints and Strangers came together to settle the dispute:

> This day before we came to harbor, observing some not well affected to unity and concord, but gave some appearance of faction, it was thought good there should be an association and agreement, that **we should combine together in one body**, and to submit to such government and governors, as we should by common consent agree to make and choose.[30]

The other primary source, *Of Plymouth Plantation*, likewise provides few specifics. In it, William Bradford only noted that the compact helped put down the nascent mutiny and also would potentially act, so the Pilgrims hoped, as a kind of replacement for their now-defective patent from the London Company:

> I shall a little turn back and begin with a **combination** made by them before they came ashore, being the first foundation of their government in this place, [which was] **occasioned partly by** the discontented and mutinous speeches that some of the [S]trangers amongst them let fall. . . . **And partly** that such act by them done (this, their condition [of not having proper authority from either the London Company or Plymouth Company] considered) might be as firm as any patent, and in some respects, more sure.[31]

The agreement was drafted and signed aboard the *Mayflower* that morning of November 11, 1620.

Concise and Singular

Born of necessity, the "combination" was brief, but remarkable. From a culture dominated by an absolute monarchy, where the origin of one's birth determined much, if not all, of one's prospects in life, these few people, beyond the edge of the only world they knew, crafted an agreement that gave everyone—every male of majority age, that is—a voice in how they would be governed. William Bradford recorded the text:

> In the name of God, Amen. We whose names are underwritten, the loyal subjects of our dread sovereign Lord, King James, by the grace of God, of Great Britain, France, and Ireland King, Defender of the Faith, etc.
>
> Having undertaken, for the glory of God, and advancement of the Christian faith, and honor of our King and Country, a voyage to plant the first colony in the northern parts of Virginia, do by these presents solemnly and mutually, in the presence of God, and one of another, covenant and combine ourselves together into a civil body politic, for our better ordering and preservation and furtherance of the ends aforesaid; and by virtue hereof to enact, constitute, and frame

·5·4·

fcte by them done (this their condition considered) might
be as firme as any patent; and in some respects more sure.
The forme was as followeth.

In ý name of god Amen. We whose names are underwriten.
the loyall subjects of our dread soueraigne Lord king James
by ý grace of god, of great Britaine, franc, & Ireland king,
defendor of ý faith, &c

Haueing undertaken, for ý glorie of god, and aduancemente
of ý christian faith, and honour of our king & countrie, a voyage to
plant ý first colonie in ý Northerne parts of Virginia. Doe
by these presents solemnly & mutualy in ý presence of god, and
one of another, couenant, & combine our selues togeather into a
ciuill body politick, for ý our better ordering, & preseruation & furtherance of ý ends aforesaid; and by vertue hearof to enacte,
constitute, and frame shuch just & equall lawes, ordinances,
Acts, constitutions, & offices, from time to time, as shall be thought
most meete & conuenient for ý generall good of ý Colonie: unto
which we promise all due submission and obedience. In witnes
wherof we haue here under subscribed our names at Cap-
Codd ý ·11· of Nouember, in ý year of ý raigne of our soueraigne
Lord king James of England, franc, & Ireland ý eighteenth
and of Scotland ý fiftie fourth. An: Dom·1620·]

After this they chose, or rather confirmed m^r John Caruer (a man
godly & well approued amongst them) their Gouernour for that
year. And after they had prouided a place for their goods, or
comone store (which were long in unlading for want of boats,
foulnes of ý winter weather, and sicknes of diuerse) and begune
some small cottages for their habitation; as time would admite
they mette and consulted of lawes, & ordors, both for their
ciuill & military gouermente, as ý necessitie of their condition did require, still adding thereunto as urgent occasion
in seuerall times, and as cases did require.

In these hard & difficulte begginings they found some discontents
& murmurings arose amongst some, and mutinous speeches & cariags
in other; but they were soone quelled, & ouercome, by ý wis-
dome, patience, and just & equall carrage of things, by ý gou^r
and better part wch clave faithfully togeather in ý maine.
But that which was most sadd, & lamentable, was, that in 2.
or ·3· monthes time halfe of their company dyed, espetialy
in Jan: & february, being ý depth of winter, and wanting
houses & other comforts; being infected with ý scuruie &

The Mayflower Compact from William Bradford's handwritten manuscript
of his *History of Plymouth Plantation*, from George Ernest Bowman,
The Mayflower Compact and Its Signers (Boston: Massachusetts Society
of Mayflower Descendants, 1920). *Courtesy of the Library of Congress*

such just and equal laws, ordinances, acts, constitutions and offices, from time to time, as shall be thought most meet and convenient for the general good of the Colony, unto which we promise all due submission and obedience. In witness whereof we have hereunder subscribed our names at Cape Cod, the eleventh of November, in the year of the reign of our sovereign lord, King James, of England, France, and Ireland, the eighteenth, and of Scotland the fifty-fourth. Anno Dom. 1620.[32]

If the meaning of a constitution in political theory includes a mechanism by which an assembly of people establishes governing principles, then the Mayflower Compact could possibly be considered at least a proto-constitution, for as Bradford described, the 1620 combination was "their first foundation of government in this place."[33] English law required the king's permission to form a new corporate body politic. The Pilgrims defied that prerequisite and created their own "civil body politic." Those who crafted the agreement might not have known all the theoretical implications of self-government, but they effectively created such a form using fewer than two hundred words.[34] They also established a polity based upon the rule of law to which all pledged obedience.

Origins of the Conflict

What provoked the insurrection? Because the primary sources provide only brief attention to the episode, we are limited to supposition. Perhaps, for example, the answer lies in the double character of the colonists: the Saints, on the one hand, and the Strangers on the other. The Saints were a cohesive group, one that was tightly knit together, according to Bradford, "in a most strict and sacred bond and covenant of the Lord."[35] They probably looked somewhat suspiciously on the entire body of Strangers. The Strangers, on the other hand, were not united, as witnessed by the breakaway group of dissenters who were challenging the status quo. They came from different backgrounds and joined the expedition for different purposes. The Saints had lived for years together in the Netherlands. The Strangers had not spent any time together before boarding the *Mayflower*. They likely didn't feel any strong obligation to each other, or to the Saints for that matter. It is possible that those clamoring for freedom did not want to be confined by the moralism imposed upon them by the Saints, whom they might have viewed as overzealous in their religious practices.

An alternative explanation involves Christopher Martin, the "governor" on the *Mayflower*.[36] Perhaps the mutinous speeches were spurred by a dislike of the man. Although a Stranger himself, he seemed to be universally scorned for his arrogance. Even before they'd left England, there were concerns about Martin, and his officiousness during the voyage was such that some of the sailors had threatened to harm him. He likely treated his fellow Strangers the same way. The idea of Martin remaining as governor of the settlement might have provoked the schism. If there were a chance that that man would continue lording over everyone once they got off the ship, the agitators might have wanted no part of it.[37]

There is a third possibility. The dispute that developed on the *Mayflower* appeared to be based on the very argument that Stephen Hopkins had advanced on Bermuda in 1609 when *he* had been charged with mutiny. On Bermuda, Hopkins had argued that Governor Gates's authority had ceased when the *Sea Venture* was wrecked. Whether intentionally or not, Hopkins had identified the central weakness of Gates's assertion of command over the castaways during their exile. Gates's authority had rested upon the London Company's charter for Virginia and didn't technically cover Bermuda.[38] Now, as the *Mayflower* swung at its anchor in Provincetown Harbor, some of the Strangers were advancing the same theory: because their charter via the London Company from the king only authorized them to settle in the area located at the mouth of the Hudson River, they were—in Cape Cod—outside the bounds of the expedition's authority. Therefore, they owed no obligations to the undertaking or its leaders, whether they be Saint or Stranger. Each could do as he pleased, and no one could command another.

Echoes from Bermuda

Because the arguments raised on the *Mayflower* so closely resembled Hopkins's words on Bermuda, it might be reasonable to assume that Hopkins was behind the insurrection, as some historians have done.[39]

There are several reasons, however, to believe that Hopkins was not one of the men who were challenging authority. First, it would have gone against common sense for him to have raised objections in Provincetown Harbor.

The first time Hopkins had advanced such theories had ended disastrously. He'd been shackled and sentenced to death. He'd been within mere moments of execution. Only tearful pleas on behalf of his faraway family had saved his life. Eleven years later, with his family now at his side, would he risk all again and use the same argument that was rejected before? The most probable answer is no.

Second, during the *Sea Venture* expedition, Hopkins had been under contract and attached to an aristocratic-acting clergyman. Now, he was one of the few Pilgrims who'd risen high enough to bring along his own servants under contract. The *Mayflower* malcontents specifically claimed that no one "had the power to command them," language which supposes a structure of dominion. Though the passengers had instituted a loose system of temporary governance during the voyage, it appeared to be a rather fluid arrangement and certainly not one of dominion. None of the settlers were from the aristocratic class. If any of them were under the "command" of others in the hierarchal sense of that in English society, it would have been the servants, a group represented in the camps of both the Saints and the Strangers.

Third, the very day upon which the conflict was resolved, Hopkins was likely part of a small group of armed men who were put on shore to gather firewood for cooking.[40] And only a few days later, Hopkins was named as one of only three special advisers to Myles Standish, who led their first expedition to find a location to settle.[41] Of those advisers, each of whom were appointed by John Carver, a leader among the Saints, Hopkins was the only Stranger. It is difficult to suppose that, had the conflict been instigated by Hopkins, he would immediately have been let off the ship carrying a musket and only a short while later would have been appointed as one of the leaders of the first real patrol into the New World.

Much more likely is that Hopkins spoke of his earlier adventures during the *Mayflower*'s Atlantic crossing. In fact, there can be little doubt that Hopkins shared his experiences on Bermuda and in Jamestown, for it was likely the reason that he was chosen to serve as one of the advisers to Standish, a selection which suggests that the others knew of Hopkins's previous experience in America. Whether Hopkins shared the details of his Bermuda insubordination publicly on the *Mayflower* or privately among his family and was overheard in the cramped quarters, where the only dividers for privacy in the cargo deck were sheets hung from the low beams overhead, some of the Strangers on board appeared to have absorbed and adopted his arguments as their own when they anchored at Cape Cod.

Servants and Servitude

William Bradford's description provides the best insight as to who might have instigated the insurrection on the *Mayflower*. The insurrectionists' concern for their "own liberty" implies a previous state of restraint or inability to choose for themselves. That they rejected others' "power to command them" likewise suggests that subordination was their prior state. Both concepts evince servitude; that is, that before the decision was made to turn back to Cape Cod, those making "mutinous speeches" were subject to the direction of others. That they contended that "none" had power over them implies that they objected to something broader than the governance of Christopher Martin. Based upon Bradford's description, therefore, it would seem most plausible that the antagonists were servants.[42]

When the *Mayflower* departed England, twenty of its passengers were either servants or underage wards under the care and supervision of other passengers.[43] With the death of William Button, nineteen were left on the ship when it anchored in Provincetown Harbor.[44] Of these individuals, only four signed the Mayflower Compact: two Saint servants, John Howland and George Soule, and Stephen Hopkins's servants, Edward Doty and Edward Leister. There were seven other male servants who were old enough to sign the agreement (that is, twenty-one years old or older),[45] yet they did not sign. Given that they all died soon after, it is likely that they were too ill to participate in either the altercation or its resolution.[46]

Doty and Leister both later had a series of clashes with authority, starting in June 1621—only seven months after the *Mayflower* anchored at Cape Cod—when the two men fought the colony's first duel, for which they were punished by being left on the ground bound to each other at the head and feet for twenty-four hours without food or water.[47] While Doty eventually became a member of the colony, he continued to become embroiled in legal controversy over allegations of slander, fighting, and contractual disputes. Leister left the colony as soon as he'd served the term of his indenture. He traveled to Jamestown, where he died.[48]

A theory advanced by some scholars concerning the four servants who signed the Mayflower Compact was that they were invited to sign either as a gesture of honor, such as in the cases of Howland and Soule (who were both servants of prominent Saints and later became prosperous voting members of the colony, with Soule becoming a large landowner and deputy for the town of Duxbury, and Howland an elected assistant to the governor),[49] or because of the additional commitment to the enterprise such an act would afford, such as was most likely the case with Doty and Leister.[50] When Edward Doty and Edward Leister signed the accord, they were the only two servants who helped enforce their own, in the words of Bradford, "due submission and obedience."[51]

That Hopkins's two servants likely instigated the dispute makes the most sense, given that they would have been in the best position to overhear anything Hopkins might have said about his one-man mutiny on Bermuda, which could easily be adopted for their own use.

Of the others who signed the Mayflower Compact,[52] the most likely to have joined in the rebellion was perhaps John Billington, who'd sailed with his wife and two teenage sons.[53] Though he traveled with his family and was not a servant, he was at odds with the leaders of the colony from the very start. In the spring of 1621 he was tried and convicted for disobeying a lawful command of Captain Standish. In 1625 he was still causing so many problems that William Bradford complained in a private letter that "he is a knave, and so will live and die." In 1630 Billington was hanged for murdering a fellow colonist, which capped a rather troubled life.[54]

Draftsmen at the Table

Regardless of whether Billington joined in the argument over authority, the dispute was something that likely concerned all the passengers on board the *Mayflower*—Saint and Stranger alike. Compromise was necessary. They were in the midst of a watershed event. Unless they could find an enduring solution, discord would inevitably return. Every decision would be open to challenge, a potential spark to a new disagreement as factions formed, dissolved, and reformed, alliances shifting according to individual whim and group circumstance. How would they decide where to settle? How would they apportion work? Who would cut timber? Who would forage for food? Who would build shelter? Who would clear fields? Unless some kind of authority or governance structure was established, all would likely fall into chaos and strife. And that would be the death of them.

If his own servants were the cause of this insurrection, Stephen Hopkins would have been extremely motivated to help resolve it. After all, he'd been the one who brought the two men aboard the *Mayflower*. He was their employer. He was responsible for them. Also, he had a larger financial interest in the enterprise, which had afforded him extra shares for his servants, shares that would be liquidated into money when their partnership with the Merchant Adventurers was dissolved after its seven-year life span. Hopkins thus risked losing more if Doty and Leister scuttled the entire thing. Even more pressing was the fact that he would lose the additional manpower of the two hirelings if they were allowed to pursue their "own liberty." He and his family of young children needed their help to cut timber, build shelter, and clear fields. Besides, Hopkins likely was not a dissolute employer. He'd walked in servant's shoes for seven long and hard years. He knew what it was like to serve a demanding master, and he would not be like Reverend Buck.[55] Had Doty and Leister been involved in the dispute, therefore, he most probably would have stepped to the forefront and attempted to mediate.

Fear of what might ensue if their company splintered also probably prompted Hopkins to try to help end the conflict. He'd seen what disastrous results could spring from such discord in Jamestown. Though now ten years past, the impact of the Starving Time likely would have come to mind. The catastrophe, of course, was ultimately brought on by the shortage of food, but that deficiency itself was exacerbated into deadly mass casualty by "misgovernment," according to William Strachey.[56] When the *Sea Venture* and Thomas Gates didn't arrive at Jamestown with the rest of the third supply mission, confusion and turmoil resulted as different groups of aristocrats vied for control, which in turn intensified the crisis over the settlement's depleted store of provisions.[57]

With firsthand knowledge of the detrimental effects of disharmony, Hopkins may have therefore stepped forward to defend their present enterprise, urging the importance for everyone to remain united. There could be countless difficulties ahead, and they'd surely fail if they split into different interest groups. He'd seen how division conspired against success. He may have told Stranger and Saint alike about the emaciated, straggling survivors of the Starving Time and how the acting leader of the devastated colony had scarcely been able to keep to his feet when he surrendered his commission to Thomas Gates.[58] Staying together was their only hope.

Of course, they carried a copy of their London Company patent with them on the *Mayflower*, but because they'd abandoned the Hudson River, legitimacy would require something new, an organic act that could establish authority.[59] None on board the *Mayflower* were politicians. None were political theorists. The idea of a social contract to create legitimacy of authority might not have immediately come to mind, especially when doing so conflicted with established English law. Without legitimacy on Bermuda, Thomas Gates had bluffed his way through by using the bullying tactics of an aristocrat, backed up by the swords of his soldiers.

Unlike on the *Sea Venture* or at Bermuda or at Jamestown, on the *Mayflower* there were no domineering aristocrats—no "persons of special eminence" in the words of John Robinson—who might step into the power vacuum and assert dominance by heritage or social position or indignant haughtiness. Though Christopher Martin had attempted to assert his superiority during his temporary administration, it appears as though most of the colonists discounted him because of his arrogance,[60] which presumably left them viewing one another more or less as equals.

This reality might have reminded the Saints of the conditions on which their church covenant was based. As Pastor Robinson had always taught, the covenant of mutual agreement was the cornerstone of every congregation, of each church.[61] Unlike the top-down structure of the Catholic Church and the Church of England, the Separatists believed that each congregation should govern its own ecclesiastical practices. A congregational covenant is what bound each individual to one another into "church estate," in the words of William Bradford.[62] And within a church estate, the authority of its officers, such as pastors, teachers, elders, and deacons, was obtained solely through their election by its members.[63] In other words, the people of the Separatist congregation were the source of an officer's authority.[64]

The Saints' Leiden pastor wrote extensively about congregational church structure. Once elected, the officers of a church estate would then be expected to govern the people and organize activities within the church via what Robinson called "lawful administration."[65] Because the authority of a church officer derived from his election by the congregants, that commission lasted only as long as they permitted. According to Robinson, "If the congregation may choose and elect their governors, then they may reject and reprobate them, for they that set up may pull down."[66]

If ecclesiastical authority under such a covenant derived from the people, perhaps, in the absence of a lawful grant from the London Company, civil authority for the Pilgrims' colony could likewise be derived from the people. But if adapting the church covenant to create a civil government seems an obvious solution in hindsight, it may not have been so to those grappling with the insurrection, for the Separatists viewed their church estate as something quite apart from the secular state. In *Of Plymouth Plantation*, William Bradford outlined the Leiden church covenant:

> And as the Lord's free people, joined themselves (by a covenant of the Lord) into a church estate, in the fellowship of the Gospel, to walk in all his ways, made known or to be made known unto them (according to their best endeavors) whatsoever it should cost them, the Lord assisting them.[67]

The actual words of a covenant for a church affiliated with Pastor Robinson's Leiden congregation provides additional details:

> We whose names are underwritten, do believe and acknowledge the truth of the doctrine and faith of our Lord, *Jesus Christ*, which is revealed unto us in the Canon of the Scriptures of the Old and New Testament. We do acknowledge that *God* in his ordinary means for the bringing us unto and keeping of us in this faith of *Christ*, and an holy *Obedience* thereof, hath set in his Church teaching and ruling *Elders*, *Deacons*, and Helpers. And that this, his *Ordinance*, is to continue unto the end of the world as well under *Christian princes*, as under *heathen Magistrates*. We do willingly join together to live as the *Church of Christ*, watching over one another, and submitting ourselves unto them to whom the Lord *Jesus* commits the oversight of his Church, guiding and censuring us according to the rule of the word of God.[68]

The impulse to apply the framework of such a covenant onto the realm of civil polity might not have been an instinctive one for the Separatists. Indeed, the more specific language just above expressly established that God's "Ordinance," i.e., his authority—which the Separatists strove to follow—stood expressly outside the civil government of both "Christian princes" and "heathen magistrates." The reason for this was because the goal of the Separatist church was singular: to walk in the way of the Lord *whatsoever it should cost*. In their theology and in their worldly conduct their primary inclination was to never compromise. It is the reason why they broke with the Church of England. It is why they fled to the Netherlands. It is why they fled ultimately to the New World. They sought to insulate themselves from the king and his government.[69]

Their focus was on the spiritual, not on the political. Thomas Prince was an early American clergyman and historical scholar who graduated from Harvard University in 1703. He wrote a seminal history of the Pilgrims using not only the primary sources *Of Plymouth Plantation* and *Mourt's Relation* but also upon other unpublished handwritten notes and journals produced by William Bradford that have since been lost.[70] In it, Prince described the Separatists on the *Mayflower* as desiring "to practice a *Separation* from the *World* and the *Works of the World*, which [were] the *Works of the Flesh*."[71] Civil justice or equity didn't figure into their dogma. Whether prompted by points raised by others or moved by their own intuition, however, the leaders from among the Separatists nonetheless thought to adapt the religious covenant and so form a secular polity in order to establish proper legitimacy.[72]

In such an instrument, each person on the *Mayflower* would acknowledge their mutual obligations to one another and form an organization whose goal was the general welfare of the colony, just as did the congregants in a Separatist church estate. Like those congregants, the Pilgrims would elect their officers, to whom they would promise obedience. And like congregants, they would have the ability to remove those same officers. The officials would answer ultimately to the members of the colony. If a person was persuaded to sign on to such an accord, they would thereafter be hard pressed to individually challenge the authority of the elected officials. Only by convincing other colonists could they effect change through a new election.

When the *Speedwell* abandoned its voyage, forcing over one-third of the Separatists to also abandon the expedition, the resulting ratio between Saint and Stranger fell to nearly equal. Had the Separatists maintained their larger numbers, the dispute that led to the Mayflower Compact might have turned out very differently. Suspicious Strangers might not have embraced the idea of an agreement clouded by undue Saintly influence, and the history of the United States might have slanted off in a very different direction. That the two blocs of colonists were nearly balanced in number probably made the ability to reach agreement in the form of the compact, where each of the signers committed to obeying the decisions of the whole, much more palatable. To craft such an accord would probably have required input from each group. As the Saints were familiar with the substance of their church covenants, from among them would likely have come the primary drafters. But unless at least some Strangers were invited to participate, the others would have looked askance at any product.

Thus, it seems reasonable that from each of the two camps emerged leaders who huddled together over a piece of parchment to draft the short resolution committing all of them to a common cause. From the Saints, it probably would have been men like William Brewster, who was the elder of their Leiden congregation. Among the passengers, he was the one man with university training, having spent a year or two at Cambridge, and he was also knowledgeable about the structure of congregational covenants and, as such, probably played a primary role in crafting the accord.[73]

Though William Bradford was a younger man, it is likely that he had already risen to some level of prominence, making it possible that he, too, provided input.[74] Both Brewster and Bradford at one point possessed books that pertained to political philosophy, which of course might have helped inform any input into the creation of a governing agreement, though it is uncertain whether either carried such volumes with them on the *Mayflower* or acquired them later in life.[75] John Carver became the governor of the colony immediately after the agreement was signed. Thus, he must have already been recognized as a leader among both the Saints and the Strangers and therefore was probably involved in drafting the compact.[76]

From the Strangers, a few people stand out as potential candidates who might have possessed a strength of character or charisma to influence their fellow Strangers. Captain Standish, who was tapped to lead the early explorations, seemed to have been a voice to which others listened. However, as he'd become acquainted with the Saints when he lived in the Netherlands, he was seen by some as more Saint than Stranger, even though he might not have been part of the Separatists' congregation in Leiden.[77] It is also probable that he had originally traveled with the Saints on the *Speedwell* to the rendezvous with the *Mayflower* at Southampton, which in the eyes of the Strangers would have even more firmly associated the military man with the religious group.[78]

Thus, the Strangers likely would not have embraced him as a spokesperson for their cause. Christopher Martin may have been governor of the *Mayflower* during its voyage, but he likewise would not have been a good representative, as he seemed to have repulsed nearly everyone.

One other potential contributor who might have emerged from the group of Strangers would have been Stephen Hopkins. As discussed previously, given his experience and the probability of his two servants' involvement in the dispute, he very likely would have taken a role in the debate. He also had some working knowledge of political theory, for William Strachey on Bermuda had found Hopkins's "substantial arguments" regarding civil authority to be of particular note. In fact, in making his arguments after the wreck of the *Sea Venture*, Hopkins had explicitly contended that Governor Thomas Gates's authority extended only to those who consented to following him. As Strachey recorded, "It was no breach . . . to decline from the obedience of the Governor, or refuse to go any further, led by his authority (except it so pleased themselves)."[79]

The idea of civil authority arising by consent of the governed, of course, is one of the fundamental features of the Mayflower Compact. The notion itself was not novel at the time,[80] but it would have neatly coincided with the structure of the Separatists' church estate, which placed power in the hands of its members. If Hopkins advanced such reasoning on the *Mayflower*, backed by the dreadful details he could have provided as an eyewitness to the destructive force of discord, it might have been seen as influential to his fellow Strangers. While any definitive proof of who drafted the famous accord remains hidden, it could very well be that Hopkins was one of those who leaned over the table in the master's cabin to discuss the compact's wording.

The First Election

Once the drafting committee was finished, they read the document out loud to the assembled company. One by one, forty-one adult men stepped to the table on the *Mayflower* and signed at the bottom of the freshly crafted agreement. Along with the others, Christopher Martin put his name to the compact, perhaps believing that his administration would be given new life by the consent of the others. If he harbored such an ambition, it was soon dispelled, for the Separatist John Carver was chosen.[81] Carver, who was well liked by everyone, had been a deacon in Leiden, a position into which he was

The Pilgrims Signing the Compact, On Board the May Flower, Nov. 11th, 1620, by T. H. Matteson; engraved by Gauthier (1859).
Courtesy of the Library of Congress

voted by the congregants, and, as such, was not new to idea of serving as an elected official.[82] And like Martin, he had apparently served as temporary governor until the *Speedwell* had withdrawn from the voyage, which made him a natural choice.

Significance of the Mayflower Compact

Neither the Saints nor the Strangers could likely have foreseen the long-lasting impact of the short agreement they created on that chilly November day. None of them were aristocrats steeped in abstract erudition fueled by the luxury of free time and expensive private tutors. They were farmers and weavers and shoemakers—ordinary people—commoners who knew the value of hard work and the need of practicality. The person or persons who were drafting the document articulated the essentials and were done with it. And the agreement's essentials, unencumbered by what might have been debated if time and temperament served, were what created one of the most consequential documents in history.

Decades before English philosophers Thomas Hobbes and John Locke argued about the social contract *theory* of government,[83] the Pilgrims actually *created* one.[84] Before they left their floating home in search of a permanent one, they bound themselves together and promised to enact and obey their own laws. In a few words, they brought into being a government by consent of the governed.

Using criteria such as historical perspective and impact, the Mayflower Compact has been listed among the most significant documents in the history of the world.[85] John Quincy Adams, the sixth president of the United States, asserted that the Mayflower Compact was "the only instance in human history of that positive, original social compact which speculative philosophers have imagined as the only legitimate source of government. Here was a unanimous and personal assent by all individuals of the community to the association by which they became a nation."[86]

Some historians and politicians have said that the Mayflower Compact inspired the Declaration of Independence and the US Constitution,[87] an interpretation supported by many separate anecdotes. In 1766, for example, as discontent grew in the American colonies over measures such as the Stamp Act, Samuel Adams and fellow colonial patriot, John Hancock, made a point of writing to the people of Plymouth in order to praise the "Spirit of our venerable Forefathers" for establishing a solid foundation for civil liberty that had been transmitted to succeeding generations of New Englanders.[88]

Samuel Adams's second cousin John Adams, who would become the second president of the United States, likewise looked to the "venerable Forefathers" of Plymouth for inspiration. The father of John Quincy Adams, John Adams was a descendant of two of the *Mayflower* colonists and was deeply influenced by their legacy. At the end of July 1780, at the height of the American Revolution, Adams traveled to the Netherlands to advocate on behalf of the colonies. During his stay he visited Leiden and the old quarter in which the Separatists had lived, where he was seen to weep while contemplating the city's famous cathedral, and he also invoked the Pilgrims in his 1781 appeal to the Dutch government to provide financial support to the colonies' fight against England.[89]

Shortly before leaving for the Netherlands, Adams had drafted Massachusetts's state constitution. Its preamble used language that is evocative of the Mayflower Compact:

The body politic is formed by a voluntary association of individuals; it is a social compact by which the whole people covenants with each citizen and each citizen with the whole people that all shall be governed by certain laws for the common good.[90]

Adams's constitution for Massachusetts served as the principal model used by the Federal Convention of 1787 that produced the US Constitution.[91]

After the Revolution and just after his second term as the third president of the United States, Thomas Jefferson in 1809 received a letter praising his public service from the "Antient Plymouth Society," an organization founded in commemoration of New England's first colony.[92] Though the issue was not raised by the society, Jefferson in his response highlighted the "blessing of self-government," making it a possible reference to the social contract created in 1620 and certainly an echo of the famous words of the second paragraph of the Declaration of Independence, which Jefferson authored.[93] The Mayflower Compact thus was perhaps one of the germinal seeds for an entire nation whose government *actually*—rather than theoretically—derived power from constituents it was created to serve, or as Abraham Lincoln observed two centuries later in his enduring Gettysburg Address, a "government of the people, by the people, for the people."[94]

The agreement helped the Pilgrims survive yet another storm. Together, they'd overcome another obstacle. But more challenges lay ahead. Winter was coming.

5 | MUTUAL SUSPICION

O, wonder!
How many goodly creatures are there here!
How beauteous mankind is! O brave new world,
That has such people in't!
—*The Tempest*, act 5, scene 1

WITH CARVER CHOSEN AS GOVERNOR, the settlers quickly organized a group of fifteen or sixteen men to go ashore and gather firewood. It was a rather more mundane task than forming the first democratic government among Europeans in North America, but it was one perhaps of equal importance in the pragmatic minds of the Pilgrims, for it'd been quite some time since anyone had had a hot meal. Wary of what might await them, everyone was armed. They weren't seeking confrontation, however. They desired the opposite.[1]

From the beginning, the Pilgrims wanted to establish a positive relationship with New England's inhabitants. The local people would, it was hoped, become trading partners, for the Pilgrims needed to produce income for their financial investors, and obtaining furs was a vital component of their plan. But the Pilgrims brought with them an apprehension of the unknown, and they arrived in an age and to an area that had already been shaped by prior contact between native and European. As it would turn out, mutual suspicion would significantly influence the interactions of Stephen Hopkins's *Mayflower* shipmates and their soon-to-be neighbors.

How the English Viewed Native Americans

The Pilgrims likely considered themselves far superior to and much farther advanced than the people who populated the shores of the continent to which they'd come, and their perceptions arose from their own circumstances in England, which were often harsh.

Thomas Hobbes, the seventeenth-century English philosopher, famously said in 1651 that because human nature was governed by rapacious appetites and desires, and because there were limited resources to satisfy such desires, in a state of nature—that is, without the governance mechanism imposed by political structure—anarchy would reign supreme. The natural state of man was a war of all against all, where people would be left to their own devices to obtain their needs and wants.[2] In this natural state, the life of man was solitary, poor, nasty, brutish, and short.[3]

Judged by today's standards, life in England—one of the most powerful countries in all of Europe during the reigns of Elizabeth and James—was still very much nasty, brutish, and short. The plague ravaged the populations in cities, killing tens of thousands every decade or so in crowded metropolises such as London. Rigid social stratification kept almost everyone locked into the economic world of opportunities and limitations into which they were born. Despite Queen Elizabeth's long and exemplary reign, women in the early seventeenth century were forced to stand in the shadows of men. Religious conflict spurred by the Protestant Reformation raged at home and abroad, pitting neighbor against neighbor in a conflagration that burned for nearly a century. When the *Mayflower* came to anchor in Provincetown Harbor, the Pilgrims brought with them individual outlooks that were informed by harsh and grim conditions. It was through such lenses that they viewed themselves, other Europeans, and Native Americans.

Much has been written about the role that infectious diseases played in European colonization of North America. Disease devastated Indians in the years before the *Mayflower*'s voyage, which helped ease the way for the influx from across the Atlantic. In fact, the Pilgrims' colony would soon be started on the grounds of a native village abandoned because its inhabitants had been wiped out by pestilence. But disease also devastated European visitors to North America, as Stephen Hopkins had seen in Virginia, and as the Pilgrims would see during their first winter in New England. And disease also devastated Old England in the late sixteenth and early seventeenth centuries.

England under Queen Elizabeth and King James was a busy, prosperous nation and London lay at its heart. Its population at the time was likely between 150,000 and 200,000.[4] Horse-drawn carts laden with goods trundled through the avenues, along with pack horses, wheelbarrows, and handcarts. The streets were narrow, lined with buildings that were generally three or more stories. Crowded lanes and dwellings and a busy port also made the city home to disease. The plague had ravaged and receded time and again over the previous centuries, taking countless lives, and frequently reoccurred in the sixteenth and early seventeenth centuries with catastrophic and widespread results.

Queen Elizabeth reigned from 1558 to 1603. Within that span of time, the plague visited London five times, with an outbreak at her death taking over thirty thousand lives, which represented up to 20 percent of the city's population.[5] It was this same outbreak that forced Elizabeth's successor, King James I, in November of 1603 to postpone the Hampton Court Conference where he threatened to harass Puritans and Separatists out of the country. The plague continued to beleaguer London throughout the twenty-two-year reign of King James, claiming thirty-five thousand lives in 1625, the year in which the king died. The plague returned to London and claimed ten thousand more lives in 1635. In 1665 it erupted again and claimed a stupendous toll—one hundred thousand people died.[6]

Each outbreak produced all the familiar signs of the disease: fever, delirium, and, of course, spots and pustules that spread over the entire body. Death usually came quickly afterward.[7] Houses with infected inhabitants were boarded up, its residents made prisoners within. Watchmen stood guard to prevent anyone escaping, or going in. Food and water were delivered by rope and bucket from an upper story window.[8] Tens of thousands of dogs and cats, believed to have carried the infection, were euthanized. Clothing and bedding and curtains were burned. Wealthy London residents fled to the countryside. Shops closed and commerce ground to a halt.[9]

When London was not being ravaged by the plague, however, it was a bustling, energetic place. Ships loaded and unloaded in the Thames's historic port, taking English goods abroad and bringing foreign goods ashore. Commerce helped make the world a smaller place, and colonialism helped bring more of the world under English control.

As England looked to expand its sphere of influence, it looked not only across the Atlantic toward the New World but also across the Irish Sea. Indeed, plans for colonizing in Ireland and in America were discussed simultaneously under Elizabeth and James. The same businessmen promoted both enterprises. For example, while Walter Raleigh was in the early stages of establishing a colony at Roanoke, Virginia, he and other promoters were securing grants of land in Ireland and trying to convince their fellow Englishmen to relocate to England's neighboring island.[10]

Since the time of William the Conqueror, Ireland had ostensibly been under some form of English rule. Relations were tempestuous and often marked with conflict. Henry VIII had tried to export the Protestant Reformation to Irish shores, but the deeply Catholic country rejected it and during Elizabeth's reign fought back. Several rebellions were started, each of which the English savagely put down.[11] The last of these began in 1593 and ran until Elizabeth's death in 1603. Known as the Nine Years' War, the clash involved the northern-most province of Ireland, Ulster. English soldiers in the campaign numbered above eighteen thousand at its height, and they marauded around the Ulster countryside, destroying crops, butchering livestock, and indiscriminately killing any Irish natives they encountered—men, women, and even children.[12] Many thousands starved because of food shortages, and the roads between abandoned towns became littered with the bodies.[13] The overall toll was devastating. Before the war, the estimated Irish population in Ulster was between thirty and thirty-five thousand.[14] In 1603, when the rebellion collapsed, around ten thousand people were left.[15] In addition to the Irish dead, some forty thousand English soldiers perished.[16] The war and its aftermath set the stage for subsequent colonization.[17]

England expropriated most of Ulster as a result and resettled the majority of the Irish natives to designated areas (similar to nineteenth-century efforts to relocate American natives to reservations) in order to free up about a quarter of Ulster—some five hundred thousand acres of good, cultivable land—for English settlers.[18] The rationale for colonizing Ireland was the very same as that put forward for America: spreading the Protestant Gospel and helping to improve the lot of the country's native people, who were viewed as primitives.[19]

Scots started migrating to Ulster in 1606, the same year that the first ships left England to establish the Jamestown colony in Virginia. People started moving to Ireland in still greater numbers in 1611.[20] Not surprisingly, the Irish weren't welcoming. Because the English believed that their intentions were benign and that their culture was superior, they viewed any opposition as disloyalty informed by barbarous stupidity. The English responded with violence, executing prisoners—again men, women, and children—by the hundreds in a brutal campaign of intimidation and terror meant to teach the native people duty and obedience. One commander bordered the path leading to his tent with human heads, which forced any local who came to petition the English overlord to walk past the heads of fathers, brothers, children, kinfolk, and friends.[21] By 1622, as many as thirty-five thousand English and Scots had settled in the war-torn province, and the impact of the forced colonization is still felt in Northern Ireland today.[22]

There were many parallels between Ireland and North America. Both lands were inhabited by people who'd lived there for thousands of years and who were dismissed by the English as "savages" in need of help—by force if necessary—to improve themselves.[23] Both were viewed as fertile fields onto which to sow and spread Protestantism.[24] Like Ireland, North America was seen as a trophy—the next frontier for English exploration, exploitation, and conquest.[25]

English promoters of colonization knew that Spain had colonized and conquered South and Central America and the islands of the Caribbean Sea by sheer force.[26] The Englishmen tried to convince themselves that it would be different for them, insisting that Native Americans would welcome the English as liberators who'd come to help them cast off the yoke of Spanish tyranny.[27] Of course, the paternalistic English could not conceive that America's inhabitants might not want their assistance.[28] As in Ireland, war between native and immigrant would eventually break out in America and claim the lives of many thousands.[29] Warfare divided the world into winners and losers and allowed the victor to define the future.[30]

The Englishman's sense of superiority in that era was not limited to the indigenous people of Ireland and America but extended to a sense of cultural elevation over his European rivals, for he came from a world founded on hierarchy in many forms. The hierarchy of birth. The hierarchy of sex, where women were treated as weaker vessels. The hierarchy of religion.

For the Separatists, people who shared their particular version of Puritanism came first. Next came their regular Puritan cousins. Then came other forms of Protestantism, such as the Anglicans of Henry VIII and his daughter Elizabeth. Then came English Catholics. After these ranked Christians from foreign shores, Protestants before Catholics, of course. After all these came those who did not worship Christ. Those that were different were treated with disdain, if not outright violence. Though there were exceptions, of course, many English of the early seventeenth century were savage and bigoted toward nearly everyone.

Religious self-righteousness was reinforced by technological dominance, and both fed the views of "natural superiority" that the European explorers and settlers held toward the people who'd inhabited the lands of America for thousands of years. Nonetheless, the Pilgrims were probably apprehensive as they looked out onto Cape Cod from the deck of the *Mayflower*. As William Bradford voiced,

> Being thus passed the vast ocean, and a sea of troubles before in their preparation . . . they had now no friends to welcome them, nor inns to entertain or refresh their weather-beaten bodies, no houses or much less towns to repair to, to seek succor. . . . What could they see but a hideous and desolate wilderness full of wild beasts and wild men? . . . The whole country, full of woods and thickets, represented a wild and savage hue. If they looked behind them, there was the mighty ocean which they had passed, and now [it] was as a main bar and gulf to separate them from all the civil parts of the world.[31]

Everything in the New World at this point held a "wild and savage hue" in the eyes of Pilgrims because it was so utterly new. How would the "wild men" react to the English interlopers? Would they extend a hand in friendship or in aggression? The colonists wanted to engage in commerce, but they also knew that the people of America might not appreciate their would-be trading partners. Suspicion swirled in their minds as the unknown raced toward them.

How the Native Americans Viewed Europeans

The people who lived along coastal New England had reason to be suspicious of this latest batch of foreigners who'd appeared on the coast of their homeland. After years of contact with earlier European visitors, they'd had their fair share of violent interactions mixed in with the more amicable ones. The impact of these prior negative encounters was long lasting and affected relations between Indians and those on board the *Mayflower*.[32]

There were five principal nations of Native Americans in New England at the time the Pilgrims arrived. In modern-day Connecticut lived the Pequot.

In Rhode Island lived the Narragansett. In the southeastern parts of Massachusetts, including Cape Cod and Martha's Vineyard and Nantucket, lived the people of the Wampanoag Confederation. Around Massachusetts Bay lived the Massachusett. North and east of Massachusetts Bay, in coastal New Hampshire and Maine, lived the fifth principal nation, the Pennacook, also known as the Pawtucket or Merrimack people, who were part of the Wabanaki Confederacy.[33] They all spoke variations of Algonquian, which was the language shared by everyone from the Gulf of St. Lawrence to the southernmost portion of Chesapeake Bay.[34]

Each of these nations was composed of regional bands, or tribal communities, of people that usually were subdivided into smaller local groups, with the essential social unit being the nuclear family.[35] For example, the Wampanoag Confederation, which dominated the area where the Pilgrims landed in November 1620, included twelve different bands of people, such as the Patuxet who lived in the area of present-day Plymouth, Massachusetts, and the Nauset, who lived on Cape Cod.

Kinship was the most fundamental and important bond of the people in the New England nations.[36] From that grew extended lineal families that in turn became connected to ever larger bands forming villages and regional communities.[37] Although the extended family groups were closely associated with each other by kinship and friendship, and might often support one another in times of need, they retained the right to determine their own affairs and were at liberty to leave the area of the larger group and to join a neighboring group, if one would accept them.[38]

While loyalty to kin was a building block of society, it was also a source of conflict, as insult or injury to kin could spark retributive violence even within a larger community. As a consequence, managing the network of relations and familial alliances required strong leadership. Balancing these often-competing interests was a task that fell primarily to a band's leadership, which was usually comprised of one or, in some cases, two people. In the southern part of New England, as in the Wampanoag Confederacy, such leaders were called *sachems*. In the north, as in the Wabanaki Confederacy, they were known as *sagamores*.[39] Each tribe within a confederacy would have its own sachem or sagamore, but these lesser leaders would be subservient to the paramount ruler of the confederacy. In 1620 the Wampanoag Confederacy was led by a leader whose name was Massasoit.[40] Massasoit lived in a place believed to be near present-day Warren and Bristol, Rhode Island, called Pokanoket, which was both the name of the place and the name of Massasoit's own tribe.[41] Thus, the Nauset on Cape Cod would have their own sachem who managed the tribe's affairs but who was also subordinate to Massasoit, who was the supreme sachem for the confederation.

Unlike their royal counterparts in Europe, who virtually without exception ruled based upon a transmission of power between generations within the same family, the authority of sachems and sagamores in New England depended on the consent of their people. Within this structure, family name was less important than leadership ability and charisma. In addition to keeping peace between the various families and factions, a sachem's main duties included leading trade and diplomacy with other nations.[42]

The relationship among the principal nations in New England—and even within each nation itself—ebbed and flowed between détente and open strife. While neighboring nations might trade with each other, they also periodically appraised the strength of their rivals and would not hesitate to exploit real or perceived weaknesses.[43] For example, the Mi'kmaq people were located in northeastern Maine and the coastal lands of Canada and were part of the Wabanaki Confederacy. Because the colder climate was less supportive of an agrarian economy, the Mi'kmaq largely cycled between the coast and inland winter camps, following the rhythms of spawning, migrating birds and roving moose and caribou. They became early traders with French fishermen and adventurers, exchanging animal furs for European goods such as hatchets, axes, swords, and knives. They also exhibited aggressiveness toward other nations, as well as against other members of their own confederacy. In 1606 they carried out raids against the Penobscot and the Kennebec, both of which were also members of the Wabanaki Confederacy.[44] Retribution killings escalated the conflict, and in 1607 the Mi'kmaq sacked the fortified village of the Abenaki—another Wabanaki Confederacy member—near present-day Saco, Maine. The Mi'kmaq also repeatedly raided their southern rivals such as the Massachusett nation.[45] These predatory forays lasted for decades, even after the waves of English started filling the coastal areas.[46]

Over the twenty years before the Pilgrims came into Provincetown Harbor in 1620, the Wampanoag and other nations of the New England region had encountered scores of ships from Spain, Portugal, France, and England that had journeyed each year to the coasts of Newfoundland, Nova Scotia, and

Maine to fish the productive waters and to trade with Indians for animal furs.[47] In 1602 Bartholomew Gosnold, an English lawyer turned explorer who later recruited John Smith and helped him establish the colony at Jamestown, visited the coast of modern-day Maine just north of its border with New Hampshire. Gosnold's first contact with the local population, ironically, was when a group of them piloted a European-made fishing boat out to greet the ship. Two of the six natives wore the trousers common to European sailors, and one even sported a waistcoat. Communicating mostly through hand gestures, the men explained to the English that they traded with fishermen from southwest France who came to these waters. Gosnold's exploratory cruise also took him to Cape Cod Bay. The English sailors fished off the northern tip of the cape, very near where the *Mayflower* anchored in 1620, and caught so many cod that after a few hours they started throwing many of them back into the sea, their bountiful catch prompting the name "Cape Cod."[48]

Gosnold sailed to the Atlantic side of Cape Cod, traced the arm of land south, and then turned westward at the elbow. After somehow surviving the dangers of the Pollock Rip, he continued and came to what he named the Elizabeth Islands, a small chain that extends southwest from present-day Woods Hole, Cape Cod. On one of the islands, he and his men established a camp and traded with Wampanoag, who brought tobacco, deer skins, and fish to barter. During their stay, Gosnold explored the area and gave the modern name to Martha's Vineyard, likely after his infant daughter. Though contacts with the Wampanoag were mostly peaceful, there was at least one incident in which natives attacked two Englishmen, injuring one of them. Gosnold flirted with the idea of establishing a permanent outpost, but in the end stayed only long enough to fill the hold of his ship with animal pelts, cedar lumber, as well as the roots, branches, and bark of the sassafras tree, which was an important commodity that the English valued for medicinal use against syphilis.[49]

Just after Queen Elizabeth died in the spring of 1603, another English explorer, Martin Pring, sailed to New England to retrace the path of Gosnold's voyage and, like him, trade with the local people and harvest sassafras.[50] Pring made landfall along the coast of Maine and followed the coastline southwest and stopped in the Cape Cod region.[51] He and his crew created an encampment, and during their stay, Wampanoag frequently visited. Pring tried to develop favorable relations by offering food and providing the Wampanoag gifts from his supply of trading merchandise. The approach seemed to work, with the two groups sharing meals and entertaining one another. One of the English-men played an instrument, and the Wampanoag "took great delight" in the music and "danced twenty in a ring" around the musician while he played.[52]

Pring's expedition carried a total of forty-three men. Only a smaller group of them would have been at the camp on shore, for at least some of them would have remained on their two ships anchored some distance off the coast. The Wampanoag came in groups of various size, sometimes numbering ten, other times between twenty and sixty, and at one time totaling one hundred and twenty. Pring specifically noted that the Wampanoag men, who were taller than the average Englishman, were strong, swift, and athletic. They were also well armed, each carrying a bow five or six feet long that could launch a yard-long arrow. The combination of the Wampanoag's superior numbers, physical size, and imposing weaponry seemed to put the English on the defensive when evening came, for they used a rather vicious method to induce the local people to leave. Pring had with him two mastiffs, a huge breed which can stand thirty-six inches tall and weigh over two hundred pounds. The dogs were greatly feared by the Wampanoag, not only because of their fearsome size and looks but also because one of them was trained to carry a six-foot-long spear in its mouth. In order to clear the camp of their visitors, Pring's men would release the two dogs, which then would chase the Wampanoag off.[53]

Pring spent seven weeks on the Massachusetts coast gathering sassafras and trading for animal skins. One afternoon, most of the Englishmen went to the forest to cut down sassafras trees. Four remained behind, standing watch within the barricaded encampment near the shore. One hundred and forty armed Wampanoag warriors approached and surrounded the camp. They entreated the guards to come out to them, but sensing something was amiss, the guards refused. The sailors minding the ships saw the Wampanoag crowd-ing around the camp and fired off one of the ship's cannons. The booming explosion startled the warriors. The ship fired again. The men in the forest ran to their camp to see why one of the ships was firing. With them came the two mastiffs, one with its long spear clamped between its jaws. When the warriors spotted the menacing dogs, "they turned all to a jest and sport and departed away in a friendly manner," according to a firsthand account. But not long after, the Wampanoag returned and set fire to the woods where the English had been harvesting sassafras. The conflagration spread and quickly consumed a massive area of forest, about one square mile. Pring evacuated his men to the

"European Camp" from *Tweede Scheeps-Togt van Martin Pring* (1707),
showing an incident from Martin Pring's expedition on Cape Cod, 1603.
Courtesy of the John Carter Brown Library at Brown University

ships. As the Englishmen assembled on board, a force of about two hundred
Wampanoag appeared on the shore. Several canoes paddled out to the ships,
and the warriors unsuccessfully tried to entice the explorers back to the beach.
Pring had made up his mind and returned to England.[54]

In 1605, three years after Pring's voyage and three years before the initial expedition that founded Jamestown Colony, Captain George Weymouth
sailed with a small crew of twenty-eight men to Maine to explore the area
and determine whether the land was suitable for a colony. A party of native
people—who were Abenaki and belonged to the Wabanaki Confederacy—
first approached the English sailors off the coast in a canoe. One of them
spoke loudly and gestured toward the open sea in a way that the Englishmen interpreted as a message to leave. The explorers tried to dissipate the
tension by offering bracelets, rings, peacock feathers, and tobacco pipes as
gifts. The gesture seemed to placate the Abenaki, who expressed gratitude
for the gifts. A few even placed peacock feathers in their hair. The tension

evaporated, and the English soon learned that the Abenaki were open minded and quick witted.[55]

Over the next few days, Weymouth's men invited natives onto the ship, escorting them below deck to feed them with pork, fish, bread, and English peas. Using sign language, the explorers traded knives and glasses and combs for the skins of beaver, otter, and sable. The two groups fished together, with the English letting the Abenaki keep most of the catch. The Abenaki, in turn, tried to teach the visitors their language, fetching various fish and fruit and identifying them in the Algonquian tongue. Sometimes natives were invited to sleep aboard the ship while sailors spent the night on shore at the Abenaki camp. Captain Weymouth even marveled them with a few tricks of magnetism using a lodestone and his sword to make a tabletop knife spin. The demonstration, like much of what the explorers did, was calculated in part "to cause them to imagine some great power in us, and for that to love and fear us," according to an account written by one of the Englishmen.[56]

The good-natured rapport didn't last. One afternoon, the Abenaki invited the English to go to the mainland to trade in fur and tobacco. Weymouth and fifteen men took one of the ship's boats and followed the Abenaki canoes. When they came closer to the shore, the Englishmen noted a change in the behavior of their guides. The fires of an encampment could be glimpsed through a screen of dense trees, and the Abenaki invited the sailors to beach their boat. Suspicious, they declined and instead offered to have one of their men go to investigate. When the sailor returned, he reported seeing no furs or pelts at the encampment. He'd seen only armed warriors, 280 by his quick count. He said that instead of pulling their boat onto the shore, the Abenaki now wanted them to paddle up a nearby creek, where the cache of furs was supposedly stashed. The explorers were doubtful. The creek was narrow, which would make the boat vulnerable to ambush, and they'd heard stories from other traders that natives might use deceit to gain a tactical advantage.[57] The English refused and returned to their vessel.

Concluding that the Abenaki plotted against them, Weymouth and his men decided to turn the tables and kidnap several natives.[58] Abduction—a tactic used during the English subjugation of the Irish in Ulster[59]—was a maneuver that Weymouth had apparently been considering for some time.[60] Despite an atmosphere of distrust that grew in the wake of the aborted trading mission, the English were able to lure three Abenaki onto the ship, where they were seized. At the same time, a group of sailors went to shore and used the offer of food to lure two more Abenaki into a trap. It took six men to get the struggling captives back to the ship.[61]

After kidnapping the five men, Weymouth returned to England. The Abenaki were not to become slaves, which considering their detention and forced transportation likely provided them little comfort. Instead, they were used by the English as sources of intelligence about North America.[62] The Abenaki's countrymen, naturally, believed that the English had killed them.[63] Although in subsequent years, three of the five were brought back to Maine, the impact of Weymouth's actions was lasting and engendered numerous retaliatory murders and massacres in the decades that followed.[64]

It wasn't only the English who descended upon the American coastline. In 1605 the famed French explorer Samuel de Champlain cruised the coast of Massachusetts, stopping in Plymouth Harbor, near the village of the Patuxet, the home of Squanto and the site where the Pilgrims would eventually establish their colony.[65] The Frenchman's contact with the Patuxet was brief and friendly, with native canoes paddling out to the ship and trading information about fishing.[66] Champlain next crossed Cape Cod Bay, rounded the peninsula's tip, and traveled down its Atlantic side, eventually stopping at Nauset Harbor. A group of Nauset paddled their canoes out to the ship and began to talk and trade while five of the French sailors went to shore to collect fresh water. While searching inland for a pond or creek, one of the Frenchmen was accosted by a Nauset, who ran up and ripped a bucket from his arms. As the sailor gave chase his companions ran back to the beach to signal to the ship.

Perhaps misunderstanding the nature of the alarm, the French on the ship seized one of the visiting Nauset while the others leaped overboard and swam for freedom. The French fired a few gunshots at the fleeing swimmers. Possibly in response to hearing the gunfire, another group of Nauset came upon the lone sailor who'd gone looking for his stolen bucket. They surrounded the man, wounded him with arrows, and dispatched him with their knives. Despite the death of the sailor, the French released their Nauset hostage. Calm returned, with the Nauset leaders apologizing for the theft and violence and the French burying their dead comrade on the sandy shore of the cape.[67]

The following year, in 1606, Champlain returned, this time anchoring in a harbor at the elbow of Cape Cod near present-day Chatham. Over a hundred Nauset gathered on the shore to greet the French. The ship had suffered some

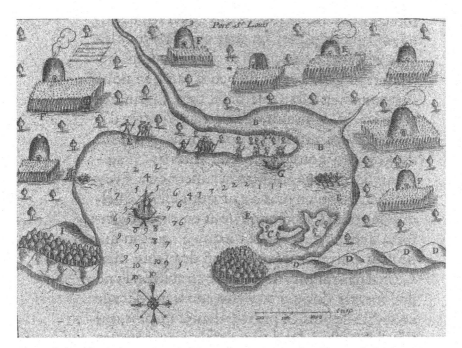

Samuel de Champlain's map of Patuxet in present-day Plymouth Bay, Massachusetts (1613). *Courtesy of the John Carter Brown Library at Brown University*

damage during their cruise, and Champlain stayed for ten days to effect repairs. The Nauset traded animal skins for food and other goods, while groups of armed Frenchmen roamed inland to explore. Whether from alarm over the roving bands of men or some other motivation, Nauset women took down their dwellings in the area. They and their children started disappearing. The French became suspicious and immediately recalled their men to the ship. Five of them were in the midst of baking bread, however, and they refused to abandon their loaves, choosing instead to spend the night on shore. The following morning the bakers woke to find themselves surrounded by four hundred Nauset warriors, who "sent them such a volley of arrows that to rise up was death," according to Champlain.[68] Four of the five Frenchmen died in the initial salvos.

The men on the ship surged into action, with fifteen jumping into one of the ship's boats and rowing to shore. They fired muskets and scattered the Nauset, which allowed them carry the dead sailors to a cross that had been erected the prior day and bury them there. After the somber task was completed, the Frenchmen returned to their ship. Only a short while later, a group of Nauset returned to the beach, where they toppled the cross, dug up the French dead, and left the corpses scattered on the dunes. The explorers were appalled and angry. An expedition set out and killed seven Nauset in retribution.[69] After the violence, Champlain and the French left Cape Cod and never returned. The Nauset still recalled the encounter with bitterness many years later when the Pilgrims arrived.

The violent confrontation would not be the Nauset's last with Europeans. In 1611 English captain Edward Harlow visited Cape Cod and kidnapped two Nauset men by using the familiar tactic of luring them onto his ship with promises of trade.[70] Shortly afterward, several sailors were attacked and wounded with arrows during a second stop. Harlow sailed south and stopped at what is believed to be Nantucket. As soon as they anchored, a group of Nauset assaulted the ship in canoes until English guns forced them back. During the battle, or perhaps afterward, the sailors captured another Nauset man. Captain Harlow next steered his ship to Martha's Vineyard, where he seized two more natives, one of whom was called Epenow. Harlow took the five men to England. Epenow had such a big, powerful physique that, according to John Smith, he was "shown up and down London for money as a wonder."[71]

Epenow was also very intelligent and charismatic and was able to convince his captors that there was gold to be found on Martha's Vineyard. He was brought back to his homeland in 1614 by Captain Nicholas Hobson.[72] Hoping to be led to the gold, Hobson anchored where Epenow instructed. Several Nauset paddled canoes out to the ship, where Hobson entertained them for a time. When they left, they promised to return the next morning with furs to trade. Twenty canoes paddled from shore the following day but paused some distance away from the ship. When the English called them closer, Epenow wrestled free from three men who were guarding him and jumped into the ocean. As soon as he hit the water, all the men in the canoes showered arrows onto the ship's deck.[73] The English grabbed their muskets and returned fire, but Epenow escaped. Hobson was wounded in the exchange, as were many of his crew.[74] The incident added to the bitterness with which the Nauset of Cape Cod, Martha's Vineyard, and Nantucket held for European interlopers, and they would ultimately focus their resentment upon the Pilgrims when they came in 1620.[75]

As the constituent tribes of the Wampanoag Confederacy regularly communicated, the Nauset's experiences would have been shared with Massasoit and his Pokanoket people, as well as with the other member tribes of the confederacy.[76] As a result, the entire confederacy became more suspicious of foreign visitors.[77] In 1614 John Smith, who'd left the Jamestown settlement in 1609, returned to America and, with two ships, cruised the coast of Maine and Massachusetts. It was during this journey that he created his book, *A Description of New England*, which would be published in 1616 and carried by William Brewster on the *Mayflower*. Smith found the people of coastal Maine, which would likely have been Abenaki or other tribes belonging to the Wabanaki Confederacy, less reticent than those of the Massachusett and the Wampanoag Confederacy. After trading in Maine for animal furs and fishing for several months, Smith took one of the ships back to England.

Thomas Hunt was in charge of the second ship. He lingered in the area under the pretense of taking on more fish. Smith had expressed a desire to establish a colony in New England. Hunt, however, wanted to keep the fertile fishing grounds and source of animal pelts to himself and decided to make the place less inviting to English immigrants by souring relations with the native population. To do this, he decided to abduct Native Americans and sell them into slavery, an act which would also feed his avarice.[78] He targeted the Wampanoag Confederacy. Using the trick that by now was so familiar to English explorers, Hunt touched at Patuxet and was able to lure twenty men aboard his ship, where he seized them. Squanto was among the prisoners. Sailing more quickly than any alarm could spread by word of mouth, Hunt rounded the tip of the cape and stopped again on its Atlantic side. Using the same deceit, Hunt kidnapped seven Nauset men. He locked up his twenty-seven prisoners and sailed to Spain. His plan to sell the men, however, was thwarted when a group of Catholic friars interrupted the slave auction.[79]

Instead of profit, Hunt earned only dishonor. His fellow Englishmen uniformly condemned the vile act.[80] On his voyage from Spain to England, Hunt himself learned about the misery of captivity when Turkish pirates captured Hunt's ship and enslaved him.[81] Hunt's raid had predictable long-term effects, alienating the members of the Wampanoag Confederacy from the English for many years to come and directly affecting the Pilgrims' first months in America.[82]

In 1617, three years after Hunt had sailed off with his Wampanoag captives and three years before the Pilgrims took to sea in the *Mayflower*, a French ship was sailing in the waters off Cape Cod when a storm engulfed it. The vessel likely struck one of the many underwater hazards and split apart. The crew somehow escaped and made it to shore. Their reception by the local people was not hospitable. As William Bradford later learned, the Nauset soon discovered the Frenchmen and hounded them until the Nauset gained the upper hand, at which point they killed all of them but three or four. The Nauset kept the few survivors and sent them from one leader to another "to make sport with, and used them worse than slaves."[83] In 1622 an English colonist named Phinehas Pratt learned from a Native American about some of the details of the Frenchmen's captivity: "There was a ship broken by a storm. . . . We made [the survivors] our servants. They wept much. . . . We gave them such meat as our dogs eat. . . . We took away their clothes. They lived but a little while."[84]

About the same time, another French ship anchored off one of the islands in Boston Harbor, intending to trade with the Massachusett people. A large number of natives loaded beaver pelts into canoes and paddled out to the ship. They carried hidden knives. The men boarded the ship ostensibly to barter, but when the leader gave a sign, they all drew their knives and struck, killing everyone on board.[85]

English Captain Thomas Dermer explored the coast of New England several times. After accompanying John Smith in 1614, he spent two years starting in 1616 based at an English fishing settlement on the island of Newfoundland located off the mainland of present-day Canada. It was there that Dermer met Squanto, who'd survived Hunt's kidnapping and, after spending time in Spain and then in England, had been sent back to America in the hope that he might help temper the animosity that his countrymen had developed for the English.

Squanto eventually convinced Dermer to launch an expedition to his homeland.[86] In May 1619 Dermer and Squanto anchored at Squanto's village of Patuxet. The place was empty, and everyone was dead.[87] Waves of grief must have swept through Squanto. The village had been a thriving place when he'd been taken by Hunt. Now, the fields lay unkempt and the homes were deserted. His family was dead. His friends, dead. No one was left.

Dermer and Squanto set off on foot to try to find out what happened. With Squanto showing the way, they walked westward, following winding native pathways through the coastal forests for about fifteen miles, where they came upon an encampment called Nemasket, which is located near modern-day Middleborough, Massachusetts. From the people in Nemasket, Squanto likely heard the sorrowful news that disease had ravaged his people, wiping out the entire population. At Nemasket, Dermer met with the sachem Massasoit, who visited with a retinue of fifty men and his brother, Quadequina.[88] According to a letter from Dermer in the possession of William Bradford, Dermer quickly learned that the Pokanoket and the other members of the Wampanoag Confederacy harbored an "inveterate malice to the English" because of Thomas Hunt.[89] Such was the generalized hatred that Massasoit threatened Dermer and "would have killed me . . . had not [Squanto] entreated hard for me."[90] Squanto accompanied Dermer to Maine, where the Patuxet parted ways with the Englishman at an Abenaki village.[91]

Thus, some five years after being violently kidnapped by Thomas Hunt and sold into slavery in Spain, after having escaped bondage and somehow gotten to London, after taking Thomas Dermer to his home at Patuxet only to find it bereft of life, Squanto was free. And while he wasn't home, he was fairly close, for from the Abenaki village it was about a five- or six-day journey overland back to the Wampanoag Confederation. It is likely at the village that he met an Abenaki man named Samoset. Samoset would accompany Squanto on his journey home within the next year or so.[92]

After seeing Squanto off, Captain Dermer sailed to Jamestown, choosing to follow the coast southward all the way to the Chesapeake Bay in order to explore and map the route. Early in the trip, a storm forced his small coastal ship onto a shoal. With wind and waves threatening to pound the grounded vessel to pieces, the sailors were obliged to dump most of their provisions to lighten the ship's weight and float clear of the sandbank. The loss of their stores forced Dermer to rely almost exclusively on the hospitality of the native communities and their willingness to trade.

But trading without their Patuxet guide proved much more hazardous than before. Stopping on the Atlantic side of Cape Cod, Dermer left his crew to mind their pinnace and went ashore, presumably in search of food. He was ambushed and taken prisoner. In an attempt to lure the sailors from the safety of their ship, the Nauset tried to ransom their captive to his countrymen. During the exchange, however, Dermer somehow managed to escape, and reunited, the Englishmen dashed away. After stopping without incident at Martha's Vineyard, Dermer sailed into Long Island Sound and reached its western end before concluding that he was embayed. Dermer sought the help of a local native with knowledge of the area, and the man guided the ship through the tidal estuary known today as the East River, which connects the western end of the Long Island Sound with the Upper New York Bay at the southern tip of Manhattan Island. During the transit, Dermer and his men came under fire two separate times when large groups of warriors shot arrows at them from the bank.[93]

When he reached Jamestown, Dermer found that, as was all too often the case in Virginia, the land was in the midst of a dangerous contagion. Dermer was stricken with the illness—in his words, "so sore shaken with a burning fever that I was brought even unto death's door"—but slowly recovered over the coming months.[94] After wintering at Jamestown, he was strong enough to return to the sea.

In the summer of 1620, just as the Pilgrims were beginning their final preparations for their voyage, Dermer sailed for New England.[95] He stopped again at Martha's Vineyard, where he met with a group of Nauset that included Epenow, the man who'd been shown as a "wonder" in London and who'd escaped captivity by diving from an English ship and surviving a hail of gunfire. Perhaps suspicious that Dermer had come to seize him, Epenow and his men acted preemptively by trying to grab Dermer. A fight broke out, and Dermer's men were killed.[96]

Dermer fought his way free, but not before he was wounded fourteen times.[97] He fled to the pinnace. The Nauset swarmed the ship, and one of them, possibly Epenow himself, lunged with a blade and would have cut off Dermer's head had a crewman left behind to mind the boat not parried the blow with his own sword. The two Englishmen somehow fended off the Nauset and escaped. Despite his injuries, Dermer and the other man were able to sail the pinnace back to Jamestown, where Dermer died.[98]

Only a few weeks after Dermer's death, the *Mayflower* hoisted anchor in England, set its sails, and began its famous voyage. Dermer's demise was the most recent example of the Wampanoag's hostile view of the English, a fact that would become a hazardous obstacle for the Pilgrims, as William Bradford later acknowledged when he noted "how far these people were from peace and with what danger this plantation was begun."[99]

Not only had English explorers killed and kidnapped people of the Wampanoag Confederacy, but they were also viewed as being responsible for an epidemic that ravaged the seaboard. Sometime between 1615 and 1618 a deadly contagion or series of contagions swept through New England, striking communities from present-day Rhode Island to Maine. Though witnesses such as Thomas Dermer, who noted the disease's impact when he explored the area in 1619 with Squanto, declared the plague was responsible, several other diseases were later suspected, including smallpox, influenza, and leptospirosis.[100] The native population had no immunological defenses.[101] The results were devastating, leaving the area a disaster zone comparable to those created by modern warfare and other mass casualty catastrophes.[102]

Dermer found some recently populous villages now utterly void of life. In others, a small remnant still clung to life, even as disease still clung to the living.[103] Some villages were abandoned, the living leaving the dead and dying behind as a feast for crows and vermin.[104] In places such as Patuxet the mortality rate was at or near 100 percent. Overall mortality estimates range from 75 percent and upward to even 90 percent.[105] A region previously described as teeming with people was now barren. The Pilgrims, too, would see the unburied bones of the victims, as recorded by William Bradford:

> They found . . . the people not many, being dead and abundantly wasted in the late, great mortality which fell in all these parts about three years before the coming of the English [Pilgrims], wherein thousands of them died. They not being able to bury one another, their skulls and bones were found in many places lying still above ground, where their houses and dwellings had been, [which was] a very sad spectacle to behold.[106]

Later colonists living on Massachusetts Bay also saw the lingering effects, seeing the bones of many who died as they lay in their houses.

Though the disease didn't discriminate, the Wampanoag were particularly ravaged. Entire villages vanished. Communities that were numbered in the thousands became communities that were counted in the dozens of inhabitants. Significantly, young men and children were most affected, a fact that contributed to changes in the political relations between rival native nations.

With fewer men, the Wampanoag Confederacy became weaker. Its neighbors took notice. And they acted. Massasoit and his people fell prey to the Narragansett, whose lands started just across the Providence River from Pokanoket and stretched westward to the border between the modern states of

Rhode Island and Connecticut.[107] Because they had had little contact with early European explorers, the Narragansett suffered relatively few deaths from the contagious outbreak that decimated the Wampanoag. As a result, they were stronger and exploited the discrepancy to demand concessions from Massasoit. With his force of warriors depleted, Massasoit was eventually driven to yield territory around Narragansett Bay to his sworn enemy.[108]

While the English viewed it as a providential sign that God was blessing their desire to colonize New England,[109] Massasoit viewed it differently. As he later recounted to Bradford, the Wampanoag sachem believed that the Europeans had unleashed disease upon his people and suspected that when the Pilgrims came, they "kept the plague buried in the ground and could send it" like a weapon against whomever they chose.[110] Massasoit's dread was made greater by a prophecy delivered by one of the French survivors of the 1617 shipwreck, as recorded by John Smith:

> [One of the Frenchmen tried to] persuade them to become Christians, showing them a Testament, expounding some parts so well as he could, but they much derided him. He told them he feared his God would destroy them, whereat the King assembled all his people about a hill, himself with the Christian standing on the top, and demanded if [the Frenchmen's] God had so many people and [would be] able to kill all those [assembled]? [The French captive] answered yes, and surely would, and bring strangers to possess their land. And not long after such a sickness came.[111]

The prophecy might have gained legitimacy because it coincided with the appearance of a comet in the sky that left a deep impression upon the native communities. Thomas Morton, an English contemporary of the Pilgrims who first visited New England in 1622 and who returned in 1624 to start his own colony, recorded the reactions to the celestial event:[112]

> Some of the ancient Indians, that are surviving at the writing hereof, do affirm that about some two or three years before the first English arrived here, they saw a blazing star, or comet, which was a forerunner of this sad mortality, for soon after it [the epidemic] came upon them in extremity.[113]

The combination of the prophecy and the comet's arrival that preceded the devastation of disease upon the Wampanoag, which forced Massasoit to cede authority to the rival Narragansett, dovetailed into and reinforced his lingering resentment over the infamy wrought by Thomas Hunt. These foreigners who wielded disease like a weapon had rendered his once-powerful nation spiritually powerless.[114]

Within a few days of the *Mayflower*'s arrival, Massasoit would likely have heard about it from the Nauset. From his base in Pokanoket, he probably sent scouts to keep an eye on the pale newcomers. He viewed them as responsible for all the tragedy that had recently befallen his proud empire. They were his adversaries, enemies of his people. He would watch. And wait for an opportunity to strike.

6 | FINDING PLYMOUTH ROCK

I would not wish
Any companion in the world but you.
—*The Tempest*, act 3, scene 1

THE FIRST INDICATION THAT the Pilgrims might not be welcome would have been clear to anyone who'd visited New England with earlier explorers like Gosnold, Pring, Weymouth, Champlain, or John Smith, for the *Mayflower* swayed on its anchor alone. As the group of men chosen to gather firewood assembled on the deck after the Mayflower Compact was completed, the beaches were empty. No one paddled out in canoes to meet their ship. When previous ships had arrived, the Wampanoag had come to trade or share food and entertainment. Now, they remained hidden on shore, angry and apprehensive over their prior encounters with Europeans.

The *Mayflower*'s longboat was lowered into the water, and the Englishmen rowed toward shore. The cold wind would have burned on their faces. Unfortunately, the bay quickly became shallow, and the longboat grounded, forcing the men to plod several hundred yards through knee-deep water to reach the beach.

After two months on a rolling deck at sea, solid ground would have made the Pilgrims reel a little. All around them were sand dunes, which reminded the Separatists of Leiden, where they'd seen similar dunes skirting the North Sea. Beyond the dunes, they found dark, rich soil populated with thick forests of trees.[1] Some varieties were familiar to the English. Others were not. The sun was sinking rapidly toward the mainland, and they didn't stay long before returning to the ship. They didn't see any natives but did have time to gather firewood. They choose one of the trees that would have been new to them: red cedar,[2] which when burned "smelled very sweet and strong," according to the firsthand account in *Mourt's Relation*.[3] Hopkins, however, was familiar with this New World cedar. For ten months on Bermuda, he'd cut down the cedar trees used to build the ships that rescued the crew and passengers of the *Sea Venture*. He'd seen the trees in Virginia too. He'd have known that the fragrant wood would be welcome on board the *Mayflower*, where it would help mask the stench of over a hundred people living in cramped, wet quarters for more than eight weeks. Indeed, the passengers liked the wood so much, they burned cedar nearly exclusively during their long layover in Provincetown Harbor.[4] Although individuals in this first foray onto Cape Cod weren't named, given their choice of firewood, Hopkins was probably one of them.

The First Exploration

The Pilgrims brought with them an open boat called a shallop, which was about thirty-five feet long and could be rowed like a longboat or fixed with a mast and set with sails. To fit the shallop into the *Mayflower*, they'd cut it into four parts, and it had been damaged during the voyage.[5] On Monday, November 13, the crew hoisted the beaten pieces out of the ship and set them on shore. The ship's carpenter declared it would take more than two weeks to make the shallop seaworthy.[6] The colonists were intending to use the shallop, with its shallow draft and room for men as well as provisions, to quickly cruise the coast and scout out possible settlement sites.

Two weeks was too long to wait. Each day reduced their dwindling supply of food. Pressure, too, was quickly mounting from the mariners, who wanted to drop their human cargo and return to England.[7] More significantly, sickness was stripping away the settlers' reserves. William Button's recent death served as a stark reminder that if they didn't quickly establish themselves, death would come again.

The *Mayflower*'s anchorage only exacerbated the situation. While Provincetown Harbor protected the ship from storms, reaching the shore proved very difficult and ultimately dangerous. The shallows reached some three-quarters of a mile from the beach, which obliged every Pilgrim who came to shore for drinking water, firewood, or to wash clothes to splash and slog through icy water. The late November weather was frigid and windy, and in combination with clothes soaked in cold water "caused many to get colds and coughs," according to *Mourt's Relation*.[8] Illness from exposure weakened many of the passengers, making them even more susceptible to scurvy, a deadly mixture that would inevitably start taking lives.[9] The survivors would have to act decisively.

From the heights of the *Mayflower*, what looked to be a river mouth could be seen some five or six miles down the inner coast of Cape Cod.[10] What the Pilgrims saw was the Pamet River that cuts through modern-day Truro. The Pamet is primarily a salt marsh, a fact, of course, that would not have been known to the settlers. To them, a river would have held the possibility of a permanent supply of fresh water, one of the critical factors for a settlement. A group of sixteen men volunteered to investigate. While the Pamet was only five or six miles away by boat, the shallop lay in pieces on the beach and getting to that point by land entailed much more distance. It would be the Pilgrims' first real exploratory effort in America. Because they didn't know what might await them, each man carried his own provisions on his back, as well as armor, a sword, and a musket.[11]

Myles Standish led the party. According to *Mourt's Relation*, three men were specially selected from among the volunteers to provide "counsel and advice" to Standish. They were Stephen Hopkins and two of the Saints, William Bradford and Edward Tilley.[12] Governor Carver appointed each of them. Standish was thirty-six at the time. Hopkins was thirty-nine. Bradford and Tilley were younger, Bradford being thirty and Tilley thirty-two. Hopkins's appointment was significant as it strongly suggests that he was already assuming a leadership role within the group of colonists. In Hopkins's appointment, Carver was perhaps also working to soothe any remaining distemper from the recent altercation over colonial authority. As Standish was associated with the Separatists because of their Netherlands connection, Hopkins was likely seen as an uncompromised representative of the Strangers, which may have helped alleviate concerns over whether the Saints would become unduly influential in the wake of Carver's election as governor.[13]

On Wednesday, November 15, the exploratory party left the *Mayflower* and sloshed ashore. It is difficult to picture the terrain four hundred years later on the ever-shifting dunes of Cape Cod. Today, this part of the cape is lined with streets and houses and modest-sized trees. In 1620, it was thickly wooded with pine, oak, ash, birch, holly, and walnut trees, and the red cedar the Pilgrims favored for firewood.[14] Walking in the soft sand of the beach with a heavy burden, the men likely tired quickly. Seeking firmer ground, they would have turned toward the hills that rose from the beach. After only a mile, which would have put them near the center of modern Provincetown, they spotted five or six men by the water's edge. They were Nauset, the first Indians seen by the Pilgrims.[15] When the smaller group saw the oncoming Englishmen, they darted into the woods.

The explorers huddled together for a tense consultation. Despite the obvious importance of relations with the native people, the Pilgrims did not appear to have had a preconceived policy.[16] They'd just gotten their first glimpse of those who would be their neighbors. Or their enemies. Now what? Should they return to the ship? Should they continue their trek toward the distant river mouth? Or should they go after the Nauset?

They chose pursuit for two reasons, which, together, reveal the conflicting attitudes of an unsettled policy. First, they were worried that more natives might be, according to Bradford's account, "lying in ambush" if they continued on their current path.[17] This rationale was likely proposed by Standish, as it was couched in the terms of an age-old military tactic. Second, the Pilgrims wanted to initiate contact with the native people, "to see if they could speak with them," as Bradford recorded.[18] This rationale was likely proposed by Hopkins. In Jamestown, he'd seen the impact of both peaceful and hostile interactions with Native Americans. When peaceful, trading for furs and food was possible. When hostile, violent conflict and starvation were probable.

For Hopkins, developing a positive relationship would have been of utmost importance. In the six years that he spent on the Chesapeake Bay, Hopkins had learned some of the language spoken by the people of the Powhatan Confederacy, who spoke a variation of the same Algonquian language as the Wampanoag.[19] He'd therefore have likely been near the front of the pack of *Mayflower* explorers, ready to try "to speak with" the Nauset. Though perhaps for different reasons, Standish and Hopkins probably agreed on the same course. They would follow the natives. If so, it would be one of many consultations between the two men, who in the months to come would both step to the fore on each of the early interactions with the people of the Wampanoag Confederacy.

The Englishmen trudged with their gear into the shadows beneath the towering trees, following the Nauset for several miles across uneven terrain, marked with dense woods, hills, and marshy ponds.[20] They eventually reached the beaches on the Atlantic side of the cape, and following the tracks in the sand, covered another ten miles or so before nightfall without catching up to the Nauset.[21] They stopped and made camp somewhere to the east of modern-day North Truro, taking turns as guards while others slept.[22]

Thursday morning, November 16, they set out as soon as there was enough light to discern the Nauset footprints in the sand. The trail led them to a creek, which they followed away from the beach into thick undergrowth in the hope of finding a native settlement. According to the unnamed authors of *Mourt's Relation*,

> We marched through boughs and bushes, and under hills and valleys, which tore our armor in pieces, and yet could meet with none of them, nor their houses, nor find any fresh water, which we greatly desired, and stood in need of, for we brought neither beer nor water with us, and our victuals was only biscuit and Holland cheese, and a little bottle of *aqua vitae* [a strong distilled spirit, such as brandy], so as we were sore athirst.[23]

By ten o'clock in the morning, they were lost, plodding through a deep valley choked with brush, scrub, and stands of long grass, following narrow, winding game paths. A startled deer bounded away. The trail of the natives they'd been following had disappeared long ago, so they took their bearings and started walking toward the western shore of the cape.[24]

Once again on the beach lining Cape Cod Bay, the group continued southward.[25] Their exertions, a sleepless night, and exposure to the frosty November weather started to take a toll. Some of the men couldn't keep the pace, and the party split into two groups, with the leading cluster pausing at times to wait for the stragglers. It would be an omen of what was to come, when the New England winter started to cull the weakest among them.

Just before the river mouth, they once more turned inland and came upon a path leading to oddly placed heaps of sand.[26] One was covered with a woven mat made of grass. They dug and determined that the mounds were graves and remade the tomb they'd disturbed "as it was, and left the rest [of the mounds] untouched because we thought it would be odious to them to ransack their sepulchers."[27]

The explorers left the graveyard and soon came upon the remnants of a small encampment and several more mounds. The Englishmen excavated, and this time, instead of a grave, they found a small basket full of Indian corn. Soon, they uncovered a larger basket containing "very fair corn of this year . . . some yellow and some red and others mixed with blue."[28] Aside from Hopkins, who would have recognized the colorful kernels from his years in Virginia, the settlers had never before seen the flint corn that the Indians cultivated. They were amazed.[29] The basket held between three and four bushels of corn.[30] Each bushel weighed about fifty pounds, and represented hours and hours of labor.

The discovery presented a dilemma. Should they take the corn, which was obviously being stored by the Nauset for use during the winter? Or should they return the food to its place, as they'd done with the graves? Again, there was a discussion, with Standish talking at length to his three advisers, Hopkins, Bradford, and Tilley.[31] Honesty demanded that they leave the corn as they found it, as did diplomacy. If their goal was to initiate positive relations with the local people, stealing from them would not be a productive first step.

Jamestown had shown Hopkins the importance of establishing goodwill, so he probably would have argued against taking the corn. While substantial, the discovery would only feed a hundred people for a few days. Instead of stealing this small amount, they should try to trade for a continuous supply, as he'd seen done in Virginia. Theft would have been the exact opposite of what he desired and thought best.

Against the demands of honesty and diplomacy weighed exigency, which suggested that they take the food, for it would be a welcome supplement to their provisions. The gray skies, cold days, and colder nights reminded the explorers of what lay ahead. Yesterday's chance meeting with the "wild men" of this land was marked by apprehension and suspicion on both sides. Relations with the sailors aboard the *Mayflower* were degenerating, and the Pilgrims feared the seamen might abandon them before they were properly established. Sickness was spreading. Food supplies were perilously low, a fact likely emphasized by pangs of hunger in their rumbling stomachs, for they hadn't eaten much on this journey.

In the end, it would have been Standish's decision as the leader of the expedition, and *Mourt's Relation* recorded the chosen course:

> After much consultation, we concluded to take the kettle and as much of the corn as we could carry away with us, and when our shallop came, if we could find any of the people, and come to parley with

them, we would give them the kettle again and satisfy them for their corn. So we took all the ears . . . [and] they that could put any into their pockets filled the same.[32]

Thus, the first act in the New World by the Pilgrims, a group whose journey was initiated by Christians so devoted to worship that they had fled their homeland, was to steal food from the people upon whose land they wished to settle. Faith alone would not feed them, and dogma apparently collapsed under the burden of extremity.

After taking the corn, the explorers marched southward toward the Pamet River. As they drew close, they spotted the remains of an old fort, which, they deduced, had been constructed by previous European visitors.[33] Though they might not have appreciated the analogy at the time, the deteriorated walls of the palisade were a memorial of the state of relations between the Nauset and Europeans. Walls and barricades signaled hostility, something that the Pilgrims would soon discover for themselves.

The river itself turned out to be a puzzle, and they couldn't confirm whether its source carried fresh water because they didn't have time to trace it far enough inland to escape brackish tidal surges. Governor Carver had commanded them back to the *Mayflower* after two days, so they resolved to return once their shallop was finished. They made camp as darkness enveloped the cape. A storm brought heavy rain and gales, and the Englishmen lit a huge fire against the cold and assembled a tall wall of logs and thick pine boughs for protection against the wind. The men again rotated in shifts that were timed by burning a length of the slow-burning cord used to fire their matchlock muskets.[34]

The next morning, Friday, November 17, they made their way northward back toward the ship. Wandering single file through a wood, they came upon something that "shrewdly puzzled" them, according to the account in *Mourt's Relation*. There was a young sapling bent double by a rope toward the ground where a few acorns were scattered. "Stephen Hopkins said it [was designed] to catch some deer." As the men gathered around to hear Hopkins explain how the trap worked, William Bradford, who was walking at the back of the group, came forward. He circled the other men to take a look and inadvertently stepped on the catch. The sapling snapped straight, and Bradford "was immediately caught up by the leg."[35] All agreed that it was an ingenious device.

After disentangling Bradford, they trekked onward. Tired and wet and cold, they eventually reached Provincetown Harbor and used musket fire to attract the attention of the ship, which sent its boat to fetch them. They were welcomed by their fellow passengers, who were happy about the stolen corn, as recorded in *Mourt's Relation*, for they "knew not how to come by any" other store of food. Perhaps out of a sense of guilt, they promised to give "large satisfaction" for the burglary as soon as they were able to make contact with the Nauset.[36]

The Second Exploration

While the ship's carpenters continued work on the shallop, the settlers kept busy collecting firewood and felling timber, for with the help of the same carpenters, they intended to build a second shallop. The weather took a turn for the worse. Temperatures dropped and frequent storms brought wind and rain. Food supplies dropped lower. As each trip to shore required the long, wet slog through the shallows, sickness deepened and spread. The shallop wasn't ready for another week and a half.

On November 27 the Pilgrims embarked on their second exploratory expedition. Twenty-four men were chosen by Governor Carver, and because the ship's master, Christopher Jones, also wanted to go, he brought with him several of his sailors, bringing the total number in the party to thirty-four.[37] Although the names of the group were not documented, it is very likely that Standish, Bradford, and Hopkins were again among them.[38] Because they were taking the shallop and the ship's boat, and because they continued to be concerned about the tensions between the passengers and sailors, Carver asked Jones to be the leader of the expedition.

The group launched into stormy seas churned up by a fierce southerly wind so strong that neither boat could make use of its sail. Undeterred, the men bent over their oars and labored eastward across Provincetown Harbor to the beach near what is now called East Harbor, a tidal estuary that four hundred years ago was open to the rest of Provincetown Harbor, but today is enclosed by a narrow neck of land. The wind became so strong, however, that the shallop risked foundering. They couldn't go on and decided to harbor there that night. Determined not to lose more time, some of the Pilgrims wallowed through thigh-deep water to shore and continued overland, with the men who stayed behind agreeing to sail southward as soon as they could to rendezvous with those on foot. The group marched for hours into the teeth of the frigid wind. The gale howled ceaselessly. The rain turned to snow, and the wintery mix battered them. By dusk, they'd gone only six or seven miles. Overnight about a half a foot of snow accumulated. The impact of the long hours of exposure would be lasting: "Some of our people that are dead took the original of their death here."[39]

The next morning, November 28, the shallop and Jones's boat were able to make headway against the wind, and by eleven o'clock in the morning, had sailed down the inner side of Cape Cod to meet up with those who'd gone ahead. From there, it was not long before they reached the mouth of the Pamet River. The explorers quickly discovered that the inlet that marked the river was too shallow to support ocean-going ships, though it would accommodate smaller boats. They landed and traced the river inland. After several hours of toiling up and down hills and valleys through the thick blanket of snow, the men were exhausted. Master Jones ordered the group to make camp. They built a fire under the pine trees, where the ground was less snowy, and by the fortune of passing flocks of birds and several well-placed musket shots, they had three fat geese and six ducks for their dinner, which according to *Mourt's Relation*, "we ate with soldier's stomachs, for we had eaten little all that day."[40]

They slept as best they could on the cold ground and in the morning continued following the river to determine whether its source was fresh, for the water was still brackish at the spot where they camped. But after some time battling the steep, slippery hills, they abandoned their quest. With a shallow harbor and hilly terrain, settlement at this place would have been difficult regardless whether it had a supply of fresh water. They chose to look elsewhere.[41]

The place where they'd taken the Nauset corn was not too distant, and since they'd seen several more mounds during their prior visit, the Pilgrims returned to look for more. As they'd already crossed the moral threshold, their second crime was done without discussion. Also, by this point, the settlers had realized that they would not be getting a friendly reception from the local people.[42] Men like Thomas Hunt had turned them against any newcomers. Still no canoes had come from the shore to visit the *Mayflower*. The first native people they'd seen had fled. It was clear that they were not enthusiastic about the Pilgrims, which perhaps made their task at least more morally palatable.

The ground was so frozen that they were forced to use their daggers and short swords to chip away the ice in order to get at the buried corn.[43] What role Stephen Hopkins played in this—whether he objected to it or resigned himself or gleefully joined the others in ransacking the mounds—was not recorded, but it was likely that he at least would have supported repaying the Nauset, which was a sentiment that William Bradford expressed several times. (Some six or so months later, the Pilgrims did ultimately reimburse those whose corn they took.)[44]

With the skies showing that more foul weather was imminent, the nominal leader of the expedition, Master Jones, decided to return to the *Mayflower*. Along with him went his sailors and from the settlers, according to *Mourt's Relation*, "our weakest people, and some that were sick." This left eighteen who "desired to make further discovery and to find out the Indians' habitation," an objective even more important given their sense that the Indians would not be seeking them out.[45] Stephen Hopkins was most probably one of the men who stayed behind.[46] After the boats left, the men camped again on the snow-crusted, frozen ground. The next morning, November 30, they continued exploring until that afternoon, when Jones returned with the shallop to retrieve them. By evening they were aboard the *Mayflower*, where they discussed whether to settle at the Pamet River location.

Despite the river's drawbacks, some of the Pilgrims argued in favor of it, listing several reasons. First, though the sheltered harbor at the mouth of the river was too shallow for ships, it was convenient for boats. Second, by the corn they pilfered nearby, the land showed promise for supporting the cultivation of crops. Third, Cape Cod was believed to be a good place for fishing. And finally, and most significant to those advocating for the place, they were running out of time. The unseasonably cold weather made it more difficult and dangerous to look for alternative sites. The danger was particularly acute because the frigid, wet lodging aboard the ship and in the field had so affected the group of settlers that nearly everyone was wracked with fits of coughing. If they continued much longer in these inhospitable conditions, the weak would die and even the strong would eventually succumb to disease and infection. Furthermore, their food supplies would only last a short while longer, and they would need much of it to fuel the hard labor of clearing land and building shelter. They were also worried that as the inventory of food *decreased*, the risk *increased* that Jones and the sailors would abandon them.[47]

The Pamet River idea didn't receive unanimous support, which led to controversy.[48] Perhaps the dispute grew out of the discord that resulted in the

Mayflower Compact. More likely, however, the altercation emerged because of the severity of spreading illness. Those who were not feeling well or who had sick loved ones would likely have argued for the river. They needed to escape the dank, wet lodging on the ship as soon as possible. Joining them would probably have been those weary of trekking about in the cold rain and sleet and snow.

Those who opposed the Pamet River location were probably not yet sick or, significantly, understood that finding the right site was, in the long term, more important than the impact that a further delay that might impose. Hopkins would probably have been in this camp. The shallow harbor would quickly become a hindrance to subsequent supply and trading missions. More important, they hadn't confirmed whether the river even carried fresh water. All their samples had been brackish, just like the James River, which had caused so much illness for the Jamestown colonists. The only obvious source of fresh water was a large pond they'd discovered nearly three miles away from the river mouth, a distance scarcely desirable for such an essential component of survival. The few small pools they'd found that were closer would require traversing steep hills and could dry up in the summer.[49]

A grim pragmatism would likely have underscored the resolution of those opposed to the Pamet River: yes, people were sick, but this was unavoidable. Whether the group settled immediately or waited to find a better site, there was a good chance that the weakest among them would die. It was part of the seasoning with which Hopkins was all too familiar. The New World was different than the Old, and not all the people of the latter would survive in the former. This place demanded its sacrifice. Jamestown proved as much.

Some of those against the Pamet River proposed that they look for a spot on the mainland far to their north. As noted before, William Brewster carried with him John Smith's *Description of New England*. In it, Smith had made note of a place called Agawom, which was located on the coast some seventy or so miles north of Cape Cod, at modern-day Ipswich, Massachusetts. Whether it was Brewster himself, or others among the Saints with whom he'd shared the book, a group of the colonists passionately urged that they sail to Agawom, for the land was believed to have, according to *Mourt's Relation*, "an excellent harbor for ships, better ground, and better fishing."[50]

Still others who disfavored the Pamet suggested that they might find better locations on and around Cape Cod.[51] They simply needed to look a little farther

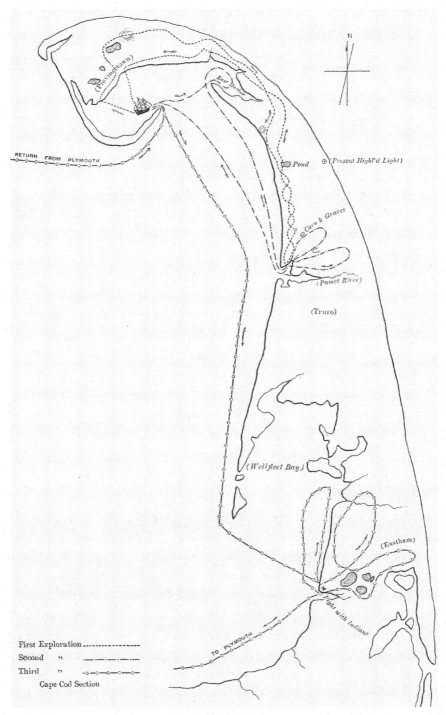

"Routes of the Three Explorations Made While in Cape Cod Harbor," from Azel Ames, *The May-Flower and Her Log* (Boston and New York: Houghton, Mifflin and Company, 1907); image digitally adapted. *Courtesy of the University of Toronto*

afield. Because the opposition to the Pamet River was split into two groups, the argument between the competing factions was involved and clearly took place over several days, as the next expedition didn't begin until six days after the shallop from the second excursion returned to the *Mayflower*.[52] The debate was also interrupted twice by sorrowful events that helped press home the urgency of their situation. Although the end of November had seen Susanna and William White celebrating the birth of the first English immigrant born in New England, by December 4 they were mourning the loss of their servant, Edward Thompson. Two days later, Jasper More, a seven-year-old boy indentured to the family of John Carver, passed away.[53]

In the end, the group that recommended continuing to search the immediate area won the day, a decision potentially encouraged by the report of one of the *Mayflower*'s pilots who'd been to the region before that there was a navigable river with a good harbor on the mainland directly across from Cape Cod.[54] Governor Carver chose a select company of ten of the Pilgrims' "principal men," in the words of William Bradford. They would go in the shallop with seven of the ship's sailors and the pilot and look for the pilot's river on the mainland.[55] Because of the pressing demands of time, they were instructed—likely by Master Jones—to go no farther.[56] It would be their last expedition before making a final decision on where to build their settlement.

The Third Exploration

Signifying the importance of the third exploration, the "principal men" included Carver himself. With him went Myles Standish and his three advisers from the prior expeditions, Stephen Hopkins, William Bradford, and Edward Tilley. The others were John Tilley (Edward's brother), Edward Winslow, John Howland (one of John Carver's servants), Richard Warren (one of the Strangers), and Edward Doty (one of Stephen Hopkins's servants). They boarded the shallop on Wednesday, December 6. The weather was harsh. It was bitterly cold and grim. A strong wind was blowing out of the northeast, which pinned them against the curling fingernail of land to the southwest of the *Mayflower*. They spent more than a day trying to clear the tip of Long Point, which lay only about two hundred yards away from the ship.[57]

Though the Pilgrims didn't know it, a nor'easter was settling into the area.[58] Named for the direction from which the wind blows, these storms are among the most destructive type of weather event in all New England because of their severity. They are complex systems and can become very large and very intense in the winter months. Oftentimes, nor'easters create blizzard conditions, with snow driven by winds over thirty miles an hour that can reduce visibility to less than one-quarter of a mile and temperatures at or below twenty degrees Fahrenheit. Coastal areas like Cape Cod might get a sloppy mix of snow, sleet, freezing rain, and rain. Tidal levels can rise several feet above the norm, and waves as high as fourteen feet can pound the shoreline.[59] In the open ocean, wave heights can jump exponentially in a matter of hours, and waves have been recorded over sixty feet high off New England and have approached one hundred feet off the coast of Nova Scotia.[60]

Thwarted by the wind and drenched with pounding rain, the Pilgrims spent the night in the open boat. Edward Tilley nearly passed out, overcome by the combination of frigid conditions and illness, and one of the sailors became so pallid that they thought he might expire. Despite deteriorating conditions and an increasing threat to their health, they were determined to press on, for they had no other choice. This was their last opportunity. If they turned back, the entire venture might collapse.

Struggling with their oars against the wind, they finally cleared Long Point on Thursday, December 7. The rain turn into sleet. They made for the inner side of the cape, which would provide them some shelter from the northeastern gales, an effort that took them two hours. Here, the water was a little smoother, which made for better sailing, but, according to *Mourt's Relation*, "it was very cold, [and] the water froze on our clothes and made them many times like coats of iron." They passed the Pamet River and spent the rest of the day exploring what is today Wellfleet Harbor, which is nearly three miles across and about three and half miles long. As the sun was setting, they came closer to shore to look for a place to camp and spotted a group of ten to twelve Nauset. As the shallop approached, one of the Nauset looked up, and the group scattered into the woods.[61]

Battered by sleet and gusting wind, the Englishmen went to the forest's edge and cut trees to construct a barricade of logs and brush. They lit a fire and set sentinels. The cold and wet weather made sleep difficult. Smoke rising from campfires only few miles distant made it impossible. The Nauset were close at hand.

By morning, the freezing rain turned to snow. The English decided to investigate whether this place might present a suitable location for settlement, and the party split up. The eight sailors took to the shallop to explore and sound the depth of the harbor to see if it was fit for shipping, and the Pilgrim group surveyed the shoreline. They focused on the most critical factors: a convenient freshwater supply and flat fields sufficient to support crops. The sailors learned that Wellfleet Harbor had deep enough water to allow ocean-going ships, but the Pilgrims found it insufficient in the other aspects.[62]

They decided to look for the Nauset, tracking their footprints inland and losing sight of the shallop. They came across a path and followed it deep into the woods, spending the day tramping through the cold and returning to the bay as the sun dropped low in the sky. They'd not eaten anything all day and were faint and weary from exertion.[63] Together with the sailors, they made camp at what is today called First Encounter Beach near the Herring River in Eastham, building a three-sided barricade of logs and tree boughs to about the height of a man. Tired, hungry, cold, and wet, the men made their only meal of the day with their meager provisions. After eating, they set the first sentinels for the night.[64] The rest of the men tried to sleep.

At about midnight, "a great and hideous cry" rose from the woods, according to *Mourt's Relation*. One of the guards called out, "Arm! Arm!" The weary explorers quickly roused themselves and grabbed their muskets. Two shot in the direction from which the noise came. Would there be a charge? The men strained to see into the black night. They listened above for any sound that seemed out of place, but there was only the wind and the rain. One of the sailors, who'd been to Newfoundland on a prior voyage, said he recognized the sound as that coming from a fox or wolf.[65] If so, perhaps the shots had scared the creature away. The adrenaline of the alarm ebbed, and the men returned to their places by the fire, trusting the guards to remain vigilant.

At about five o'clock in the morning, December 9, the company started stirring. Two or three men fired their matchlock muskets into the woods to test that they worked, for wet weather often fouled the gunpowder. Those that prayed gathered together for a quick devotion. It was still dark out. They stoked the fire. All but four of them carried their armor and muskets down to the shallop at the water's edge, which was some distance from their campsite clearing, before returning to eat what breakfast they could.[66] The meal was soon interrupted.

Perhaps the shots fired earlier in the morning, though done with innocent intent, were misinterpreted as a hostile act, or perhaps the Nauset had been lying in wait. Whatever the case might have been, the Nauset now attacked. As one of the contributors of *Mourt's Relation* recorded,

> Anon, all of a sudden, we heard a great and strange cry, which we knew to be the same voices [that had been heard at midnight], though they varied their notes. One of our company, being abroad [i.e., outside the barricade], came running in and cried, *They are men, Indians, Indians.* And withal, their arrows came flying amongst us.[67]

The shadows under the trees were deep and dark, making it very difficult to locate their attackers, a condition made worse by the glare of the campfire, which both ruined their night vision and illuminated the Englishmen, making them easy targets. By the noise of their cries, the Pilgrims estimated that there were thirty or even forty, although some thought that there were many more hidden by the predawn gloom.[68]

The Nauset screamed as they attacked, a sound that "was dreadful" to the Englishmen, according to *Mourt's Relation.* The men who'd taken their muskets to the shallop raced through the hail of arrows to retrieve their arms. The movement was met with intensified cries from the Nauset, a group of whom wheeled toward the fleeing Englishmen, trying to keep them from reaching the shallop. The first few to reach the boat quickly grabbed their swords and slipped into their coats of mail, which helped to protect them against arrows. Thus armed, they charged the oncoming Nauset warriors, holding them at bay and creating a screen for the others running for their muskets. The guns of three of these men were primed and ready. They fired wildly at the swarming Nauset, which scattered them for the moment.[69]

The four men who'd retained their muskets were now alone at the barricade. Not all of the Nauset had followed the large group that'd run for the boat. Many of them were still arranged around the barricade. Using trees for cover, they continued to send arrows toward those at the barricade. One of the four men was Myles Standish. The other three were not identified, but they were likely those who'd earlier fired their weapons to check them against the elements. Standish was the only member of the party who owned a snaphance musket, which unlike the matchlocks with their unwieldy burning match, fired a shot by driving a flint onto steel to spark and ignite the main charge, a feature which made the weapon more easily prepared for use.

Standish aimed and fired into the shadows. One of the other three remaining men was faster than the others at readying his matchlock musket and soon followed suit. By this time, the other two men had prepared their weapons, but Standish shouted to them to hold their fire, according to *Mourt's Relation*, "until we could take aim, for we knew not what need we should have, and there were four only of us [that] had our arms there [and] ready."[70]

Given his extensive experience in Virginia, where he'd lived through a war with the Powhatan, Stephen Hopkins may have been one of the three men with Standish. Though his personal objective was to make peace with their future neighbors, Hopkins was not naive. He understood the reality that violence might not be avoided when people of different cultures met under the cloud of suspicion. In Virginia, Powhatan's policy had been hostile when the survivors of the *Sea Venture* had arrived. His people attacked any English boat on the river within bowshot. Within five days of their coming from Bermuda, the Powhatan had shot and killed two of Hopkins's shipmates. Despite such attacks, Thomas Gates—Jamestown's then-governor and the man who'd condemned Hopkins to death—had at first pursued peace with the Powhatan, believing that if the English were more acquiescent they would be able to "win [the Powhatan] to a better position," in the words of William Strachey. Only after repeated skirmishes, and several more English deaths, had Gates launched his own attacks.[71]

Hopkins had absorbed all the lessons of this pull and push of diplomacy and violence in Virginia. During that morning on Cape Cod, he would have understood the risks and would have understood, too, that their interactions thus far with the Nauset had not been friendly. Having lived so long in the frontier, he may have been on edge after the strange midnight cry they'd heard. Perhaps he'd kept his musket and remained at the barricade with Standish.

While the two men who'd held their fire stood guard, gripping their muskets tensely, the other two raced to reload. Loading a seventeenth-century musket was an involved affair that required anywhere from ten to twelve independent steps, and it would have taken the two men at least a minute to reload. First, they'd have poured a little of the black gunpowder into the firing pan. This was the small charge that was lit by the burning match that swung down—or flint when it struck steel in Standish's case—when the trigger was pulled. Once ignited, the charge in the pan would kindle the larger charge of gunpowder that would be placed in the bottom of the gun's barrel, which in turn would launch the ball. With the pan primed, the shooter would swing closed a metal plate called a frizzen, which would hold the primer in place and protect it from premature ignition. Putting the butt of the gun on the ground, the shooter would next pour the main charge of gunpowder into the muzzle of the barrel. Then, he'd reach for a musket ball and wadding, which was necessary to seal the ball in the barrel—otherwise the ball could roll out of the barrel as the weapon was lifted and leveled for firing. With fingers likely still numb from the cold, Standish and the other would have lifted their ramrods free from their place under the barrel and used them to tamp down the wadding, ball, and gunpowder to the bottom of the barrel. With the gun charged, Standish's snaphance musket would have been ready. The second man would have then had to take the additional step of setting the wick of the burning match cord, which was secured by a thumbscrew to the metal serpentine activated by the trigger, at the right length so that it would reach the priming powder in the firing pan when the trigger was pulled.

As they prepared their weapons, they called down to the men who'd gone to the shallop, which was obscured by the terrain and trees, for they'd heard the crescendo of cries and shooting. The men at the water's edge shouted back that they were unharmed, but they asked for help. While three of the men had lit their match cords before bringing their muskets to the shallop, the rest had not. They therefore needed a burning brand from the campfire. Without a way to light their match cords, the muskets were useless. The four men at the barricade likely exchanged quick glances. One of them handed over his musket, bent to the campfire, and grabbed a rather large burning log. Hoisting it to his shoulder, he ran down to the shallop, an incredibly brave act, which in the words of the man who wrote this part of *Mourt's Relation*, "was thought [to] not a little discourage our enemies."[72] The remaining three exchanged fire until one musket shot tore into a tree near the head of the Nauset's leader, sending up a shower of bark and wooden splinters.[73] The man gave "an extraordinary cry" and fled, which triggered a retreat of the rest of the Nauset.[74]

The men from the shallop charged up to the barricade, and with the others decided to pursue the Nauset in order to discourage them from regrouping for another assault. Leaving six men behind to guard the shallop, the rest raced for about a quarter of a mile into the woods on the heels of their attackers. They stopped, caught their breaths, and gave a collective roar to let the Nauset know, according to *Mourt's Relation*, "we were not afraid of them," a gesture they repeated one or two times more, firing a couple of musket shots for emphasis. The encounter was over. None of the Englishmen had been injured, though their camp was littered with arrows. A few coats that'd been hanging on the barricade were "shot through and through."[75]

With the anxiety of the confrontation subsiding, the explorers packed and loaded into the shallop and returned to their task of finding the harbor that had prompted this third exploration. They steered westward for the mainland. After only a couple of hours on the water, the weather became a pummeling mix of snow and rain. By midafternoon, the wind was howling, and the seas turned incredibly rough. The strain of conflicting forces soon proved too great for the shallop. Its rudder broke. Without steerage, there was a real risk that the shallop would swing its beam to the swells and be overwhelmed and over- turned, a danger even greater than that faced by both the *Mayflower* and the *Sea Venture* because of its much smaller size. If the northeastern gales didn't overset the shallop, they might just be able drive it onto the lee shore around modern-day Sandwich, Massachusetts.

Facing such grim prospects, two of the sailors managed—after great effort in freezing conditions and the lurching boat—to rig a couple of the boat's oars together and fashion a steering oar, a crude proto-rudder put over the side of the vessel like those used on ancient ships. The shallop again had steerage, but the weather deteriorated still more. The waves grew steeper and steeper, and the men grew worried. They were in grave danger.[76] Making matters worse, night was coming.

Through tearing sheets of rain and snow, however, the pilot who'd told them of the harbor spotted a landmark, likely Manomet Point on the south- ern edge of Plymouth Bay. They made for the opening into the bay, but the furious wind proved too much. The mast split into three pieces, sending the sail overboard and the wreckage toppling onto the men.[77] After clearing away the mess, the men took up oars. Somehow, with the aid of a flooding tide and the added strength of the nor'easter's storm surge, they made it into Plym- outh Bay, which provided some shelter to the towering waves rolling across the expanse of Cape Cod Bay. But in the gathering darkness and masked by shrouds of rain, the harbor proved to be unfamiliar to the pilot.[78]

They were lost.

The gale forced them onward. An island appeared out of the gloom, and they made for a cove on its windward side. As they got closer, a new roar rose above the blasting wind. The cove was filled with huge, crashing waves. With the wind driving them onto the breaking whitewater, they'd be smashed to pieces. The sailor at the steering oar shouted above the combined din to the men to heave with all they could. Otherwise, they were doomed. The explorers strained to their utmost at their oars, and the sailor struggled to force the makeshift rudder to push them into a turn, and somehow the shallop cleared the danger. They steered for the lee side of the island.

Darkness was now complete. The nor'easter dumped heavy, cold rain.[79] The wind howled about them. There was no relief to be found in the open boat, and the men bent over their oars with water whipped and streaming everywhere. The island's coast was ringed with dangerous rocks, affording them no place to shelter. Still they rowed, searching for some safe haven. At last, they found a sandy inlet protected from the wind and high surf. They anchored and spent the rest of the night in the shallop, unsheltered from the penetrating rain and cold.[80] The men spent the next two days on the small island recuperating from the ordeal.[81]

On Monday, December 11, they climbed again into their sturdy shallop and explored Plymouth Bay, which was promising, according to *Mourt's Relation*:

> We sounded the harbor and found it a very good harbor for our shipping. We marched also into the land and found diverse cornfields and little running brooks, a place very good for situation [i.e., locating the settlement], so we returned to our ship again with good news to the rest of our people, which did much comfort their hearts.[82]

Though the explorers brought back good news with them, they returned to the *Mayflower* to find more bad news. While they'd been gone, two more had succumbed. On December 7 William Bradford's young wife, Dorothy, who was twenty-three, had died after falling over the side of the ship.[83] Bradford revealed nothing more than recording the simple fact of his wife's death in a personal journal. Whether the episode was an accident or intentional suicide brought on by the stress of their dire predicament has been the subject of debate over the ensuing centuries. Because Bradford never mentioned her again, some historians have concluded it likely that Dorothy committed suicide.[84] Since taking one's own life was considered among Christians at the time a terrible sin and an act of blasphemy, Bradford's shame, remorse, or regret of such an act would help explain why he never wrote again of her after her death.[85]

Dorothy wasn't the only casualty. James Chilton, another Separatist, had died on December 8.[86] His wife and thirteen-year-old daughter were left to mourn. And to prepare for the coming New England winter.

Making a Decision

As Plymouth Bay was some thirty miles from Provincetown Harbor, the Pilgrims decided to move the *Mayflower* to an anchorage in the new harbor to better explore the place.[87] The ship arrived on December 16, which was a Saturday, and they found the waterway to be "a most hopeful place," filled with waterfowl and fish and surrounded by "goodly land."[88] The harbor itself was larger than Provincetown Harbor, and it contained two islands.[89] At least eight freshwater brooks emptied into the bay at various places along the six miles of mainland shoreline protected by two headlands that partially enclosed it.[90] Plymouth Bay looked very promising.

On Monday, December 18, a party went ashore and scoured the coastline. They found an area that had once been a village, with fields for growing corn, but there were no signs of recent native habitation. Later, they would learn that the village had been Patuxet, which had been devastated by the

The Mayflower in Plymouth Harbor, by William Formby Halsall (1882).
Courtesy of the Library of Congress

deadly pestilence that had swept through New England a few years before. The land was indeed "goodly" and would support agriculture, and there were deposits of clay, which was important for the manufacture of housing. The coastal forests contained many different varieties of trees, including fruit-bearing specimens. Herbs were plentiful and, significantly, they found the brooks to carry "the best water that ever we drunk."[91]

The next day, Tuesday, December 19, they split into groups, the first again walking the countryside by foot, the other in the shallop, which could cover more area by sea. Those in the shallop found another stream near modern-day Kingston, Massachusetts, that flowed into Plymouth Bay. The river is now called the Jones River after the *Mayflower's* captain.

When the parties returned to the ship that evening to share their discoveries, many voiced support for the Jones River as a place to settle. Others preferred the safety of the island on which the men of the third exploratory expedition had sheltered from the nor'easter, for the island would protect them against sudden attacks by the native people, as had happened on Cape Cod. Both of these spots, however, had drawbacks, and the Pilgrims resolved to discuss and settle upon a final location in the morning.[92]

Throughout the previous four weeks of exploration, they'd been looking for several features: a freshwater supply; land fit for raising crops; proximity to the ocean, where they would catch fish to sell into England to meet their financial obligations to the Merchant Adventurers; a harbor fit for deep water shipping, which was necessary for resupply missions and exportation of commodities such as fish; a defensible location to safeguard against any native assaults as well as against potentially hostile foreign powers, such as the French or Spanish; and natural resources, such as trees, which were necessary both for construction of their encampment and potential export.[93] Several possible spots had been identified, including the abandoned village of Patuxet, the mouth of the Jones River, the island in Plymouth Bay, and the Pamet River mouth on Cape Cod.

On December 20 the Pilgrims debated. It was time to decide, for, as recorded in *Mourt's Relation*, "we could not now take time for further search or consideration, our victuals being much spent, especially our beer."[94] The decision engendered much discussion, with advocates for each of the several prospective sites trying to convince others. Several leaders probably directed the discussion. John Carver was the duly-elected governor of the combined community of Saints and Strangers. People would have heeded his opinion. Myles Standish, of course, had led most of the campaigns thus far and had shown his courage and leadership in the face of the Nauset attack on Cape Cod. William Bradford and Edward Winslow were becoming more and more prominent.[95] Christopher Martin, whose star had faded considerably since the *Mayflower's* arrival to North America, would likely have been involved, if only because he seemed to enjoy the sound of his own voice.

Stephen Hopkins also may have played a role in the discussion and decision about where to situate the Pilgrims' colony. That he'd already been identified as one of the "principal men" of the company lends additional credence to the theory.[96] He'd been to this land before. He'd helped rebuild Jamestown. He'd labored under Thomas Dale to create the settlement of Henrico in a spot chosen because of its superior location. Perhaps his experience would have been given some weight during the discussions aboard the *Mayflower*.

The final decision about where to settle was neither unanimous nor uncontested, yet the former native village of Patuxet found the most support for reasons that one of the contributors to *Mourt's Relation* documented:

> [Patuxet was located] **on a high ground**, where there is a great deal of land cleared and **has been planted with corn** three or four years ago, and there is **a very sweet brook** [that] runs under the hillside and many delicate springs of as good water as can be drunk, and [it is near] where we may harbor our shallops and boats exceedingly well.[97]

The deserted Native American village was situated on ground that rose from the shore to a 165-foot hill, high above stagnant coastal marshes and their unhealthy perils. From it, the settlers on a clear day could see Cape Cod some thirty miles away across the waters of Cape Cod Bay, which meant that they would be able to discern whether incoming ships were English or foreign.[98] The coastal forests had been cleared from the area by the Patuxet, which accelerated their ability to plant crops. The brook—which the English started to call Town Brook—ran down the hillside just steps away from where the Pilgrims would build their homes.

If the argument that Hopkins was listened to during the debate is credible based on his prior experience in America, the description in *Mourt's Relation*,

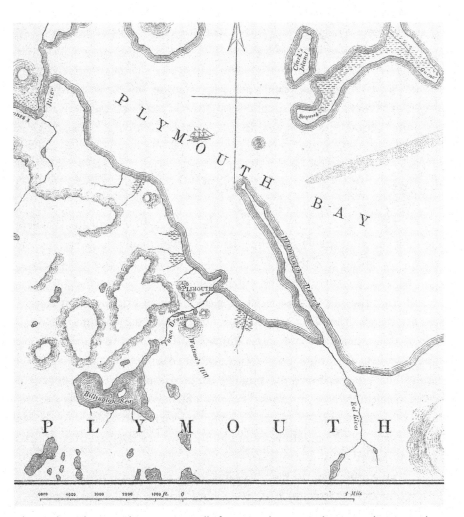

Plymouth Colony and Watson's Hill, from Azel Ames, *The May-Flower and Her Log* (Boston and New York: Houghton, Mifflin and Company, 1907); image digitally adapted. *Courtesy of the University of Toronto*

quoted here, provides more support, for it is uncannily reminiscent of language used by William Strachey—who'd seen the same things that Hopkins had in Virginia—when Strachey wistfully reflected upon the swampy location chosen for Jamestown:

> If it had been our fortune to have **seated upon some hill**, accom-
> modated with **fresh springs** and clear air, **as do the natives of the**

country, we might have, I believe, well escaped [the misfortunes that the residents of Jamestown suffered].[99]

In Patuxet, Hopkins would have seen what he and Strachey had envisioned as they watched the countless victims succumb to Jamestown's brutal seasoning period. Not only was the site situated on high ground and close to uncontaminated water supplies *like* those chosen by the "natives of the country," it had been an *actual* site of a native village. The two passages are too similar to dismiss as coincidence. In the choice of Patuxet, the Hopkins influence seems reasonably apparent.

Patuxet, of course, was the site of the famous Plymouth Rock, where the Pilgrims purportedly first touched land when finally disembarking the *Mayflower*. Because of the *Mayflower*'s deep draft, its anchorage in Plymouth Bay was almost a mile and a half from the shore. Nevertheless, access to and from the ship was easier than it had been in Provincetown Harbor because the shallows were not as restrictive.[100] Here, the Pilgrims could sail or row their shallop or the ship's longboat all the way to shore, and use the convenient Plymouth Rock as a dock for loading and unloading. As a result, the stone has become a singular landmark in American history that has been celebrated for centuries.[101] Without Stephen Hopkins likely steering the majority in favor of Patuxet, the Pilgrims very well could have chosen another spot, and Plymouth Rock might not have become part of America's foundational mythos.

As living proof that the Pilgrims came to the right decision, one need only look at a modern map of the eastern seaboard of the United States. Some four hundred years later, Plymouth, Massachusetts, is a vibrant city of over fifty thousand residents. The street along which Hopkins and the other Pilgrims first built their dwellings—today called Leyden Street—is lined with picturesque New England clapboard houses and buildings. Jamestown, Virginia, on the other hand, was finally abandoned by the opening of the eighteenth century. By the mid-1800s only ruins remained. Today, it is a national historical park and tourism site, where archaeologists struggle to recover more information about America's oldest English settlement in the face of an ecosystem that over time had reabsorbed the old colony.

Jamestown provided Hopkins with an object lesson of where *not* to locate a colony, a lesson reinforced when he helped Thomas Dale build a new settlement at Henrico. He would have learned from the experience, and it was likely his firsthand knowledge that helped the Pilgrims make a better decision in 1620 than did John Smith and his compatriots when they founded Jamestown in 1607.

7 | A DEADLY, DISCONTENTED WINTER

Let them be hunted soundly. At this hour
Lie at my mercy all mine enemies.

—*The Tempest*, act 4, scene 1

WHILE MASSASOIT AND THE WAMPANOAG watched with distrust, the English continued their race against the triple threat of winter, disease, and dwindling supplies. They'd been in America for a month and had little to show for it.

While John Smith had not joined the expedition after being approached by the Saints, he did keep track of their endeavors, writing about their trip to America in a 1622 publication, quoting extensively from *Mourt's Relation* in a 1624 publication, and including more information about them in a work published in 1631.[1] Perhaps piqued over his own exclusion, he criticized their delays spent "wandering up and down in frost and snow, wind and rain, among the woods, creeks, and swamps" of Cape Cod before they finally settled upon the site of Patuxet.[2]

The bitterness of the winter surprised the Pilgrims. Measured by lines of latitude, this part of the coast of Massachusetts lay far to the south of London. In fact, it was closer to the same parallel as Rome. But while Patuxet stood on the shores of the same ocean as their point of departure at Plymouth, England, the regional weather patterns led to quite different extremes.[3] The New England cold penetrated everything, further weakening compromised immune systems. Disease was becoming rampant, and it combined with illness

140

from exposure to form a deadly calamity. Nearly half the Pilgrims would die in a span best measured in weeks.

On Wednesday, December 20, the day on which they'd decided upon Patuxet, a group of about twenty made a camp on shore. Others planned to join them the following morning and so begin the work of constructing dwellings. The weather didn't cooperate, as recorded in *Mourt's Relation*:

> All night it blew and rained extremely. It was so tempestuous that the shallop could not [reach the] land so soon as was [necessary], for they had no victuals on land. At 11 o'clock the shallop went off with much ado with provision, but could not return it blew so strong and was such foul weather that we were forced to let fall our anchor and ride with three anchors.[4]

Overnight, one of the men on the *Mayflower* died. Richard Britteridge, a Stranger recruited by Thomas Weston and one of the men who'd signed the Mayflower Compact only a few weeks before, was the first person to die in Plymouth Bay.[5] Winds prevented anyone on the ship from making the long trip by boat to Patuxet. The twenty men on shore were trapped. The storm was so fierce and daylight on the winter solstice was so short that they were unable to begin work on shelters. They could do nothing but endure the cold and wet as best they were able.[6]

The tempest continued in force the next day, Friday, December 22. Those on shore were again stranded, still without food, for the people on the *Mayflower* couldn't hazard the journey. They huddled below decks in their awkward quarters. With only a few sheets hung for privacy, with the *Mayflower* bucking against its anchor, with their main-deck ceiling likely dripping from the deluge, Mary, the wife of Separatist Isaac Allerton, gave birth in the candlelight to a boy. He was stillborn.[7]

On Saturday, the weather cleared enough to allow a group of men to leave the ship. Because of spreading disease and illness, however, only a small number traveled to the mainland. After presumably distributing food to those who'd been trapped on shore, the assembled men got to work. The first objective was to build a common shelter, and the settlers spent the day felling trees and carrying timber from the forest to the clearing of the old native village. This activity highlighted the only drawback to using the abandoned Native

American village: since the Patuxet had cleared the area of trees, the English had to walk about an eighth of a mile to the closest woodland.[8] Such a distance would clearly be an inconvenience for gathering firewood, especially without the benefit of any draft animals, a luxury the colonists would not enjoy for a number of years. It made the task of building a compound—in late December in New England—even more difficult, for it required that they drag by hand the heavy trunks and long branches through the slush and mud and muck to the building site, a task that would have taken a team of several men.[9]

The sailors would have stayed on the *Mayflower*, leaving the work to the settlers. But with the recent deaths, the Pilgrims counted a little over forty adult men and teenage boys old enough to share in such demanding labor. The number actually able to help was no doubt much smaller because of sickness. A person fevered and weak either from the flu or from scurvy, no matter what size or age, would have been unable to handle the exposure from cold rain and wind during journey to the shore, let alone try to trudge in the same miserable conditions into the forest to help drag logs to the building site.

Of course, it was not only the weather and the arduous task of harvesting timber that concerned the Pilgrims. Many other questions produced anxiety. How many more would die before they could build enough dwellings to shelter their loved ones? How long would their food last? And, finally, what would the next encounter with native people produce? The early-morning battle on Cape Cod told the colonists that relations with the people of the Wampanoag Confederacy would remain a challenging problem with no easy resolution.

Sunday, December 24, was Christmas Eve. It was also the Sabbath. The Saints, who strictly observed the Lord's Day, likely worshipped in the hold of the *Mayflower*.[10] Some of the company, likely Strangers such as Stephen Hopkins, as well as Myles Standish, remained on shore and labored.[11] Anglicans like Hopkins would probably have held a more pragmatic view of the Sabbath than did their Separatist counterparts. People were dying, and there was work to be done. He would probably have remembered from his parish clerk duties that labor on the Sabbath was lawful if it was necessary, just as Jesus taught when the Pharisees challenged his disciples for plucking corn on the Sabbath Day.[12] Hopkins's wife and children needed shelter. They all did.

As they toiled on shore, the men heard a cry from the woodlands. The Englishmen had been fooled before on Cape Cod when a midnight sound had been dismissed as the call of a wolf. They'd not be fooled again. They expected an assault. An alarm was raised, and every man jumped to his musket. Likely fighting the ache of cold fingers, they fumbled to ready their matchlocks, lighting their match cords from the nearby campfire, measuring its length and securing it to the serpentine. Tension mounted, but the attack they feared never came.[13]

Though they lost no one to the native people that day, their more prominent enemy, disease, claimed another life: Solomon Prower, who was about twenty-four years old and Christopher Martin's stepson, died.[14]

The Separatists did not celebrate Christmas Day, as they held that such celebrations were unbiblical and amounted to blasphemy against the true meaning of Christ.[15] Neither did the Strangers. Instead, everyone worked. Some went to the forest to cut down trees. Others split timber into planks. Some carried logs and planks. *Mourt's Relation* recorded that "no man rested all that day."[16] Working together, they began to erect the settlement's first building.[17] It would be a modest dwelling, a square of about twenty feet by twenty feet,[18] and would take them another two weeks to finish.[19] The floor would be dirt, for there was neither time nor sufficient manpower to set a proper foundation. For the walls, the Pilgrims likely used thick planks riven from trunks—a laborious process that required a series of metal wedges to be tapped along a straight line into the length of a trunk; as the wedges were driven deeper, the wood split along its grain leaving a roughly flat plank; a single trunk of an oak tree might thus have been split into several planks. Gaps between the mounted planks were filled with interlacing twigs and branches that were cemented together with clay, a process called wattle-and-daub construction, which was the typical style for building cottages in rural England. After the roof was framed, it would be covered with thatch made of cattails and reeds gathered from nearby marshes.[20]

As night was falling, the workers heard "a noise of some Indians," according to *Mourt's Relation*. The alarm went out and everyone scrambled to their muskets. Clutching them tightly, they probably took up defensive positions and stared out into the dark gloom, where the distant tree line marked the edge of the unknown. The fire crackled and snapped. A little farther off, Town Brook murmured. At the bottom of the hill, the surf ground onto the shore. Out in the bay, the lights glimmered on the distant *Mayflower*. The men waited, their breath likely quickened with anxiety.

Concluding finally that no attack was imminent, they organized themselves for the night. About half the company rowed back to the relative comfort of the ship. The rest—about twenty men—stayed by their construction project to protect it against a possible raid. Another storm settled over Plymouth Bay, bringing rain and wind. The settlers on shore likely huddled in the wet and cold, stoking the campfire to an enormous size, and set sentinels for the long night ahead. Those who returned to the ship were surprised with a small holiday treat. Because the supply of beer was running perilously low, everyone was drinking water, but because it was Christmas, Master Jones, who was jealously rationing the supply of beer in order to keep some for the *Mayflower*'s return voyage, gave his passengers a small allowance, a refreshment enjoyed by even the anti-Christmas Separatists.[21]

The storm grew overnight. The next morning, those who had returned to the *Mayflower* couldn't reach the shore, leaving the twenty-person contingent who'd remained behind to fend for themselves. On Wednesday, however, the weather cleared, allowing work to resume on the common building.

By Thursday, December 28, the first dwelling was far enough completed that consideration turned to the second-highest priority: creating a defensive position to help protect them against native animosity. They'd brought a few cannons in the *Mayflower* for use at the settlement and chose the highpoint on their hill as the place to construct a platform, from which they'd be able to protect their settlement from an overland attack as well as command the bay should any hostile ship appear. They also started considering a plan for the settlement, dividing the colonists into their respective families in order to count the number of homes that were needed. There were nineteen families, which meant a minimum of nineteen dwellings.

Because of the labor involved, as well as the constraints of time, illness, and food supply levels, a decision was made to require any single men to be housed with a family in order to reduce the number of homes that were needed.[22] Thus, men like William Bradford, who'd lost his wife only a few weeks before, might have been assigned to live with a family like that of William Brewster, with whom Bradford had lived when he first moved to the Netherlands as a much younger man.[23] Likewise, the household of Stephen Hopkins would take in his servants, Edward Doty and Edward Leister.

Lots for each house were assigned by the size of the household, and each was staked out on the hillside along what is today called Leyden Street in Plymouth. They decided to arrange the houses in two rows on either side of the street so that the settlement would be fairly compact, and thus more easily defended by the cannons that were going to be installed on the hilltop.[24] Despite the eventual success of the colony, the Pilgrims at this point acknowledged the precariousness of their situation. While they laid out a plat for all nineteen homes, there was an understanding that the assignments might not be permanent, as was recorded in *Mourt's Relation*:

> considering the weakness of our people, many of them growing ill with colds [from] our former Discoveries [i.e., the three exploratory expeditions] in frost and storms and the wading [in Provincetown Harbor, both of which] had brought much weakness amongst us, which increased so every day more and more, and after was the cause of many deaths.[25]

That would prove to be the case in the coming weeks, for instead of nineteen homes, only seven would be built in the first year of the colony as the mounting number of dead forced them to radically change their initial plan.[26]

The next two days were so stormy and frigid that the Pilgrims were too "troubled and discouraged" to force themselves to work. Adding to the general feeling of hopelessness was the renewed fear of native hostility, for huge plumes of smoke, which indicated large campfires, were seen only six or seven miles to the south of their settlement site.[27] The native people tending the unseen fires were likely not only Nauset from Cape Cod. This part of the mainland was populated by other tributary tribes of the Wampanoag Confederacy, such as the Nemasket and Manomet people. More likely, the obscured gathering was a combination of Wampanoag tributaries that included some Nauset and some Pokanoket, for the Nauset would have spread the word when the *Mayflower* was first spied in Provincetown Harbor. The presence of the English would have been seen as a threat to the entire region.

As they watched the smoke rise in the distance, the Pilgrims would have likely asked themselves whether the natives were gathering for an all-out assault. That the natives were nearby but had not yet approached the settlement would have most reasonably been taken by the English as a sign of ill will. Though they'd decided on a location for their cannons, none had yet been placed. And though they'd nearly completed their first building, they were very exposed. Would the natives sense this weakness and attack?

Meanwhile, the year drew to a close. New Year's Eve fell on a Sunday. Some of the company kept the Sabbath on the *Mayflower*, while others kept it at the place of their settlement, which they began to call Plymouth.[28] New Year's Day, 1621, only added to the company's melancholy, for another of the Saints passed away. Degory Priest, who'd made and sold hats in Leiden, was about forty-one years old when he fell victim to the sickness that was picking off the settlers.[29]

On January 3 a group of men were out looking for plant material suitable for thatching the roof of the common building. They wandered far enough afield to find cornfields, and they saw, according to *Mourt's Relation*, "great fires of the Indians," yet they saw no people, for the native people had probably been alert to the Englishmen's movements and had scattered before their arrival.

The following day, a band of five or six Pilgrims returned to the spot to see if they could locate any of the Native Americans, for despite their anxiety about possible hostility, their purpose remained to establish contact with the people on whose land they wished to settle.[30] The party was led by Myles Standish. Although none of the other men were identified by name, it is probable that Stephen Hopkins would have been one of them, as this mission to meet with the natives was identical to their first exploratory mission on Cape Cod, when Hopkins was special adviser to Standish. Thrown together by happenstance on the *Mayflower*, the two men appeared in the records together more often than not in the early days of the colony.

While they shared some similar characteristics, they likely approached the world from different perspectives, each of which complemented that of the other man in the unique conditions in which they found themselves. Short in stature, Standish was a man of action with an infamously short fuse.[31] Seventeenth-century historian William Hubbard described him as

> a little chimney soon fired; so was the Plymouth Captain, a man of very little stature, yet of a very hot and angry temper. The fire of his passion [could] soon [be] kindled and blown up into a flame by hot words, [and] might easily . . . [have] consumed all, [if it could not be] seasonably quenched.[32]

He was a soldier cut from the same cloth of the Dutch war against Spain, as were the harsh governors of Jamestown, Thomas Gates and Thomas Dale. As a soldier, Standish would probably have viewed any native person first as a hostile, for to do otherwise would have given them the advantage.

The fact that on January 4 Standish's party traveled to the Indian encampment to seek peace, rather than spending the valuable time working on shelter or improving their defenses—which was a critical priority, especially for someone of Standish's background—indicates that some person or persons among the Pilgrims might have influenced Standish. As the group's military leader he presumably could have insisted on pushing forward with deploying their cannons, which were at this point still in the hold of the *Mayflower*. His training, background, and instincts would have advised such an approach. But he instead spent the day searching for Native Americans. If someone convinced him to take this course, Hopkins is the obvious candidate.

Hopkins would likely have been perfect counterweight to Standish, a man who perhaps could quench the fiery captain's temper, for Hopkins was inclined to the abstract, a cool thinker who "could reason well," in the words of his *Sea Venture* shipmate, William Strachey.[33] Where Standish likely viewed the Wampanoag as hostile based upon their only interactions thus far, Hopkins probably still believed in the possibility of peace, for he'd seen how Pocahontas's union with John Rolfe quickly resolved the long-running war between the Powhatan and the Jamestown colonists. Standish leaned toward confrontation. Hopkins leaned toward conciliation. Hopkins probably helped to balance Standish's tendency to overreact, and as a result, the two men would have stood in a sort of counterpoise to each other. When it came to navigating relationships with the Native Americans, it makes sense that Standish would have respect for Hopkins's judgment based upon his prior experiences in the New World.

Standish and his small party of men went to the cornfields discovered the previous day. They found the place where the Wampanoag had camped but could find no one. Since arriving in Patuxet, they'd not seen a single native person.[34] Distrust and enmity kept Massasoit from engaging with the foreigners. He continued the watchful wait. Standish and his men returned home with the threat of the natives still looming.

As they fretted about the Wampanoag, illness continued to carry the English away. By Saturday, January 6, Christopher Martin was very ill.[35] By Monday, he was dead.[36] His wife, Mary, was left to grieve over the deaths of her son, Solomon, and now her husband.

The day after Martin passed away, the settlers continued work on the encampment.[37] The common house was almost done and lacked only a thatch roof. Construction progressed slowly, however, taking them four days to complete only half the covering. Frost and foul weather were to blame, hindering the settlers so that they were seldom able to work more than half the days out of a given week.[38]

Thursday, January 11, was one of the fairer days that didn't prevent the men from working. William Bradford engaged in heavy labor when he was suddenly seized by a violent pain that, according to Mourt's Relation, "shot to his huckle-bone"—that is, his hipbone. During the various explorations on Cape Cod, Bradford was one of the many men who'd taken ill, especially during the third exploration that began with the Nauset attack and ended with the discovery of Plymouth Bay. During these exertions, he'd felt some discomfort in his ankles in addition to the normal aches and pains that might accompany a viral infection, but this present pain was very different. At first, they suspected that Bradford was at death's door. He survived, but it took him over two months to recover.[39]

Also on January 11, four men left the encampment to harvest more reed thatching to add to the common building's still-unfinished roof. The men separated during the day and two of the four disappeared. Given their state of anxiety, the Pilgrims immediately assumed that the missing men had been set upon by Wampanoag. The next day, a group of ten or twelve men put on their armor and took their muskets to look for the missing men. Standish and Hopkins were very likely members of the search party. They marched for seven or eight miles around the countryside trying to pick up the trail that the men—and their captors—might have left, but found nothing. The grim news distressed everyone at the encampment, as they suspected the men had either been killed or abducted, which provides a clear indication of how the English viewed the state of their relations with the Wampanoag.[40]

As it turned out, the two thatch gatherers had become hopelessly lost, and it took them a whole other day before they finally managed to find the settlement, ready to faint from hunger and exhaustion.[41] The day after the two had limped into camp, the common house, with its roof finally finished, burst into flames. A stray spark from the building's fireplace flew into the thatch, which ignited instantly. Governor Carver and William Bradford were both lying sick in the dwelling. With the roof on fire, they rolled out of their beds out of fear that they might be blown up, for each of them kept their fully-charged muskets near their sickbeds in case an alarm was raised. But the fire was doused before the blaze did irreparable damage.

The Pilgrims patched the charred roof and, to create more space in the crowded dwelling for the increasing number of sick, they built a shed nearby to store their equipment and supplies.[42] Work continued without much incident, but the end of January brought another sobering event. Rose Standish, the wife of the captain, died. Altogether, eight members of the company died that month.[43]

Another fierce storm hit the area in the first week in February, bringing intense rain and winds that were stronger than any the Pilgrims had encountered in North America. Though the *Mayflower* rode at anchor in the protected harbor, she and all those on board her were in danger. At this point, many of the colony's stores had been unloaded, and the ship therefore rode high and light in the water, which made her more vulnerable to being upset by the strong gales. On shore, the winds were equally threatening and grew so powerful that they stripped the daubing from the seams of the buildings. The storm continued for several days, forcing everyone to hunker down where they were. The common house, which was nearly full with ill people, caught on fire again—an ever-present hazard in the poorly ventilated single-room building because a fire was always burning for heat and for cooking—but little damage was done before the flames were extinguished.[44]

After the storm started to abate, Master Jones went on shore to hunt and came upon a wolf hunched over the body of a deer. Jones scared the wolf away and saw that the stag had been killed by the Wampanoag, who'd cut off its antlers and left the rest for carrion. As Stephen Hopkins would likely have known, antlers had many uses, one of which was to fashion weapons. In fact, after the assault on Cape Cod, Hopkins and the others collected and examined the arrows that the Nauset had shot into the English encampment. Many of them were tipped with stag horns.[45]

The possibility that the Wampanoag were harvesting material to make war would have been understood by the Pilgrims as a probability under the circumstances, for leaving the valuable meat of a deer behind for wolves in the deep of winter when food was especially scarce left little room for doubt. Jones's discovery would therefore have likely increased the tension among the settlers. Signs of animus kept increasing, while signs of friendship were nonexistent.

By the middle of February, a persistent wind was blowing from the north, bringing cold and frost, which prevented the Pilgrims from doing much work. One man took the lull as an opportunity to hunt for waterfowl. He hiked about a mile and a half from Plymouth and settled into a bed of high reeds near a creek to conceal himself as he waited for a flight of birds. A noise drew his attention away from the water, and he held himself still while a group of Wampanoag warriors marched by. He counted twelve of them and could hear the sound of many more who didn't pass through his field of vision. They were heading toward the settlement. Nervous, he waited, crouching in the thicket, until the Wampanoag were gone. Then, moving as stealthily as possible to avoid detection, he returned as fast as he could to Plymouth to raise the alarm.[46]

The warning reached two of the settlers who, despite the conditions, had gone into the forest to harvest timber. They dropped their cutting tools and rushed back the camp to arm themselves, as they believed an assault might be imminent. None came. But while the Englishmen were rushing to join the others in the settlement, the Wampanoag stole the tools they'd left behind. That evening the settlers saw the ominous smoke of another huge Wampanoag campfire.[47]

Whether stealing the cutting tools was merely a response to the thefts by the English on Cape Cod or another overture of hostility was, of course, uncertain, but it was likely a combination of both. Massasoit's warriors had gathered in the area to maintain a constant surveillance of the English. Spying while shying from contact and now stealing their axes were unmistakable indications of aggression. This is clearly how the Englishmen viewed the latest incident, for immediately afterward they resolved to "keep more strict watch" and to make greater efforts to keep their muskets in working order and ready, no small task in the frequent rain, which made it difficult to keep the match cords of muskets lit and could likewise render gunpowder ineffective.[48]

The scare was such that the following day, Saturday, February 17, the Pilgrim men who were well enough convened "a meeting for the establishing of military orders," according to the author of *Mourt's Relation*. Perhaps because Governor Carver was still confined to a sickbed, and thus incapable of making an appointment, the assembled group of men voted to formally invest Myles Standish with authority to command the colony's military affairs, a role he'd in substance already been fulfilling since the earliest forays on Cape Cod some two months before. While Standish and the others discussed how best to defend themselves against the perceived antagonism of the Wampanoag, one of the men noticed movement on a hilltop—today known as Watson's Hill—less than a quarter of a mile away. According to *Mourt's Relation*, two native men appeared "and made signs unto us to come unto them."[49]

It was an extraordinary development. After months of estrangement, this appeared to be the Wampanoag's first effort to start a dialogue. Perhaps peace was at hand, after all. The hill on which the Pilgrim's settlement was located was on one side of Town Brook. Watson's Hill stood on the other side. Perhaps fearing a trap if any of them were to approach the newly arrived visitors, the English "likewise made signs unto them to come to us." The Wampanoag declined.

The impasse aroused suspicion in the minds of the colonists. Why wouldn't the natives come forward? The gathered men grabbed their muskets. Just the day before, they'd resolved to keep their weapons prepared for use. If, however, any of the match cords were unlit, one of the men would have raced to get a burning brand. Together, they "stood ready."[50] Smoke from the muskets' slow-burning matches drifted upward into the morning sky. The two men on Watson's Hill didn't move.

After a few moments of tense indecision, Myles Standish and Stephen Hopkins stepped forward. For different reasons, they were the two best equipped for the situation, Standish for providing protection with his military prowess, Hopkins for using his prior experience and language skills to potentially play the spokesman. History did not record how the decision was made, whether it was by acclamation of those who'd gathered, or an executive decision made if Governor Carver were present, or simply an organic resolution offered by the two men themselves. But given recent history, their undertaking the task made sense. Standish and Hopkins had been in the vanguard on Cape Cod. They'd be in the vanguard now and act as the colony's first emissaries.

The two Englishmen walked down the hill from the settlement toward Town Brook. Only one of them carried a weapon.[51] Though the primary sources did not identify which man it was, their backgrounds and the context of everything that happened before make it most plausible that Standish carried the gun.[52] This, of course, would have left Hopkins unarmed, which would have corresponded to his likely role as spokesperson. Approaching without a weapon was an indication that he intended peace. By leaving his musket behind, he again played the counterbalance to Standish. Together, they formed an ideal team for the encounter, projecting both power and the promise of goodwill.

Most likely keeping their eyes on the Wampanoag standing on the hilltop above them, Standish and Hopkins slowly splashed across Town Brook. Surging adrenaline would have probably muffled the piercing chill of the icy waters. The two warriors remained on the summit of the hill. Some movement toward the two approaching Englishmen would have seemed a natural gesture of friendliness. That they didn't move forward to close the gap might have aroused suspicion. What lay beyond the men on the hidden side of the summit?

As the Englishmen mounted the bank on the brook's far side, their senses probably would have become even more alert to the dangers of an ambush. They were alone now, out of the range of their compatriots' muskets. Their breathing would have accelerated. Standish's mind might have raced to solve the complex puzzle of anticipated moves and countermoves that would be required if something happened. Hopkins's mind might have flashed back to all his encounters in Virginia. Did any of those experiences yield a clue about what might come next?

Despite the real risk that this might be a trap, Standish and Hopkins paused after taking a few steps up the hill toward the watching natives, and the musket was placed on the ground. Whether the two men had agreed beforehand or whether a quick discussion prompted it, the act was intended as a "sign of peace," according to *Mourt's Relation*. It was a deliberate signal that Standish and Hopkins had come "to parley with them."[53] Having now committed themselves, the Pilgrims continued their ascent of the hill, perhaps holding their hands out, palms forward, to try to reassure the waiting warriors.

The Wampanoag, of course, had their own reasons to be wary. After all, these men now walking up the hill were like the foreigners of the past who'd brought violent confrontation to the shores of Cape Cod and Patuxet. Foreigners who'd kidnapped their relatives and friends. Indeed, these were the very men who only weeks before had stolen precious grain from the Nauset. They'd rifled through sacred tombs. They'd fired their guns recklessly into the forests, which may have been seen as the provocation to the Nauset attack that morning on Cape Cod.

Standish and Hopkins came closer, but suddenly the two warriors turned away and disappeared down the hidden backside of the hill.[54] Standish and Hopkins likely froze in their tracks. What would come next? Standish might have looked back to his musket, calculating his chances of reaching his weapon. In the interval, the two Englishmen heard the cry of a great number of men from the other side of the hill, a noise so loud that it was heard by the group of Pilgrims nervously waiting back in the settlement.

The roar was taken as a threat. The two men leaped down the hill toward safety. Reaching his gun, Standish probably twirled to see if there would be a charge of warriors. For the moment, the hilltop was still clear. The two men splashed back across the brook. On the far side, they'd likely have stopped and checked again for pursuit. Still nothing. No one came charging after them. They fell back into the settlement, and with the rest of the able men of the colony, they waited. None of the warriors appeared on the hill again. The Wampanoag stayed out of sight, retreating once more into cover of the woodlands.[55]

Over the next few days, the Pilgrims dropped all their building activities and came together to work on the colony's defenses. By Wednesday, February 21, Master Jones with the help of many of his sailors brought to shore the Pilgrims' heavy cannons. The barrel of the first was over seven feet long, and it could shoot a three-pound ball nearly three-quarters of a mile. It could also be loaded with several hundred pistol balls, an ammunition known as "case shot" and used as an antipersonnel weapon. The big gun could launch the case shot, which would spray out to create a broad killing field of fire, about 250 yards. Though it wouldn't have reached the top of Watson's Hill with case shot, it could certainly provide sufficient coverage against anyone trying to approach Plymouth after crossing Town Brook.

The second cannon that Jones and the sailors unloaded from the *Mayflower* was even bigger, with a barrel over nine feet long. It could shoot a five-pound ball over a mile, depending on the trajectory, though its chief purpose was to fire its shot low to the ground, where the cannonball was to bounce around, thus causing as much damage as possible to anything in its path. The sailors brought two smaller cannons as well. Working with the mariners, the Pilgrims mounted the four cannons, plus one that had already been brought ashore, at the high point of the settlement's hill, just where Captain Standish had desired.[56] The visit from the Wampanoag had indeed been momentous. It had pushed apprehension to new heights.

The Pilgrims' reaction to the Watson's Hill episode reveals that they considered it a hostile act.[57] Indeed, based on the conduct of the warriors and the subsequent eruption of angry cries, it was very likely an attempted ambush.[58] In such a scenario, the two warriors who showed themselves on the hill would have been bait. This would explain why they refused to come over to Plymouth when the Pilgrims signaled to them. They were trying to draw some of the English away from the safety of their encampment.

If so, the baiting worked, for Standish and Hopkins came to Watson's Hill to investigate. The trap was probably intended to be sprung once the Englishmen got close to the two Wampanoag, for the large group hidden on the back slope of the hill could have then pounced, killing or taking the two settlers captive. If it was an ambush, it had gone awry, for courageous though the two warriors had been, they'd apparently bolted a few moments too early, before any of their fellows were able to seize the Pilgrims. Hopkins had seen similar ruses in Virginia, where the Powhatan were quite adept in practicing deception.[59] The incident inflamed more fear among the Plymouth colonists.

The day they dragged the cannons up from shore to the top of the hill, disease struck again. Four people died. One victim was William White, one of the Separatists—whose sister was married to the congregation's Leiden pastor, John Robinson. He left his wife, Susanna, behind to cope with two young boys, one aged five and the other, who'd been born in November while the *Mayflower* was anchored in Provincetown Harbor, only a few months old. Another was William Mullins, one of the Strangers.[60] He'd been a man of some means who'd made a good living as a shoemaker in London and brought with him on the voyage over 250 pairs of shoes, toward what purpose can only be guessed. His wife, Alice, was left to mourn his death with their eighteen-year-old daughter and fourteen-year-old son. White and Mullins had both signed the Mayflower Compact.[61] The names of the other two Pilgrims who died at the same time were not recorded. Only a few days later, Mary Allerton, who'd given birth to a stillborn son in December, passed away too, leaving her husband, Isaac, to care for three young children, ages three to seven, and a thirteen-year-old boy who'd been apprenticed to him. The total death toll for February was seventeen.[62]

Massasoit Gathers the *Powwáws*

As the English finished their fortifications and buried their dead, the leader of the Wampanoag Confederacy considered all his options. It was likely Massasoit's idea to try to draw the invaders into a trap, but that had failed. Now the foreigners were bringing even larger guns into their settlement. Massasoit had met with Europeans before and had probably witnessed the power of their weapons, which in an instant could strike a warrior down over a hundred paces away. To counter this power, Massasoit sought power of his own. He convened a religious ceremony to summon the spirit powers of his people, intending to bring a curse upon the English intruders.[63]

There was a belief among the Native Americans that the supernatural dwelt within and took part in everyday life. They saw the divine in many things, both in nature and in humans. This form of animism viewed the immaterial world as a complex and diverse web of power that dwelt within every aspect of the natural world. Christians such as the Pilgrims believed that God had given humanity the power and duty to dominate nature, but the native people of North America believed nature itself was imbued with spiritual power and might fight back. The relationship was holistic. Sometimes nature's spirits demanded human restraint. At other times, the situation provided opportunities for exploitation.[64]

Everything on earth was part of a complex tapestry that transcended the boundaries between physical and spiritual. Spiritual power could be found everywhere, from plants and animals to rocks to the wind and clouds and bodies of water.[65] Roger Williams, a Puritan minister who later developed close and friendly ties with Massasoit and the Wampanoag, counted the names of thirty-seven individual gods, ranging from points on the compass, such as Wompanánd (the Eastern God); to their dwellings, such as Wetuómanit (the House God); to various parts of nature, such as Keesuckquánd (the Sun God), Paumpágussit (the Sea God), and Yotáanit (the Fire God).

Though power was in everything, its concentration varied, thus requiring different measures of respect or caution. For example, Williams reported that the Wampanoag held black foxes in special esteem and would never hunt them specifically because of their divine power. The supernatural was even to be found within different biological functions of the human body: one spiritual power controlled a person's pulse, another his lungs, and so on.[66] Not only did power surge within everything, it also ebbed and flowed through interactions between different components of nature.

Native Americans attempted to tap into this power and exploit it to their own purposes via rituals. Thus, a spirit within a plant or animal might be approached and flattered or even deceived in order to help people find, catch, or kill for food.[67] Such powers might also be induced to inflict harm upon one's enemies, as Massasoit undertook to do.

He first sent summons to the priests from all the tribes in the Wampanoag Confederacy.[68] These priests were called *powwáws*, according to Roger Williams.[69] The English came to regard *powwáws* with a combination of contempt and outright fear, for though they acknowledged the *powwáws'* abilities in the healing arts, they believed the native priests to be in consort with Satan.[70]

The rituals that these priests performed ultimately became known to the English as *powwows* by the name of those who directed them and were marked by invocations to the spiritual powers interconnected with the object of their pleas. According to Williams, the priest or priests would lead a vigorous, physical service in which the people of the community would participate, all of them combining to entice the spirits to do the called-upon act.[71]

After assembling all the Wampanoag *powwáws*, Massasoit and his people held a massive ritual in a secret, impenetrable part of the forest. They called upon the spirit world to place a curse upon the English and thus clear them from Wampanoag lands.[72] It was an exceptional event, for only rarely did the leader of a confederacy as large as the Wampanoag convene such a gathering. Though in theory a sachem like Massasoit had absolute sovereignty over the constituent tribes of the confederacy, in practice only his powers of persuasion could bring his people to act.[73] That the furtive assembly occurred at all is perhaps a testament to the near-universal dread with which the Wampanoag Confederacy viewed the English as much as it is to Massasoit's personal charisma. Led by the *powwáws*, Massasoit and his people spent three intensive days calling on the spirit world to drive the English from their lands.[74]

It was an approach other native leaders employed. For example, some ten to twenty years later, the Pennacook, who lived along the Merrimack River between Massachusetts and New Hampshire, also tried to summon the spirits of their people to drive away the settlers of the Massachusetts Bay Colony.[75] After Massasoit's ritual, he watched to see its impact on the foreigners in Patuxet.

The Awful Toll of Disease

Had Massasoit been able to infiltrate Plymouth, he might have taken some heart that his *powwáws'* invocations seemed to be working, for the Pilgrims had sunk further into distress. Since arriving in the *Mayflower* some four months ago, they'd never been in a weaker position. Just as Stephen Hopkins had seen in Virginia, the seasoning was inflicting dreadful losses; William Bradford recorded, "That which was most sad and lamentable was that in 2 or 3 months' time, half of their company died, especially in January and February." Scurvy from their long diet of salted foods from the *Mayflower*'s stores had weakened people to the point of death. Pneumonia and possible tuberculosis from months of exposure during the inhospitable New England winter finished many of them off. Two and even three people died in a single day during the darkest weeks, a period Bradford called "the first sickness."[76]

At one point, only a handful of people were able to function, according to Bradford:

> [In the] time of most distress, there was but 6 or 7 sound persons, who, to their great commendations be it spoken, spared no pains, night nor day, but with abundance of toil and hazard to their own health, fetched them wood, made them fires, dressed them meat, made their beds, washed their loathsome clothes, clothed and unclothed them. In a word, [they] did all the homely and necessary offices for them which dainty and queasy stomachs cannot endure to hear named, and all this [they did] willingly and cheerfully, without any grudging in the least, shewing herein their true love unto their friends and brethren.[77]

Bradford was one of the sick and had been bedridden since mid-January with a condition so dire that he still hadn't recovered his strength by April.[78]

So great was the loss of life during these bleak times that the Pilgrims tried to disguise the numbers of dead by burying them surreptitiously, concealing all traces and certainly not erecting any monuments to note their passing, so that the Wampanoag might not perceive how truly vulnerable the English were.[79] Whenever a threat was perceived, the Pilgrims rallied everyone to produce a show of force, with even the sickest playing a role. The healthy would help the ailing out of bed, lean them against a nearby tree, and put a musket in their hands, using them like a prop in an attempt to disguise the truth.[80]

Death did not discriminate, taking men, women, and children, employers and servants, the strong and the weak. Nearly everyone lost someone dear.

Entire families were wiped out. Others left only orphans, who were taken in by the remaining families.[81] Only four of the married women survived, among them Stephen Hopkins's wife, Elizabeth. In all, 52 of the 102 passengers who'd made it to Cape Cod would be dead by springtime.[82]

At the outset of this most acute period, the *Mayflower*'s sailors maintained their traditional disdain for the landsmen, even though at that point they'd spent over half a year together. For example, they continued to hoard their beer, even denying a miserably sick William Bradford the request of even a small serving. One sailor's response to Bradford was "that if [Bradford] were his own father he should have none."

Eventually, however, disease and infection spread among the seamen and turned them against each other. Where before they'd been a tightknit bunch, they now began to abandon one another, not willing to get close to their sick friends for fear of infection and so leaving them in their cabins or cots to die alone. Before they finally left the colony on April 5, 1621, the crew of the *Mayflower* would lose almost half their company, thus nearly matching the mortality rate of the Pilgrims.[83]

The spread of disease finally even caused a change of heart over precious beer when Christopher Jones himself took ill. Because the common house of the colony was much more comfortable than his small, cold cabin on the *Mayflower*, he desired to come to shore, where the Pilgrims welcomed him. In return for the favor, Master Jones told Governor Carver that anyone who wanted beer need only request it, and Jones would have it brought from the ship, even if it meant that the surviving crew had to drink only water during their homeward voyage.[84]

Perhaps not surprisingly, murmurs of discontent started to arise among the Pilgrims during these horrible weeks, with some even giving "mutinous speeches," according to William Bradford.[85] Neither the sowers of discord nor their arguments were identified, thus making it difficult to try to discern who was involved, but Bradford was probably referring to an incident on March 24 when John Billington refused to perform sentry duty as requested by Captain Standish, choosing instead to slander the captain with insolent words.[86]

Standish, naturally enough, would have been offended by derogatory remarks by a man such as Billington, and no doubt his temper flared. The strife was soon quelled, however, by a combination of Governor Carver and the "better part" of the company, according to Bradford.[87] As punishment,

Governor Carver ordered that Billington's feet be tied to his neck only to commute the sentence, as it was the factious man's first offense.[88] The punishment likely helped to satisfy Standish's honor, and its commutation likely helped keep Billington in line. After all, it shouldn't have taken much to convince both men that the only way to survive was to stick together and see the effort through.

Massasoit Watches, Waits

Massasoit had been keeping close tabs on the English settlers, who often spotted his warriors. Sometimes they would intentionally show themselves, as they'd done on Watson's Hill in February, only to flee if any of the Pilgrims even started to approach. Other times, they were only seen indirectly, as when their campfires were marked by columns of smoke rising into the sky. Since the arrival of the *Mayflower*, Massasoit been gathering a steady stream of information and had even learned that the Pilgrims were Englishmen, which meant that his observers had been close enough to the settlers to overhear their speech and thus determine their nationality, for Massasoit and the Wampanoag were familiar enough with both English and French that they could discern between the two languages.[89]

Despite Massasoit's appeal to the spiritual powers, however, his men also would have probably reported back to their leader that the *powwáws* had not eradicated the nascent colony. The English were still laboring on their dwellings. They continued to bring provisions and supplies off the towering ship floating in the harbor. Whenever the English noticed their observers, they raised an alarm, and men noisily organized themselves in defensive positions.

But Massasoit's religious ceremonies hadn't failed altogether, either. As the cold weeks progressed, Massasoit's watchers would have likely noted that the English worked more slowly. The weather often interrupted their work, and their numbers seemed to be in flux. Some days his men would have been able to count one number of people dragging timber from the forest and laboring about their large square structures, but other days—for long stretches of time—there would have been noticeably fewer people active at the settlement. There would have been an unmistakable lull, for example, when all but six or seven Pilgrims were bedridden. If they could get close enough to hear the foreigners speak, Massasoit's men would have probably gotten close enough to see how weak or ill many of the men looked when responding to an alarm.

Other than short hunting forays into the surrounding woodlands, the newcomers stayed close to their encampment. Even the big ship in the harbor did not move. Perhaps the *powwáws* were having an impact, after all.

Since the primary sources were written by Englishmen, there is no record of everything the Wampanoag did or didn't do as they watched the colony. All that remains is what was shared by the natives to the Pilgrims after the fact. Thus, Massasoit's mind-set during this period is unknown. But some sense of his attitude can be reconstructed by the activity that was recorded, and it seems clear that Massasoit was not well disposed toward the Pilgrims in early 1621, a view reinforced by the *powwáws'* ritual and the attempted ambush, as well as by the violence experienced in the recent history between the Wampanoag and European explorers. Indeed, it would have been difficult to imagine him openly embracing any Englishmen.[90]

In fact, the Wampanoag believed that the *Mayflower* had come to seek revenge.[91] And the way the Pilgrims conducted themselves probably reinforced such a belief. First, they chased the small group of Nauset who'd been innocently wandering the beach at the tip of Cape Cod. Then, they ransacked graves and stole corn. Next, in December, they fired their muskets in the middle of the night toward Nauset who'd been watching them from a distance. The Nauset had done nothing to provoke the reckless discharge. This likely indicated to the natives that the English intended bloodshed. How could it be taken any other way? The violent gesture likely incensed the Nauset, who then gathered a force to protect their villages against further English marauding. This would explain why a group of Nauset warriors were assembled on the morning of the first encounter between the Pilgrims and Indians. That morning, before dawn, the Nauset were waiting in the forest shadows outside the ring of light made by the invaders' campfire. Did the Nauset attack first? No, again, they were merely watching, waiting to see what these people would do next. But, again, the English attacked first, firing their guns into the woods where the Nauset warriors were arranged. Of course, the Pilgrims did not intend the shots to do harm. A few of the men were merely testing their weapons against the wet conditions; they didn't know that anyone was nearby. But the Nauset could not have known this. It would have been reasonable for the group to consider the shots as a provocation. The English had apparently come to fight, and thus the Nauset started fighting back that morning on Cape Cod.

When he learned of that skirmish, Massasoit probably became convinced in his belief that the English were coming for revenge. This would also explain what most probably was an attempted ambush of Standish and Hopkins on Watson's Hill in February. It was a sign that Massasoit was probably determined to gain the upper hand, a sign that he was not fearful. His warriors outnumbered their people, but he would have known that they possessed weapons that were superior to those carried by his men. The previous exchanges between the Wampanoag and English and French exploratory voyages would have shown him the danger of those guns. The brief fight on Cape Cod reinforced that fact, for the Nauset had sent several dozen warriors against only eighteen Englishmen yet were driven back to the safety of the forest by only a few shots from their muskets. Because of this imbalance of power, Massasoit had likely tried subterfuge at Watson's Hill. In doing so, he employed an often-used tactic.

Though called barbarous and savage by the Europeans, the Indians they encountered were not dull or simple people. Rather, they were sophisticated and ingenious. Thomas Morton, the Pilgrim contemporary who started a colony in Massachusetts in 1624, became an avid student of the Native American people, finding them "most full of humanity and more friendly than" the Separatists at Plymouth. He wrote and published in 1637 a tract entitled *New English Canaan* about his experiences among the Wampanoag and Massachusett. Morton devoted one of the chapters of his book to "their subtlety," in which he described how it was typical for native sachems to use "subtle stratagem" against more powerful rival clans when brute force would not work, employing deception and ruses to achieve desired ends.[92] Such an approach also suited the situation that the Wampanoag faced with the English and their more potent firepower.

Though the probable ambush on Watson's Hill had failed, there is no evidence that Massasoit was ready to yield. The *powwáws* he'd convened proved that much. The enemy on his doorstep likely appeared to him more powerful with their guns, but he was experienced and had an active mind. He probably would have replayed the Watson's Hill incident. When the two warriors presented themselves, only two Englishmen had approached—an equal number—leaving the rest of their men behind. What's more, they'd carried only one weapon between them and put that down a short distance away. This might have indicated to the Wampanoag sachem that the English, though seemingly predisposed to violence, were also curious. Perhaps they would also be approachable, like some of the earlier European visitors to his land. He would have likely recalled his visit with Squanto's traveling mate Thomas Dermer.

Though he'd been inclined to harm the Englishman, Massasoit also would have remembered all the questions that the explorer asked about the country and the Wampanoag, a sure sign of inquisitiveness.[93] Perhaps these newcomers could be similarly enticed with the promise of information. Perhaps he could send an envoy into their very midst, ostensibly to answer their questions but also to gather more information about their situation: their numbers, their health, their defenses. What better way to understand their true strength and to search for exploitable weaknesses than to send a man under the appearance of friendly visit? With a "subtle stratagem," he would likely gather invaluable intelligence, which he then might use to determine how best to strike and eliminate his foe.[94]

Massasoit had just such a man for the job: his name was Samoset.

Ironically, had Massasoit waited longer, he'd likely have concluded that the *powwáws* were successful, for without his intervention that began with his use of Samoset, the English colonists most probably would have perished before the first anniversary of their landing at Cape Cod.[95] But Massasoit didn't wait, and what happened next was a pivotal meeting between the Pilgrims and Massasoit's first emissary, one in which Stephen Hopkins played the essential role.

8 | SAMOSET AND THE SPRING THAW

Now I will believe
That there are unicorns . . . .
—*The Tempest*, act 3, scene 3

FRIDAY, MARCH 16, WAS FAIR AND WARM, and the Pilgrims were determined to finish discussing the military plans that they'd started the month before, when their meeting had been interrupted by the Watson's Hill incident. Now they were interrupted again. While the settlers were gathered on Standish's platform of cannons, a man appeared. He wasn't spied on the distant summit across the creek. He was *in* their settlement. He was boldly walking up the colony's narrow lane—where he must have drawn the rapt attention of any settlers working around their houses. Naked but for a piece of fringed leather tied at his waist, he was a tall, fit warrior. His hair was black, cut with bangs across his forehead, but long in back.[1] He carried a bow and wore a sheath for arrows over his shoulder, and he was in their midst, approaching their fortification.

The men at the cannons were stunned. Here they were meeting about the colony's defenses, and they'd let one of their potential enemies slip among them, within an arm's reach of their children, who likely stood wide-eyed in amazement at the tall "savage," as he was described in *Mourt's Relation*. A cry went up, and the Englishmen rushed to intercept the warrior so that he could not reach their heavy weaponry, which they feared he might do "out of his boldness."[2]

As the men came scrambling down the hill toward him, Samoset offered his famous salutation: "Welcome, Englishmen! Welcome, Englishmen!," as Thomas Prince recorded it.[3]

163

If the Pilgrims were astonished before, they probably were doubly so now. They'd been in North America for over four months, unable to approach a native without an eruption of violence or subterfuge. This man was the first. And he spoke English. How could this be? Despite being armed, they quickly concluded that their visitor did not, at least immediately, wish to harm them. In fact, he seemed rather interested in communicating with them.

Samoset's English was limited, but he was willing to talk.[4] After months of silence, the settlers jumped at the chance. Samoset told them that he was not from this area. He was a sagamore of the Abenaki nation—that is, a man who had command over others, a position akin to what was called a sachem in this part of New England[5]—and he lived in present-day Maine, some five days travel by land or one day by sail with a powerful and steady wind. He told the Pilgrims about the English fishermen that he knew, listing the names of many of the captains and masters of the fishing vessels that had visited the shores of his homeland. It was from these fishermen that he'd learned "some broken English," as it was put in *Mourt's Relation*. Samoset also told the settlers about the region in which they'd chosen to settle and spoke about the various native people and their leaders and even details about their military strength. He told them that the place on which they'd built their houses had been Patuxet and how an unprecedented plague had wiped out the villagers about four years earlier.[6]

Though Abenaki, Samoset, like all the native people on the eastern seaboard from Canada to Virginia, spoke in a dialect of the Algonquian language. To the untrained English ear, Algonquian was "very copious, large, and difficult," according to Pilgrim Edward Winslow, who later admitted that the language was so challenging that even after many years he still could not understand much without the help of interpreters.[7] Samoset's limited grasp of the English language and the chasm between his native tongue and the English ear has caused some historians to question how so much information was conveyed during this first interaction between native and Pilgrim.[8]

The answer that immediately suggests itself is that Stephen Hopkins also played a part in the interview. Though its accents and intonations were different, Hopkins's knowledge of the language spoken by Powhatan in Virginia would have helped him understand Samoset when English failed the native. He likely used this knowledge to bridge any gaps in comprehension. At any rate, a conversation took place that lasted for hours and transmitted vital information as well as informal social exchanges about food and drink.

During the course of the afternoon, the Pilgrims offered Samoset food, for which he was appreciative. And in a sign of his familiarity with English fishermen, Samoset asked for a drink of beer, which the settlers did not have, as any remainder of the precious stuff was locked on board the *Mayflower*. They gave him instead some of their liquor, which they'd used to brace themselves against the cold during their first exploration on Cape Cod. As the sun shifted into the west, the wind started to rise. While the day had been fairly mild, the wind brought with it a chill, and the Pilgrims offered Samoset a heavy horseman's coat to wear against the cold.[9]

Though the conversation was informative and seemingly congenial, the general atmosphere of distrust had not been dispelled. When night approached, the English wanted Samoset to leave. Out of fear that he might wreak havoc while they slept, they wouldn't suffer his presence in the settlement overnight and presumed that he would likewise desire to leave. But Samoset, to everyone's surprise, refused. His defiance would have likely made the settlers even more wary. Any sense of familiarity from their earlier exchange of information would have probably dissolved into tension.

Casting about for a solution, someone suggested that he spend the night aboard the *Mayflower*, which at this point was still anchored out in the middle of the bay. Samoset, perhaps again perplexing his hosts, agreed and willingly walked down to the shallop tied off near Plymouth Rock. He and a crew of Pilgrims boarded the boat, intending to row out to the distant ship, but the wind was continuing to strengthen and the tide was ebbing. A dropping tide would help them going to the ship, but would impede their progress on the return trip. With the hazardous wind and a contrary tide, they feared that they wouldn't be able to regain the shore if they took Samoset to the *Mayflower*, so the idea was abandoned.[10]

The situation had come to an impasse. What would they do with this imposing man? The past four months had taught them that the local people were generally not receptive to the presence of the English. In fact, their only interactions had been hostile. On top of that, the settlers as a group were still very weak and vulnerable. Their numbers were severely depleted, and though January and February had been deadly months, many were still very ill. Edward Winslow's wife, Elizabeth, would die within a matter of days. Thirteen people total would die by the end of the month.[11] In such a state, where so many of the well had to focus on tending to the unwell, the settlers didn't trust this "savage" to stay among them while they slept, close to their sickly invalids and to their women and children. What could they do?

The standoff might have quickly degenerated into a confrontation, but Stephen Hopkins intervened. To the probable astonishment of his fellow Englishmen, he asked Samoset to spend the night with him and his family in the home that he'd had just finished building.[12] At this critical juncture, Hopkins became the most significant ambassador of the Pilgrims. He'd suffer the company of this "savage" and let him into his house, let him share close quarters with Elizabeth and their young children.

It is quite possible that this was the kind of opportunity that drove Hopkins to take his family on this dangerous adventure across the ocean, so far away from their homeland. This seemingly was what Stephen Hopkins wanted. It was the chance to bridge differences and potentially forge a relationship with the native people of America. Whether it'd been the impact of the "nonpareil" Pocahontas or the sum total of his immersion in Virginia, something about these Americans seemed to have captivated him.

As such, Hopkins likely stepped forward with some amount of eagerness to dispel the tension by Samoset's intransigence. It was Hopkins's time. It was his moment. The decision was singularly consequential, for during that night, Hopkins and Samoset somehow changed the dynamic of the relationship between the Wampanoag and the English settlers. The night began with suspicion. Dawn brought with it a hope that would be realized in the coming days as an alliance that would last for decades to come.

Of particular note is the fact that Samoset accepted staying with Hopkins. As a sagamore, Samoset probably would not have endured the company of just any person. Indeed, sagamores would scarcely even "speak to an ordinary man," according to one English contemporary of the Pilgrims who spent time among the Abenaki. If circumstances demanded communication with someone beneath him, a sagamore would appoint one of his own men to speak to the person. In other words, a sagamore wouldn't lower himself. Sagamores spoke only to other sagamores.[13]

Samoset must have gotten the impression during the day's interview that Hopkins was one of the leaders of the colony, an observation that would have been supported by what was likely Hopkins's primary role in the day's events given his familiarity with Algonquian, as well as by any possible deference that other Pilgrims paid to him. If Samoset hadn't obtained such an understanding, the Abenaki sagamore likely would have refused to spend the night with Hopkins and his family.

Samoset in Hopkins's Home

So Samoset followed Hopkins to his home, and each of the other Pilgrims retired to their own. In *Mourt's Relation*, it is reported that Samoset was "watched" during his stay with Hopkins, which might imply that there was an additional guard set outside the house.[14] Perhaps it was one or both of Hopkins's servants, Doty and Leister, who may not have shared Hopkins's enthusiasm for sharing quarters with a "savage." Or perhaps they "watched" from within Hopkins's house, which is, after all, where they lived. Or perhaps the note in *Mourt's Relation* simply means that it was Hopkins who was the watcher. Regardless, the main body of the Pilgrims settled into their own homes for the night, and Stephen Hopkins sat down with Samoset.

There is no record of what was said between the two men, but it would have been natural for Hopkins to introduce his wife and children, who then might have retreated as well as they could in the simple dwelling. Using Samoset's knowledge of English and Hopkins's knowledge of Algonquian, the two men probably talked well into the night. Samoset, if indeed he'd been sent by Massasoit to spy on the colonists, would have pressed for information about the settlement. Because of Hopkins's experience with the Powhatan's use of "subtle stratagems," he might have seen such inquiries for what they were and demurred. Hopkins likewise would have wanted to know as much as possible about the intentions of Massasoit and the Wampanoag, so perhaps the two men danced around one another into the early hours of the morning, neither letting down his guard.

But this is not the most likely scenario. Considering the events that took place in the wake of Samoset's stay, it is more likely that the two men broke through the barrier of distrust and found common ground upon which they—and the two peoples they represented—could build. During the still of the night, Hopkins and Samoset seemed to have developed a rapport and nurtured fragile bonds. The Abenaki shared tight quarters with the English family, and in the faces of Hopkins's wife and children, Samoset might have seen a mixture of desperation and hope. Hopkins probably explained to Samoset that the Pilgrims did not want hostility. They wanted peace. They wanted to become friends.

They wanted to trade to the mutual benefit of both people. They wanted to become steadfast partners. They wanted to become allies. And they could be powerful allies to Massasoit.

Hopkins probably told Samoset about his many years in Virginia. He'd have likely spoken about Pocahontas and the peace that developed between the Powhatan and the English. And he'd also probably have related how, when at war, a force of Englishmen of several dozen fought to a stalemate a mighty confederacy of twenty thousand people. The implication would have been clear: *we can be powerful allies, or we can be powerful enemies.*

When he first approached the English, Samoset had gotten close to their cannons. He'd probably have understood what force they could project, for he'd seen one or two of them no doubt on English fishing ships that he'd visited. With their cannons and muskets, these English settlers were a force to reckon with, regardless of their number. And their number could increase at any moment if more of their big ships appeared on the horizon.

That Hopkins and Samoset changed the dynamic overnight is indirectly supported by the written accounts of Samoset's historic visit to Plymouth, for it appears as though during the night Samoset revealed details to Hopkins that he hadn't shared with the larger group of Pilgrims earlier in the day. According to *Mourt's Relation*, the most detailed firsthand account, and to *Of Plymouth Plantation*, there is a certain order to the presentation of information that Samoset provided to the English during his visit.[15] On the day he walked into Plymouth, he first spoke about where he came from, where it was situated, and how he'd learned some of the English language. Then he'd talked about the various provinces in what the settlers called New England, identifying leaders and estimating the number of people affiliated with each native nation or community.[16] After this, they ate, and Samoset spoke about Patuxet and how, sadly, it had come to have been wiped clean of its inhabitants. Then came nightfall and the dispute over lodging and Hopkins's offer.

It was only after Samoset spent the night with Hopkins that the Pilgrims learned more about their nearest neighbors, Massasoit and his Wampanoag Confederacy and its tributary, the Nauset. It was only in the morning that they learned an incredible amount of detail not shared before. For the first time, they learned that the Nauset on Cape Cod were still very angry at the English because of Thomas Hunt's 1614 kidnapping raid. They learned, too, that the Nauset had taken revenge only a few months before the *Mayflower* arrived by killing three Englishmen—the men who'd been with Thomas Dermer in the summer of 1620. This would likely have helped the Pilgrims understand why the people on the cape stayed aloof from contact: they feared that the Pilgrims had come seeking retribution. For the first time, they learned that it was the Nauset who'd attacked them in December, a confrontation no doubt that was born from misunderstanding stemming from the Dermer incident. For the first time, they learned that Massasoit could field a band sixty warriors strong and that the Nauset had a force of one hundred.[17] The timing of these disclosures is consequential because it underscores the probability that Hopkins had overnight achieved some sort of breakthrough with Samoset. The two men had likely forged the beginning of a relationship that would alter the course of events and turn Massasoit from an enemy into a steadfast ally.

Massasoit's choice to send Samoset was interesting for a few reasons. First, he wasn't a Wampanoag. Second, Samoset at best understood and spoke only scraps of broken English that he'd learned from fishing ships.[18] There was another person with Massasoit who would seemingly have been much better suited to communicate with the Pilgrims. His name, of course, was Squanto, a man who not only could speak better English but who'd also even lived in England for a time. Unlike Samoset, Squanto was born and grew up on the very spot where the Pilgrims had started their colony.[19] He was a Wampanoag. Patuxet was his home. Why would Massasoit use as his first ambassador to the foreigners a man who was a stranger in his own right, a man who spoke the language of the settlers with less fluency than did Massasoit's own subject, Squanto?

Thomas Morton, the Pilgrim contemporary who was also devoted to the Indians of New England, may have provided the best answer to the question. Writing in 1637, Morton stated that the man who first walked into the Pilgrims' encampment had been a captive of the Wampanoag. Massasoit had promised the captive his freedom if he would risk putting "his person amongst these new-come inhabitants."[20] While Morton's account has been criticized for certain inaccuracies, it remains an intriguing explanation for Massasoit's choice of sending Samoset first, instead of Squanto.[21] In this theory, the Wampanoag sachem was so wary of the Pilgrims that he sent someone who was, in effect, disposable.[22]

While Massasoit had purportedly promised Samoset freedom in exchange for approaching the English, Samoset would not likely have trusted Massasoit following through with the commitment. Following this scenario, Samoset therefore opened the possibility of trying his luck with the English, whom he'd seemingly come to know as reasonable people through his prior dealings with the fishing ships. This interpretation is supported by the fact that he refused to leave the Pilgrims when the sun went down during his first visit to Plymouth even after the English let him know that they wanted him to leave. It is further supported by the fact that he eagerly agreed to spend the night on the *Mayflower* instead of returning to Massasoit. Possibly the English intended to scare Samoset off with their offer to have him sleep aboard the *Mayflower*, as he certainly knew that it might be a ploy, one used by the English again and again to trap and kidnap Native Americans.[23] Despite knowing about the underlying threat of an "invitation" to sleep on an English ship sitting more than a mile off shore in Plymouth Bay, Samoset *still* refused to leave the colony.[24]

The overnight stay with Hopkins was pivotal, for afterward, Samoset agreed to speak on their behalf to Massasoit. He left Hopkins and the Pilgrims on Saturday morning, March 17. The Pilgrims gave him a knife, a bracelet, and a ring, ostensibly to encourage his advocacy on their behalf. Samoset promised to return in the next couple of days with some of the Wampanoag, telling the English that the natives would bring beaver skins for trading, a topic likely raised with Samoset by Hopkins.[25] The overnight change in dynamics was dramatic. An atmosphere marked only by antagonism was suddenly turning toward one filled with the possibilities of mutual reliance and benefit.

Aside from his famous visit to Plymouth in 1621, little is known about Samoset. He may have been related to two of the Abenaki who were seized in 1605 by George Weymouth. He'd survived the vicious war between the Mi'kmaq and their neighbors, as well as the pandemics that swept the coastal region in the subsequent years.

Sometime after his role in the sequence of events that led to the peace treaty between Massasoit and the Pilgrims, Samoset left Plymouth and returned to his people near Pemaquid, Maine.[26] By 1623 or 1624, he was certainly home, for he met there an English sailor, Captain Christopher Levett.[27] In a voyage that started in 1623 and ended the following year, Levett sailed from England to explore the shores of Maine, much like Weymouth and the others had nearly two decades before. Unlike his earlier countrymen, however, Levett sought only positive relations with the Abenaki and—somewhat peculiarly for an Englishman—considered them to be the rightful heirs of their lands in the New World.[28] At one point Levett described meeting a man who was likely Samoset:

> There I stayed four nights, in which time, there came many [native people, among them] *Somerset*, a Sagamore, one that has been found very faithful to the English and has saved the lives of many of our nation, some from starving, others from killing.[29]

Although Levett transcribed his name as "Somerset," this Abenaki sagamore was indeed Samoset.[30] Also of little doubt is that Levett was referring to the Pilgrims at Plymouth when he noted Samoset's help that saved many English "from starving" and "from killing." That Levett—a contemporary of the Pilgrims—had already heard about Samoset's history with the English speaks to the importance that the Pilgrims placed on the role that Samoset played, a fact that points to the significance of his initial interactions with Stephen Hopkins.[31]

In noting the importance of Samoset's part in the survival of the Pilgrims, Levett apparently understood the impact that individuals could have on larger events and trends. What contemporaries knew to be achieved by the participants, many early historians painted as divine intervention, arguing simply that God was responsible for the Wampanoag's change in heart toward the Pilgrims.[32]

Some modern historians have done little better, attributing Massasoit's abrupt swing from hostility to friendship to another form of deus ex machina—namely, that the insufferable arrogance of his rival Narragansett prompted the Wampanoag sachem to befriend the Pilgrims as the lesser of two evils.[33] Under this theory, the purpose of the *powwáws'* ritual that Massasoit held was not to curse the Pilgrims, as recorded by William Bradford, but rather, to ritually cleanse the Wampanoag of their enmity toward the English as a prelude to an abrupt diplomatic reversal.[34]

While the English participants who wrote of the events, such as Bradford, were no doubt influenced by their own biases in what they documented, it would seem unduly cavalier to entirely dismiss Bradford's description of what he was told by Massasoit himself (or perhaps by Squanto or Samoset), which was that the ritual of the *powwáws* had been an attempt by Massasoit to drive the invaders from the shores of his domain.[35]

Perhaps, then, the words of Levett about the power of individual impact should be reconsidered and held in higher regard. Just as the actions of an individual such as Thomas Hunt alienated the Wampanoag against the English, the actions of two individuals—Stephen Hopkins and Samoset—seemed to have inspired a reconciliation, for when Samoset left Hopkins's house, he initiated a chain of events that quickly brought Massasoit himself to Plymouth to enter into a peace treaty.

Samoset and Massasoit Have a Talk

Samoset left the English on Saturday morning, March 17, promising to come back with some of the Wampanoag as well as with beaver skins for trading. Although Hopkins would have reported to his fellow colonists how his evening with Samoset had gone, the Pilgrims were still apparently very wary. The initial contact had yielded positive news, but much more was needed to truly develop a sense of trust.

At this point, there was still no true relationship. Accordingly, they instructed Samoset that any visitors to Plymouth must leave their weapons a quarter of a mile from the English settlement. Samoset returned the very next day with five of Massasoit's warriors, who must have been waiting nearby, most likely watching and waiting to see the outcome of Samoset's visit. The Wampanoag complied with the Pilgrims' demands, putting down their bows and arrows before entering the town.[36]

The men brought with them three or four animal skins, but because it was Sunday, the Pilgrims would not engage in any trading. In any event, the number of furs was insignificant—the English "wished them to bring more," according to *Mourt's Relation*—which is yet more evidence that the Wampanoag had sent Samoset to visit without a predetermined outcome in mind.[37] If the goal had been to embrace the English from the beginning because Massasoit had undergone some providential change of heart, they most likely would have been better prepared to open the relationship with trade, which historically had been the primary reason for European sojourns to their shores.[38] The Pilgrims offered the warriors food. For their part, the Wampanoag "made semblance unto us of friendship and amity," but there was an undercurrent of anxiety. As a result, the meeting was brief, and the English "dismissed them so soon as we could."[39]

A group of armed Pilgrims started to lead the Wampanoag back to the place where they'd left their weapons. Once outside the settlement, two of the men tried to slip away from their escorts, most likely out of the atmosphere of fear that had persisted throughout the encounter. After all, they were being led away under guard by men perceived as aggressors—not only historically but in recent months as well. It would have thus been a natural reaction to flee at the first opportunity. One of their peers called the runners back, however, and according to *Mourt's Relation*, all the Wampanoag "were amazed" and "glad" when they were brought to the place where they'd laid their bows and arrows, for they apparently presumed a less agreeable outcome.[40] The incident and the reactions of the Wampanoag highlight the lingering suspicion of the Wampanoag toward the Englishmen, which in turn provides further insight into the mind of Massasoit. The shows of friendship and amity were just that, an artifice. There was no immediate rush to embrace the English.

So the Wampanoag left, but Samoset did not. According to *Mourt's Relation,* he "would not go with them," which provides yet another hint that the Abenaki had been held against his will by Massasoit. Samoset stayed in Plymouth for the remainder of the day on Sunday. He spent the night again, presumably with Stephen Hopkins, and was a guest for three more days, not leaving the colony again until Wednesday, March 21.[41]

As before, there is no record of the details surrounding Samoset's second visit to Plymouth, but several things may be inferred from surrounding events. Back on Saturday morning, March 17, when Samoset had left Hopkins after his first visit, he met with several Wampanoag who'd been waiting for him in the forests outside the settlement. They returned under the guise of trading as a delaying tactic while one or more of the men who'd been waiting for Samoset raced to Massasoit, who was in Pokanoket about forty miles away.[42] They carried a message from Samoset, who now had detailed information about the English. The message prompted Massasoit himself, with his brother and an entourage of sixty warriors, as well as Squanto, to travel to Plymouth. He arrived on Wednesday, March 21, and made camp in the forest out of the view of the settlers.

The time line and distance to Pokanoket and Samoset's departure from Plymouth again on March 21 suggest that Samoset knew when Massasoit would arrive in the area. He found and met with Massasoit and his entourage. The Abenaki sagamore and the Wampanoag sachem discussed Samoset's visit to the English. At this point, Massasoit's best intelligence about the Pilgrims came from Samoset. And Samoset's knowledge of the Pilgrims was certainly influenced by Stephen Hopkins, the man with whom he'd lived for five out of the past six days. Samoset probably explained the situation in person to Massasoit, likely relating that the English wanted peace, not war, but that they were fully prepared for war if need be. Massasoit needed only to walk to the forest's edge and see the display of cannons on the Pilgrims' hill for himself to confirm the validity of the Abenaki's words. As Hopkins probably shared stories of his time at Jamestown, Samoset also likely explained to Massasoit how his English host had lived for years in Virginia and how a small group of them resisted many thousands of Powhatan warriors. Information like this might have impressed Massasoit and helped him consider how the English could become useful allies to the Wampanoag.

There is no evidence of the particulars of Samoset's meeting with the Wampanoag sachem, but the outcome allows for the foregoing interpretation, for the following day, Thursday, March 22, Massasoit walked into Plymouth to sign a peace treaty. He apparently spent less than twenty-four hours in the area before walking across Town Brook to meet with the English and come to terms. This implies that Samoset presumably gave Massasoit such a favorable description of the Pilgrims that he turned away from animosity and decided to form an alliance and work with the English to the benefit of his confederacy. With the power of their guns on his side, he would be in a much stronger position vis-à-vis his rivals, the Narraganset and Massachusett.

A curious incident underscores that Massasoit's mind was not made up until he met with Samoset. On that Wednesday, March 21, while Samoset and Massasoit were likely meeting, the settlers in Plymouth noticed two or three Wampanoag on Watson's Hill. Unlike the previous appearance, these men didn't signal in a manner to invite the English to them; instead, they made aggressive gestures, or so they were interpreted by the Pilgrims.[43] According to *Mourt's Relation*, Myles Standish and "another" went to investigate. Though the second man was not identified, the most probable candidate would have been Stephen Hopkins, given his role in the prior Watson's Hill visitation and also his role in the discussions with Samoset. At this point, William Bradford was still bedridden because of his January injury, leaving Edward Winslow as the probable author of this section of *Mourt's Relation*. In at least one other instance, Winslow referred in early accounts specifically to Hopkins as "another."[44]

Because the Wampanoag on the hill did not appear peaceful and because of their last experience, both carried weapons.[45] The two men splashed across Town Brook, just as they'd done before. The warriors at the crest of the hill looked scornfully down at them and, according to *Mourt's Relation*, "whetted and rubbed their arrows and strings" in a "show of defiance." The Pilgrims likely paused, perhaps sharing a word about strategy and fingering the triggers of their muskets. Thus far, all signs were pointing toward confrontation. Nevertheless, the Englishmen continued up the hill, likely trusting in the superiority of their firepower. As they drew near, the natives fled.[46]

An interpretation of the episode doesn't easily appear from the primary sources, for none of the Wampanoag apparently ever discussed the event with the Pilgrims. But most likely, the display coincided with Massasoit's final decision after meeting with Samoset. At some point the Wampanoag leader must have announced his determination to pursue peace with the English, informing his people that he'd approach the settlement himself the very next day. A few of his warriors, impatient for a fight, probably disliked the decision and raced to Watson's Hill in a show of courage and anger, a final gesture of defiance against their would-be enemies. They were angry at these Englishmen, for the evils that Thomas Hunt had committed left lasting damage to so many Wampanoag families. It was time for revenge, not peace. Their sachem's decision, therefore, might have become a source of frustration, which they then vented on Watson's Hill.

Thursday, March 22, was a fair and warm day, showing that spring was starting to get a firm grip on New England. Shortly after noon, Samoset walked up to the colony, and he brought with him Squanto, the sole survivor of the Patuxet people. Three other Wampanoag also accompanied them, this time bringing several furs and even a few freshly caught and dried fish for trading. Squanto was more capable with English than Samoset, yet communication still proved an arduous and time-consuming task. Squanto told the English that Massasoit and his brother had traveled to the area and were waiting nearby. Toward what end, however, the English had difficulty determining. Did he wish peace? Or did he have a complaint? About an hour into the interview, there was activity on Watson's Hill.[47]

On the summit appeared Massasoit along with his entourage of sixty men.[48] The English could muster perhaps twenty adult men at this point, although many of them were sick, which meant that the Wampanoag outnumbered them three to one.[49] Unable to completely understand the purpose of the visit and probably apprehensive because of the disparity in strength, they were unwilling to send anyone over to speak with the sachem. Massasoit, likewise, was cautious. He stood with his men, unmoving.[50] On their opposite hilltops, the two groups fell into a kind of standoff.

Squanto crossed Town Brook to sort it out with his leader. Returning, he suggested that the Pilgrims send an ambassador to speak with Massasoit and determine how best to proceed. They sent Edward Winslow. He brought gifts to present to Massasoit and his brother and, according to *Mourt's Relation*, "to signify the mind and will of our governor, which was to have trading and peace with him." Squanto likely translated. In the end, it was agreed that Winslow would stay on the hill in the custody of Massasoit's brother as an assurance for the safe passage of Massasoit, who himself would come into Plymouth to speak with Governor Carver. He walked down the hill with twenty of his men.

Myles Standish and William Brewster met and saluted Massasoit at Town Brook. There, the English kept several of the sachem's men as hostages to ensure that Winslow was returned unharmed. With an escort of six other Pilgrims armed with muskets, Standish and Brewster conducted the Wampanoag leader and his remaining men to one of the dwellings in the settlement that was then still under construction.[51]

Why was Winslow chosen as the diplomat over Stephen Hopkins? The primary sources do not explain. Perhaps it was simply that Winslow volunteered and Hopkins did not. Winslow was a much younger man than Hopkins. At the time, he was about twenty-six years old. Hopkins was by now about forty. Winslow had been born into an affluent family, was formally educated, and in Leiden he'd worked with church elder William Brewster in the printing business.[52] Perhaps the group trusted Winslow more than Hopkins, even though both were considered among the "principal men" of the company.[53] Or perhaps Hopkins was considered more valuable back at the settlement. As was the case with Winslow, Governor Carver would have needed the assistance of translators to help him with any negotiations. Understanding one another was still difficult, even with Squanto's arrival, so Carver would have benefited from Hopkins's aptitude with the Algonquian tongue to help ensure that both sides understood relatively abstract principles necessary to establishing a peace accord.[54] It was one thing to point to an animal pelt and use hand signs to negotiate an exchange for knives or jewelry. It was quite another to try to communicate about one side coming to the aid of another in the case of war, or about how to ensure that all the different tribes of the Wampanoag Confederacy, such as the Nauset on Cape Cod, would comply with the terms of an accord.

There was also the issue of preparing an uncompleted home as the location for the meeting between Carver and Massasoit. Unfinished, the house would have been unfurnished. Hopkins seems to have been involved in preparing the site for the meeting. The sudden and unexpected appearance of Massasoit probably sent the English settlement into somewhat of a scramble. With Winslow remaining on Watson's Hill as hostage, with Standish and Brewster and the honor guard leaving for Town Brook to meet Massasoit, and with William Bradford and others debilitated by sickness, there were precious few to help Carver prepare. Hopkins apparently ran to his own house and got a green rug and some cushions.[55] It was upon this rug and these cushions that he and Samoset had likely reclined during the Abenaki's stay in Plymouth. It would have been a natural selection to use the same setting for Massasoit.

Massasoit and the First Treaty

Massasoit and Governor Carver sat down together on the rug. They saluted each other with a drink of aqua vitae, shared a bite of food, and with the help of the interpreters, negotiated terms of peace between the Wampanoag and the colonists of Plymouth. The treaty included narrow provisions, such as requiring the return of goods taken by either group of people, as well as more consequential provisions, such as the promise by both sides to come to the other's aid if attacked by anyone else.

Curiously, in addition to a promise that the Wampanoag would not, according to *Mourt's Relation*, "injure or do hurt" to any of the English settlers, Massasoit also agreed to a provision requiring that if any of his people did injure an Englishman, he would send the offender to the English for punishment.[56] While such a condition might seem like a natural addendum to the promise against harm, it was also suspiciously like a provision that Lord De la Warr suggested to the Powhatan during Stephen Hopkins's tenure in Jamestown, which raises the possibility that Hopkins lent more to the peace process than mere translation skills.[57]

"The Treaty Between Governor Carver and Massasoit," from John Clark
Ridpath, *A Popular History of the United States of America* (New York:
Phillips & Hunt, 1887). *Courtesy of the Library of Congress*

When they concluded the accord, Massasoit took from his neck a bag of
tobacco. He filled his pipe and smoked and then leaned over and presented
the pipe to Governor Carver, who also smoked.[58] Perhaps unknown to the
Pilgrims at that time, the sharing of tobacco at this point was significant, for
tobacco held a special place in native social and ceremonial culture.[59]

Thus, the two groups of people, who up until now had interacted under
a cloud of mutual suspicion, formed a strategic alliance. This relationship
founded by treaty saved Plymouth Colony and thus ushered in the course of
events that eventually gave rise to the United States of America. The partnership would last for over fifty years. Massasoit lived until 1661, and according
to *Mourt's Relation*, during the rest of his life "always scrupulously, and most
honorably, kept his treaty" with the English. It would not be until 1675 that
the alliance would finally unravel and turn to conflict.[60]

Following the ceremony, Massasoit and his men retired to their camp in
the forest. Despite the promise of the treaty, that evening the English posted
sentinels in the settlement to guard against a surprise attack, as the pressure

from months of suspicion and enmity was not immediately mitigated. Samoset and Squanto, however, stayed behind in Plymouth.[61] Given the settlers' ongoing apprehension as evidenced by the posting of lookouts, it is almost certain that both men spent the night as guests in Stephen Hopkins's home.[62] Because he'd previously hosted Samoset and because he alone among the Pilgrims had any understanding of their native tongue, the two native men likely saw in Hopkins their closest ally among the English. In Squanto, Hopkins would probably have found a lively interlocutor, and they likely shared stories about London, for during his time there Squanto had happened to live very close to Hopkins. Only a nine-minute stroll had separated them, thus providing the men with literal common ground.[63]

Massasoit and his warriors soon returned to Pokanoket, but tensions remained high in Plymouth. Under Myles Standish's command, the men in the colony took turns as sentries keeping a watchful eye on the countryside.[64] Whenever one or two of the settlers went into the woods to gather thatch or cut more timber or to hunt for waterfowl, they remained vigilant. Occasionally, they saw Wampanoag, likely men ranging through the forest. Because of lingering uncertainty over the relationship, the Pilgrims likely experienced an upsurge of fear over these encounters. They were far from their encampment. Far from the support of their friends. What would native people do? Only once the band of Wampanoag moved on would the settler likely regain some confidence. They wouldn't be accosted today. It took several such episodes in the weeks after Massasoit's visit for the English, according to *Mourt's Relation*, to finally "conceive . . . that [Massasoit was] willing to have peace with us."[65]

At this point, Samoset dropped out of the records made by the Plymouth settlers, which indicates that he was finally free to return to Maine and his people. He played a vital part in bridging the mistrust between the Wampanoag and the English. As William Bradford related, the two sides had been "far . . . from peace" when Samoset appeared in Plymouth.[66] Stephen Hopkins played a key role in winning Samoset's trust and enlisting him to help bring Massasoit to Plymouth to negotiate an accord. Without these two men, the history of the settlement probably would have taken a very different course, for the English were in an increasingly weak position owing to the disease that was still rampant among them and would have been ill prepared for battle.

Only two days after Massasoit and Carver met to discuss the terms of a treaty, Elizabeth Winslow, wife of Edward, died. She was one of thirteen Pilgrims that died in the month of March. And though as the warmer days of spring took hold, the rate of mortality finally started to abate, there was still the question of food.[67]

Squanto Lends a Hand

The Plymouth settlers had brought seeds of the English crops of wheat and peas, which they planted. The crops failed.[68] Whether it was the climate or the soil, New England would not support these mainstays from old England.

In the first week of April the surviving members of crew of the *Mayflower* had recovered enough for Master Jones to put the ship to sea, finally, for its return voyage.[69] With the ship went the supply of food. The Pilgrims were now utterly on their own. But they did have a new friend, for even after Samoset departed for his homeland, Squanto remained in Plymouth, and he probably stayed with Stephen Hopkins. How long that arrangement lasted is unknown, but it is very likely that he lived there for some time, as there were still only seven homes in the entire settlement.[70]

What is quite certain is that Squanto soon taught the Pilgrims how to plant and fertilize native corn, he showed them where to catch fish, and he told them how to procure other necessities critical for maintaining and sustaining their settlement.[71] According to William Bradford, who over time became especially close to the Native American, Squanto "was a special instrument sent of God for their good beyond their expectation."[72]

The Patuxet man died in November 1622, only twenty-two months after he met Hopkins and the other English settlers, but he lived long enough to help the staggering colony onto its feet during its most vulnerable time.[73] A Pokanoket warrior named Hobbamock assumed the role of primary guide to the Pilgrims in the wake of Squanto's death. Perhaps not surprisingly, he and his family lived on land next to the Hopkins family for twenty years.[74]

Of course, the Pilgrims' future was still fraught with obstacles and hardship. Later in April 1621, while they were working their crops with the knowledge imparted by Squanto, Governor Carver came out of the fields feeling unwell. He complained of an intense headache and lay down. Within a few hours, it appears as though he slipped into a coma. He died a few days later.[75] His wife, Katherine, would follow about a month afterward.[76]

Carver's death hit the colony particularly hard, as he was well liked by both Saint and Stranger. Every man who could lift a musket to his shoulder formed an honor guard and fired a volley over Carver's grave. By this time, the Pilgrims had probably come to understand that in this ruthless country death was as much a part of the landscape as was life. There was little time for mourning. After burying Carver, they gathered and chose William Bradford as their new governor.[77] It would be a position he'd be elected to more often than not for the rest of his life.

Journey to Pokanoket

Though the immediate threat to the settlement by the Wampanoag appeared to have passed, by the summer of 1621, the Pilgrims decided to send a diplomatic mission to Pokanoket to visit Massasoit. There were several reasons for the trip. None of the colonists had traveled more than a few miles from Plymouth, and it was determined that they should explore farther afield. They also wanted to know exactly where Pokanoket was located, for should the need arise, they might need to quickly send a messenger to their new ally.

A visit would also give the English a better sense of the strength of Massasoit's Pokanoket forces. What Samoset had revealed after his first night with Stephen Hopkins had corresponded to the number of men who had appeared with Massasoit on Watson's Hill, but they wanted to see Massasoit's base of power for themselves. Furthermore, Plymouth had been receiving a somewhat chaotic train of visiting natives, and the English wanted to establish a more formal system to ensure that there were no miscommunications between them and their neighbors that might jeopardize their nascent relationship. The Pilgrims also wanted to start making amends for their early malfeasances on Cape Cod, such as stealing the corn of the Nauset.

Most significantly, however, the Pilgrims wanted to use the visit to strengthen their ties with the Wampanoag.[78] While they had a piece of paper with formal terms to which Massasoit had agreed, what was a piece of paper to one who did not write? Prudence dictated that they take affirmative steps to nurture the relationship to make certain that the agreement wouldn't be forgotten or dismissed. In short, they wanted, in the words of William Bradford, "to bind [Massasoit] faster unto them."[79] The mission represented an important undertaking for the English. Governor Bradford selected two of the colony's key men for the critical job: Stephen Hopkins and Edward Winslow.[80] Squanto accompanied them as guide and interpreter.

Winslow's wife of three years, Elizabeth, had died in March. About six weeks later, he'd married Susanna White, the widow of Separatist William White, who'd died in February. Theirs was the first wedding of the Plymouth colonists in the New World.[81] Winslow had previously shown fortitude when he'd met Massasoit on Watson's Hill and waited as a hostage while the Wampanoag sachem entered Plymouth to negotiate the treaty. In the coming years, he would become a principal diplomat for the Pilgrims as well as a trade negotiator. He also would serve as governor of the colony for several terms. In 1646, two years after Hopkins's death, Winslow would sail to England to support Oliver Cromwell's Puritan Commonwealth and would never return to the colony.[82]

In early July 1621, with Squanto leading the way, Hopkins and Winslow left Plymouth on the momentous visit to Massasoit. The forty-mile journey to Pokanoket, which was situated along the northern shores of Narragansett Bay in modern-day Rhode Island, took two days, and the group traveled past villages and settlements that had been devastated by the plague that had swept through New England some three years before.[83]

As they approached Pokanoket, much of the land had been cleared of trees, but where crops once stood now was mottled with weeds that grew head high.[84] A stony hill called Mount Hope rose about three hundred feet above the otherwise flat green terrain. Covered with boulders exposed by glaciers, it was an important gathering place for the Wampanoag Confederacy.[85]

The settlement was likely a typical village of the day with wigwams of various sizes covered in woven mats and bark from chestnut and birch trees situated in a clearing near freshwater springs.[86] Cooking fires would have sent smoke spiraling into the sky. Women, men, and children would have stood and turned to look when Englishmen arrived. For many of the villagers, the two Pilgrims might have been the first Europeans they had ever encountered.

The travelers quickly learned that Massasoit was out in the country. Word was sent to the Wampanoag leader, and while they waited Squanto advised Winslow and Hopkins to salute Massasoit on his return with a volley from their muskets. The two men started the laborious process of loading the cumbersome matchlocks, but the sight proved too much for some of the women and children, who fled believing—likely because, until recently, the English were viewed as enemies—that the visitors were about to attack. According to *Mourt's Relation*, the frightened villagers "could not be pacified" until the guns were lowered to the ground and Squanto personally explained to them that no ill will was intended.[87]

Winslow and Hopkins took up their arms again when Massasoit arrived, and after their loud salute, he invited them into his home. The Pilgrims presented several gifts, including a red horseman's coat and a copper chain to be carried by any visitors from Massasoit to Plymouth so that the colonists would know that the person spoke on behalf of the Wampanoag leader.[88] Hopkins was the most likely source of these ideas, for he'd seen them used in Virginia.[89] The gifts were well received, for as recorded in *Mourt's Relation*, when Massasoit put on the coat and chain, "he was not a little proud to behold himself, and his men also to see their King so bravely attired."

With Squanto's help, the two ambassadors reiterated to the Wampanoag leader the English settlers' desire "that the peace and amity that was between them and us might be continued . . . because we [desired] to live peaceably, and as with all men, so especially with them our nearest neighbors." They also raised the issue of the corn stolen from Cape Cod and enlisted Massasoit's help so that the English could repay the Nauset, which they did later in the month.[90]

Although his Pokanoket people had been greatly diminished by the plague, Massasoit still commanded some five hundred square miles of New England stretching from Narragansett Bay in Rhode Island to Cape Cod, and held sway over several constituent tribes.[91] He was still a proud leader of a proud nation. Massasoit told the Pilgrims that "he would gladly continue that Peace and Friendship which was between him and us." He then called a gathering of his warriors who were in the village. They came, and he stood before them "and made a great speech," pausing at times when the crowd applauded.[92] In a series of questions, Massasoit elicited responses from his people:

> Was not he, Massasoit, commander of the country about them? Was not such a town [as the one they were in] his [as well as] the people of it? Should they not bring their [animal] skins to us [i.e., the English at their colony]? To which they answered [that] they were his and would be at peace with us and bring their skins to us.[93]

Using the same question-and-answer format, Massasoit "named at least thirty" other places within the Wampanoag Confederacy, a process that was necessarily lengthy because of the breadth of his dominion.[94]

After the speech, he sat down with Hopkins and Winslow, and as he did in Plymouth after consummating the agreement with then governor Carver, Massasoit lit his pipe and shared tobacco with the two Englishmen.[95] The ritual sharing of tobacco indicated that Massasoit saw this exchange on the same level as that which had taken place several months before in Plymouth.[96]

In perhaps a special nod to Hopkins, who'd hosted his emissaries in Plymouth, Massasoit insisted that both visitors spend the night with him in his dwelling. As described in *Mourt's Relation*, "He laid us on the bed with himself and his wife, they at the one end and we at the other."[97] That as a sachem Massasoit entertained them indicates that he viewed both men as leaders among their people. As such, he regarded them much as his equals; otherwise, he likely would not have condescended to even speak with them.[98] That he allowed them to sleep in his home, especially with his wife present, further suggests that he held them both in special esteem, for the Indian women in coastal New England were usually rather guarded about their interactions with Europeans.[99]

Hopkins and Winslow stayed in Pokanoket for two days. When they left, Squanto stayed behind to follow up on the notion of commerce, which had been one of the issues they'd discussed. More trade would not only bring the two peoples closer together but would also help the Pilgrims in their efforts to repay their financial backers in London. To this end, Massasoit sent Squanto to the area's villages to promote the idea of trading furs with the English at Plymouth.[100]

With an escort of six men from Pokanoket, Hopkins and Winslow started the long hike back to the colony. Without Squanto, they had no translator other than Hopkins, for as noted earlier, Winslow found even after several years that the Algonquian language was impossible to "attain to any great measure" of understanding without help.[101] Along the way, they encountered Wampanoag, with whom they bartered for bits of food, for they had none. What they traded for they shared with their Pokanoket escort, but they were soon limited to a spoonful of cornmeal taken with a pipe of tobacco to dull the pangs of hunger. The tobacco was rapidly exhausted, and the Pokanoket led them five miles out of the way to a dwelling where they hoped to find food. The residents were not home, however, and the men were forced to retrace their steps, even hungrier now for their efforts. Winslow and Hopkins sent one of their guides ahead to look for food; others abandoned the party, probably deciding that they'd be better able to find a meal on their own, leaving the two Pilgrims by the end of the day with only two Pokanoket.[102]

They stopped for the night near the midpoint of their journey at a river where the local people fished. Though it was typically an active fishing spot, there were no people present and there was no shelter, so they slept on the ground in the open around a campfire. A storm swept into the area, and by two o'clock in the morning the wind turned violent. Lightening flashed, thunder rolled, and heavy rain came pummeling down. The fire sputtered out.

The rain continued in force, and the men resumed their journey as soon as light allowed. Coming to a village, they stopped, seeking shelter and food, and were invited into a bark-covered wigwam crowded with native people waiting for the storm to break. Winslow and Hopkins handed out gifts to all those who "showed us any kindness," according to *Mourt's Relation*. One of their Pokanoket escorts who'd abandoned them the day before was among the people resting in the wigwam. The man protested when the Pilgrims did not give him a gift as they'd done to others, "marvel[ing that] we gave him nothing and told us what he had done for us." The English responded by listing "some of the discourtesies he [had] offered us," insisting therefore that "he deserved nothing." Nevertheless, they presented him with a "small trifle," and in return he offered them tobacco as an offering of amity. The Pilgrims immediately became suspicious, though, because the man had been with them when they'd consumed the last of their shared tobacco.[103] They confronted him in front of everyone in the wigwam, explaining that he must have stolen the tobacco, and if that were the case,

> We would not take it, for we would not receive that which was sto-
> len upon any terms. If we did, our God would be angry with us and
> destroy us. This abashed him and gave the rest great content.[104]

Though the group implored the two Pilgrims to stay because the weather was unrelenting, they decided to press on, finally making it home to the Plymouth settlement late that night—wet, weary, and with aching feet. Their ability to communicate during the return journey was no doubt because of Hopkins's facility with the Algonquian tongue, a point highlighted by the rather complicated discussion with the Pokanoket about discourtesy, thievery, and the punishment of God.[105]

Giving Thanks Together

The settlers spent other parts of the summer exploring the region, and a group sailed with Squanto in the shallop up to Massachusetts Bay to establish relations with the natives in that area. It is not known whether Stephen Hopkins was part of these exploratory ventures, but given his past involvement it is rather likely that he, in addition to Myles Standish, were participants.[106] Other colonists fished the coastal waters, finding more success now than they had earlier in the year, while still others hunted for game, such as venison, and fowl, such as wild turkey, geese, and ducks.

As fall began to shorten the days, the Pilgrims, according to William Bradford, began "to gather in the small harvest they had" and set about preparing their dwellings for the coming winter.[107] It had been a plentiful season, and the Pilgrims invited their allies, the Wampanoag, to join them in celebration. Massasoit returned to Plymouth with about ninety of his people, and they and the Pilgrims spent three days together entertaining and feasting.[108] The relationship was growing into more than a strategic alliance; the two peoples were becoming close and amiable, as recorded in *Mourt's Relation*:

> And although it be not always so plentiful, as it was at this time with us, yet by the goodness of God, we are so far from want. . . . We have found the Indians very faithful in their Covenant of Peace with us; very loving and ready to [please] us. We often go to them, and they come to us. . . . [T]here is now a great peace amongst the Indians themselves, which was not formerly [and] neither would have been but for us, and we for our parts walk as peaceably and safely in the wood as in the highways of England. We entertain them familiarly in our houses, and they as friendly bestowing their venison on us. They are a people without any religion or knowledge of any God, yet very trust[worthy], quick of apprehension, ripe-witted, [and] just.[109]

Thus, friendship was a hallmark of the First Thanksgiving. Without this friendship, the Pilgrims would likely not have survived that first year.

The diplomatic partnership that blossomed into friendship had required a dramatic shift in the attitude of Massasoit, who according to the available evidence was not inclined toward peace until Samoset's famous visit to Plymouth. His courageous walk into the settlement helped to bridge the chasm that had divided the English and the Wampanoag. And Samoset might not have been as persuasive an advocate of peace without the influence of Stephen Hopkins. When Hopkins opened the door of his home to Samoset—when no one else would—he opened the door to the prospect of prosperity that came with peace.

9 | A MELANCHOLY UNRAVELING

> The cloud-capped towers, the gorgeous palaces,
> The solemn temples, the great globe itself—
> Yea, all which it inherit—shall dissolve,
> And like this insubstantial pageant faded,
> Leave not a rack behind.
> —*The Tempest*, act 4, scene 1

IN NOVEMBER 1621—ONE YEAR AFTER THE *MAYFLOWER* anchored in Provincetown Harbor—a ship arrived from England carrying thirty-five more settlers.[1] Plymouth Colony still had only seven houses, and Governor Bradford distributed the newcomers among the existing families.[2] The vessel departed a month later carrying clapboard cut from New World trees, as well as a very small supply of beaver skins, the financial fruit of the Pilgrims' labors. The cargo wouldn't do much to recoup the original investments of their London backers, but it was a start. Unfortunately, the ship was seized by the French just off the English coast, and the entire consignment was lost.[3]

The Wampanoag alliance with the English had sent ripples through the network of relations between the various native nations in New England. Massasoit's closest rivals, the Narragansett in Rhode Island and the Massachusett in the coastal region around Massachusetts Bay, were particularly piqued. In December 1621 or January 1622 Canonicus, the leader of the Narragansett, sent a messenger bearing a bundle of arrows wrapped in a snakeskin. Squanto was temporarily unavailable, but Hopkins was able to gather details about the Narragansett's intentions, namely that while Canonicus had initially desired peace with the Pilgrims after learning of their accord with Massasoit, he was now provoked against them. Although the messenger explained that someone had inappropriately influenced Canonicus to turn on the settlers and assured Hopkins that he could convince Canonicus of the benefits of peace, the people of Plymouth were still concerned.[4] With the possibility of conflict rising, the Pilgrims decided to fortify Plymouth, and they built a wall around the settlement much like the one that protected Jamestown. The work took them until March 1622 to complete.

The spring planting season that year didn't yield as much bounty as the previous year. By summer, with less food and more mouths to feed, famine began to pinch the stomachs of the English, for by this point the colony had about a hundred people. English boats visiting the fisheries off the coast of New England brought news of a massacre in Jamestown. The peace struck with the Powhatan during Stephen Hopkins's time there had completely disintegrated. About 350 English settlers—including men, women, and children—had been killed that March.[5] The massacre in Virginia and the scarcity of food in Plymouth served as ominous reminders that life in the New World remained dangerous.

New English Settlements: Weston, Morton, and the Massachusetts Bay Colony

Though the men and women of Plymouth Colony suffered through setbacks, others in England took heart from the Pilgrims' resiliency and launched their own colonial endeavors, and they acknowledged that the Pilgrims' alliance with the Wampanoag was one of the primary influences. For example, John Pory, a three-term secretary to the governor of the colony at Jamestown, visited Plymouth in late 1622. He wrote in January 1623 to the London Company about the status of the Pilgrims' colony. With the tremendous loss of life in Jamestown from the massacre still fresh in mind, Pory noted that the Pilgrims' peaceful relations with the native people were unprecedented:

> They both quietly and justly sat down without either dispossessing any of the natives, or being resisted by them, and without shedding so much as one drop of blood. Which felicity of theirs is confirmed unto them even by the voices of the savages themselves, who generally do acknowledge not only the seat but [also] the whole siegniory [an archaic term from feudal times meaning dominion] thereto belonging, to be, and do themselves disclaim all title from it, so that the right of

those planters [i.e., the Pilgrims] to it is altogether unquestionable—a favor which, since the first discovery of America, God has not vouchsafed, so far as ever I could learn, upon any Christian nation within that continent.[6]

Plymouth's lasting peace helped draw successive waves of new colonists to New England, as explained by Benjamin Trumbull, an eighteenth-century historian who in 1797 published what has been described as the most thorough chronicle of the colonial history of the state of Connecticut:[7]

By making permanent settlements, to which others might resort on their first arrival in New England, or afterwards in times of distress; **by making treaties with the Indians, by which the peace of the country was preserved**; by their knowledge of it and the experience which they had gained, [the Plymouth colonists] were of peculiar advantage to those who came over and made settlements after them.[8]

The first two colonial attempts inspired by Plymouth fizzled out. In 1622 Thomas Weston sent a group of men to settle at a place called Wessagussett, which was located about twenty-two miles north of Plymouth in modern-day Weymouth, Massachusetts. The Wessagussett settlement was more like Jamestown than like Plymouth in that it was composed of unattached men who shared little in common with each other. And like the first settlers in Jamestown, they built a fort but did little else to establish themselves, such as creating a reliable source of food or seeking a peaceable relationship with the Massachusett, who dominated that part of the coast.[9] Though the Pilgrims in Plymouth reluctantly lent some assistance to their countrymen, the settlement quickly failed and was abandoned.[10]

In 1624 Thomas Morton came with a group of thirty indentured servants to start his settlement in modern-day Quincy, Massachusetts. The colony lasted only until 1630.[11]

In that same year, a huge convoy of seventeen ships anchored in Massachusetts Bay. Within a few months about a thousand English men, women, and children arrived and started to create a series of Puritan settlements that together constituted what was called the Massachusetts Bay Colony. At its inception, it already had more than three times the number of settlers as did Plymouth.

In 1636 Roger Williams founded what would become the religiously toler-
ant colony of Rhode Island.[12] The flow of new settlers would come to have an
enormous impact on the region and would also directly influence the direction
of the last years of Stephen Hopkins's life.

Hopkins Continues to Lead

Despite the singular importance of creating peace with the Wampanoag, historians seemed to have missed Hopkins's influence in the early survival and
ultimate success of Plymouth Colony.[13] His fellow settlers, however, understood
and appreciated his contributions from the very outset. For example, the preface
to *Mourt's Relation*, the first published account of the Pilgrims' experiences in
the New World, specifically promoted the value of the knowledge of "such as
have been there **a first and second time**," a probable reference to Hopkins,
for whom the *Mayflower*'s voyage was indeed a second trip to America.[14] He
remained a member of the colony's leadership, and his influence can be seen
at various times as the years passed. In 1623 Governor Bradford decided to
abandon the colony's approach to communal food production and transitioned
to individual family plots, a conversion that Hopkins had seen happen successfully in Virginia.[15]

In the colony's second decade, the voting men of the settlement repeatedly asked Hopkins to serve in an official capacity. In January 1633 he was
selected as an assistant to just-elected Governor Edward Winslow. Serving with
Hopkins as assistants were William Bradford, who'd just completed serving
twelve consecutive terms as governor, and Myles Standish.[16] Hopkins served
as an assistant to the governor for the following four years, through 1636, and
appears to have been much employed in public affairs during this period.[17] For
example, in 1633 he and Myles Standish were appointed to handle the estate
of a man who died in debt so as to satisfy his creditors and protect his widow.
And in January 1636 he was asked by the colony's leadership to resolve a collection claim against a Plymouth debtor on behalf of Jane Warden, a single
woman who lived in a settlement in Connecticut.[18]

The position of an assistant to the governor wielded significant authority.
The assistants sat with the governor on the colony's General Court, which
functioned as both the settlement's legislative body as well as its judicial court.
As such, this group directed much of the colony's business, including allocating

land to families and resolving disputes among the various settlers, a task that became more important as the number of colonists increased, which naturally caused an increase in the number of disputes.

In addition to serving on the General Court, each assistant to the governor was, according to contemporaneous records of the colony, to give "his best advice both in public court and private counsel with the governor for the good of the colonies." As an assistant, Hopkins was privy to confidential matters that "concern[ed] the public good." He had "a special hand in the examination" of anyone accused of violating the colony's laws, and played a special role "in contriving the affairs of the colony." If the governor was absent from the colony, an assistant might be deputed to govern during the absence. Assistants also had the power to issue arrest warrants and to imprison anyone suspected of a crime until an appropriate hearing could be arranged. In the case of imminent danger to the colony, an assistant to the governor even had the authority to press fellow colonists into service in the defense of the colony.[19] Hopkins's multiyear service in this capacity confirms that his early role in the colony was considered significant by his peers.

The Pivotal Years of the Pequot War: 1636 and 1637

From their earliest days exploring Cape Cod through the beginning of 1636, Stephen Hopkins had been a model citizen and leader of the colony. But in the middle of that year, everything changed.

It began in June when Hopkins was brought before the General Court— which was composed of Governor Winslow and Hopkins's fellow assistants— for assaulting a fellow colonist. John Tisdale, a farmer, complained to the court that Hopkins had attacked and "dangerously wounded" him, according to colonial records.[20] Tisdale was new to the colony, likely having arrived from England earlier that year.[21] At the time, Hopkins was fifty-five years old. Tisdale was twenty-two.[22]

The case was tried before a jury that included Myles Standish and others who'd sailed with Hopkins on the *Mayflower*. John and Kenelm Winslow, brothers of Governor Edward Winslow, also served on the jury. At trial, Tisdale still bore the wounds from the confrontation with Hopkins, and the jury found that Hopkins had breached the king's peace, "which [as an assistant to the governor] he ought after a special manner to have kept," as noted in colony records. Hopkins was fined five pounds and ordered to pay Tisdale another two pounds as recompense for his injuries.[23]

The incident was the first of what would become several controversies putting Hopkins on the wrong side of the colony's laws. All of them likely shared a similar genesis arising from Hopkins's attitude about Native Americans and a string of events involving Connecticut, the Pequot people, and war. The period was not only a pivotal one for Stephen Hopkins; it was pivotal for all of New England.

After its founding in 1630, the Massachusetts Bay Colony kept growing as more and more Puritans arrived from England. Over the course of only a few years, settlers pushed inland into Massachusetts, establishing some twenty towns. As new towns became crowded—limited in their capacity by geography and distance because each family needed enough acreage to farm for sustenance and for cattle to graze—settlers kept pressing into new regions "like swarms of bees," according to seventeenth-century historian William Hubbard.[24] Colonists rationalized that expansion was desirable and beneficial to the native populations, to whom the English hoped to impart more efficient agricultural methods and religion. New England natives were understandably less optimistic about this inexorable acquisition of land.[25]

Hopkins probably did not approve of the new settlements because of the additional strain they put upon the delicate ecosystem of the region. Plymouth's economy depended upon peaceful trade, and the Pilgrims had taken great care to establish and strengthen ties with the Wampanoag and other local natives. The flood of new arrivals from England threatened the balance of relations that the Pilgrims had so labored to maintain. The New World was more than beaver pelts and clapboard and other commodities. It was a place made unique in no small part by its inhabitants, a fact that Hopkins seemed to deeply appreciate. The native people were not barbarous. They were intelligent and thoughtful and clever and humorous. They were a people to be respected and treated like equals.[26]

The Puritans of the Bay Colony did not seem to view the region in the same way. They took the much more traditional English view of the world and approached America as a place to be conquered, just as Ireland had been. Most of the leaders in the Bay Colony saw the world in absolute terms and embraced the notion that God wanted them to possess New England, seeing, for example, a 1633 smallpox outbreak that decimated native populations as evidence of divine will.[27]

The Bay Colony swarm eventually turned southward. Several settlements were established in the lower Connecticut River Valley at modern-day Windsor and Hartford, Connecticut.[28] The Windsor location included a trading house established by Plymouth Colony, which was led by Jonathan Brewster, the forty-three-year-old son of *Mayflower* passenger William Brewster.[29]

But the European settlers weren't the only inhabitants of the area. The Pequot nation had migrated down the Connecticut River in the years before the English started arriving and had intermittent conflict with other native people in the lower river valley, including the Narragansett to the east, the Wampanoag to the north, and the Mohegan to the west.[30] In 1634 Pequot warriors murdered Bay Colony trader John Stone and his crew along the banks of the Connecticut River.[31]

By the summer of 1636, the river valley was simmering with hostility, and as an assistant to the governor, Hopkins would have been well acquainted with the situation.[32] The English settlements and trading outposts along the river had engendered heightened animosity between native nations, which competed for control over the best trapping grounds and for exclusive trading relationships with the English. Competition led to bickering. Bickering led to skirmishes. Skirmishes led to warfare.[33] Settlers were not immune from spreading conflict.[34] A broader clash between the English and the Pequot became a distinct possibility.

The June 1636 incident between Hopkins and John Tisdale coincided with the tectonic changes underway in the region because of the increasing number of English immigrants. The contemporaneous records didn't account for why Hopkins attacked one of his own countrymen, but Tisdale's life after the encounter provides clues as to what might have transpired between the two men. As it turned out, Tisdale held a very different view of Indians than did Hopkins. Where Hopkins saw them as equals—as partners in peace—Tisdale supported "every course of the English to keep them in subjection," according to a family history written by one of his descendants.[35] Later in life Tisdale became the leader of a militia group organized to bully a tribe within the Wampanoag Confederacy into a new pledge of fidelity to the colony.[36]

Tisdale's attitude ultimately led to his death. On June 27, 1675, in the opening days of the conflict that would become known as King Philip's

War, Wampanoag warriors—the sons and grandsons of men like Massasoit, Squanto, and Hobbamock—killed John Tisdale and burned his farmhouse to the ground in revenge for his involvement in an earlier effort to confiscate firearms from them.[37]

Hopkins no doubt was in the wrong for attacking Tisdale, but since he'd not previously been involved in any kind of physical altercation in Plymouth, it would be reasonable to assume that he was somehow provoked by the younger man. Tisdale was a newcomer, one of the bees in the swarm that was quite literally changing the face of the New England landscape. As talk in Plymouth in 1636 would have included conversations about the possibility of war with the Pequot in Connecticut, perhaps Tisdale made some stray remark that revealed his disdain toward the native people upon whose lands they now lived.

Whatever precipitated the fight, Hopkins must have been truly offended, a premise supported by several reasons. First, he broke with his prior record of peaceable conduct. He wasn't a temperamental man. He was the opposite. He'd been able to get along with both Saints and Strangers under the incredibly challenging circumstances not only of a transatlantic voyage but also the exploration and establishment of a settlement on a foreign shore in the dead of winter while disease ravaged both friend and family. He'd gotten along with profane men such as John Billington.[38] He'd been teamed with Myles Standish, a man who *did* possess an irascible temperament, and had worked with the captain under intensely stressful conditions, yet not once did he and the fiery Standish ever fight. In fact, he seemed to be a calm counterbalance to Standish's impulsiveness.

Second, Hopkins knew that as an assistant to the governor, he owed a higher duty to keep the king's peace than other colonists because he held a special position of prominence in the community. He was one of only a few men who held the powerful position at the time and understood his responsibilities.

Third, at age fifty-five, he was elderly in an era when the average lifespan for a man might be only fifty-nine years. Tisdale was less than half Hopkins's age and in the physical prime of his life. Given Tisdale's later colonial role as a constable and his avid participation in the militia, he did not seem like one who was physically limited or timid, which would preclude a situation where someone older might still be able to harass someone who was weaker. Despite his governmental position, despite knowing better, Hopkins thrashed Tisdale.

Soon afterward, war broke out.

Jonathan Brewster reported later in June that conditions in Connecticut were deteriorating. He'd learned that the Pequot had come to believe that the English were planning to attack them. As a result, they were plotting a general campaign against both the English and their primary rival in the Connecticut River Valley—the Mohegan people—and were planning to strike first. Brewster described the plan as one of "desperate madness."[39]

Although the Mohegan shared ancestral ties with the Pequot, the Mohegan's leader, Uncas, wanted to expand their influence and his own power.[40] Because the Mohegan were not as strong as the Pequot, Uncas had turned to the English.[41] It was Uncas who told Brewster about the Pequot's contemplated attack, though an unrelated event actually triggered war.

On July 20, 1636, an English trader named John Oldham, brother-in-law of Jonathan Brewster,[42] was attacked and killed on Block Island, which is located off the coast of Rhode Island and was home to people of the Narragansett nation.[43] Oldham had arrived with his family in Plymouth in 1623 but had a troubled relationship with the colony.[44] By around 1630, he had moved to the Massachusetts Bay Colony, where he became wealthy trading with Indians along the New England coast.[45] Oldham was conducting business with Narragansett when he was killed.[46]

Though the Block Islanders belonged to the greater Narragansett nation, they answered directly to their own petty sachem, and the chief sachem of the Narragansett disavowed knowledge of any preconceived plot to kill the Englishman. The fact that some of the warriors who'd been involved in the attack fled to the Pequot, who harbored them against the demands from the Bay Colony, supported the chief sachem's claim.[47] To the great dismay of those in Plymouth—and particularly so, in all likelihood, to Stephen Hopkins—the English in Boston saw the murder as an act of war and decided to attack.[48]

In August, the Bay Colony sent a force of ninety men under John Endicott who, according to John Winthrop, a prominent leader of the colony, were instructed to "put to death the men of Block Island, but to spare the women and children," who were to be taken captive. Narragansett defended against the English as they landed on the island but soon dispersed, leaving the Puritans to march around the place in search of a foe. One Narragansett died in the initial skirmish, and one was taken captive later. The Englishmen found no more and satisfied themselves by burning two empty villages.

From Block Island, the men sailed to Pequot lands near the mouth of the Connecticut River, where they demanded that the Pequot turn over the Narragansett men who'd killed John Stone two years before. A fight broke out. Thirteen Pequot were killed, and forty were wounded. Two Englishmen died. Before returning to Boston, Endicott ordered the nearest villages to be burned.[49]

In October, the Pequot attacked an English fort at the river's mouth. They also repeatedly attacked English settlers up and down the river valley over the next several months, killing over thirty people.[50] As the conflict escalated, the Bay Colony sought the assistance of its smaller neighbor to the south. Plymouth demurred, complaining that the Puritans were responsible for starting war and insisting that the "war did not concern them [i.e., the Plymouth colonists], seeing the Pequot had not killed any of theirs."[51]

In January 1637 Stephen Hopkins's string of years as an assistant to the governor came to an end, likely due in part to the Tisdale incident. In April, the Pequot attacked another English settlement on the Connecticut River, just twelve miles downriver from Windsor where Plymouth Colony's trading house was located. Three women and six men were killed in the assault, and the Pequot carried off two young girls.[52]

Given the fight's proximity to Plymouth's Connecticut interests, Bradford sent Edward Winslow to Boston in May to discuss the situation. Winslow told the Bay Colony that Plymouth was now willing to lend aid in the fight but also expressed that the colony had several reservations and objections. Boston's leaders responded that they expected Plymouth's help against the Pequot, whom they considered a common enemy, and warned Winslow that if the Pequot were to prevail, it would cause all the New England natives to join together against the English.[53]

Winslow took the message back to Plymouth so that they could make a decision. Shortly after he returned, Governor Bradford convened a meeting of the colony's voting men in Plymouth to debate what course to take.[54] Should they join with their countrymen in the war against the Pequot? Or should they remain neutral and hope that the conflagration did not spread and threaten their very existence?

Without waiting for Plymouth's response, the Bay Colony struck again at the Pequot. On May 26, the English, led by John Mason, a veteran of the brutal Protestant-against-Catholic Thirty Years' War, attacked a fortified village of the Pequot near modern-day Mystic, Connecticut. Using a tactic from the continental religious wars, where burning towns and killing women and children was fairly common, Mason set fire to the Pequot settlement. Between four hundred and seven hundred men, women, and children were killed.[55] The violence was horrific: "It was a fearful sight to see them thus frying in the fire, and the streams of blood quenching the same, and horrible was the stink and scent thereof."[56]

On June 7, after learning of the massacre, Plymouth voted, deciding to assemble a militia force of thirty men to support the Bay Colony's war.[57] Curiously, Hopkins volunteered to serve in the militia contingent that Plymouth raised for the war. Why? If Hopkins was supposedly a steadfast friend to the native people, why would he have signed up to fight? One possibility is that despite the relationships that he'd helped to nurture, Hopkins's loyalties ultimately lay with his fellow English colonists. Refusing to join his fellow colonists wasn't going to undo what had happened to the Pequot settlement. Plus, the violence wasn't one-sided. Dozens of settlers had been killed in the Connecticut River Valley, and perhaps Hopkins enlisted to help protect them against further violence.

Another potential explanation is that Hopkins considered the aggressive Pequot a threat to Plymouth's longtime ally, Massasoit. If left unchecked, the Pequot would presumably have continued clashing with neighboring nations, including the Wampanoag Confederacy. Massasoit had been faithful in upholding the peace accord with the Plymouth colonists that Hopkins had helped establish.[58] If the Pequot presented a danger to the Wampanoag, then Hopkins probably would have been motivated to assist Plymouth's native neighbors and friends.

Another possibility is that Hopkins understood that in the wake of the Pequot massacre in Mystic, the risk of combat was negligible. The muster roll of the Plymouth force provides potential support for this interpretation, for it included both of Hopkins's sons. Giles, who'd sailed on the *Mayflower*, was about thirty years old, but Caleb was only about thirteen or fourteen.[59] That Hopkins let a child of such a young age join a conflict that had already produced the horror of the Pequot massacre—over the likely protests of his wife, Elizabeth—implies that he might have believed the chances of actually joining the fight were not high. If so, he would have been right. According to William Bradford, before the volunteers were even ready to march from Plymouth, they received word "to stay, for the enemy was as good as vanquished."[60]

The Mystic carnage had shattered the Pequot. Surviving remnants scattered, some being absorbed into the Mohegan nation, others into the Narragansett nation. The Pequot sachem, Sassacus, fled far to the west to the Mohawk people, who cut off his head and sent his scalp to Boston.[61] The Pequot were effectively no more.[62]

In the war's aftermath, the Bay Colony started a new policy, one that would have a lasting impact on the relations between Native Americans and Europeans for centuries to come. During the fighting, many Pequot women and children were captured. The Puritans sold them into slavery. Some were shipped some off to the Caribbean, where English sugar plantations were relying on enslaved Africans for labor. Some were disbursed to the various Bay Colony settlements, where they served Puritan households.[63] In the view of the Bay Colony, selling captives raised funds to help pay for the war, and the practice removed what they perceived to be a dangerous people from the region. The policy also cleared the Pequot's lands of inhabitants, which in turn opened them for more English settlements.[64]

The Bay Colony by this time had become the dominant force in New England, and Plymouth Colony was relegated more and more into the larger colony's shadow.[65] Some of the Pilgrims, such as Edward Winslow, embraced the change. Winslow, of course, was the man who'd volunteered to walk to Watson's Hill in March 1621 when Massasoit first appeared at Plymouth. He'd remained in the custody of the sachem's warriors while Massasoit negotiated the historic peace treaty. He'd been Hopkins's companion on the first Pilgrim excursion into the mainland wilderness when the two were sent as envoys in the summer of 1621 to Pokanoket to ratify the treaty. He'd traveled there again in 1623 when Massasoit fell ill and had scraped a noisome film from the feverous sachem's tongue, perhaps saving his life.[66]

Winslow had worked hard to help establish peace in the region that the Bay Colony and its attendant influx of settlers were disrupting. Nevertheless, he seemed to gravitate toward the Puritans. By May 1637, Winslow had recently moved his family to the town of Marshfield, putting him nearly equidistant from Plymouth as he was from the southernmost towns of the Bay Colony.[67] Being so close to the new colony, he soon established personal financial ties with its prominent merchants.[68] He even obtained one of the Pequot children seized as a spoil of war. The youth, who was given the name Hope, apparently remained bonded to the Winslow household for some ten years, at which point the Winslow family sold him to a planter in Barbados.[69] The contract of sale stipulated that Hope, now an adult, was to remain with the planter for another ten years.[70] Although Hope was then to be freed—twenty years after being captured and two thousand miles from his homeland—it is unknown whether the planter in fact did so.

At the time Hope was sold, Winslow was on a trip to England as an agent of the Bay Colony without the consent of Plymouth's leadership, a fact about which William Bradford later complained.[71] England at the time was mired in political controversy that had grown into civil war. A Puritan named Oliver Cromwell had become one of the leaders of an insurrection against the government of King Charles, who in 1625 had succeeded his father, King James. Winslow joined Cromwell's government after the king was deposed and beheaded. He never returned to America.[72]

As Plymouth's fate became more closely enmeshed with that of the Bay Colony, relations between the Pilgrims and their native neighbors became less affable. Native Americans themselves had historically turned defeated foes into slaves, but the Bay Colony's actions against the vanquished Pequot became somewhat of a tipping point. Other native leaders took note. If the fierce Pequot could be turned into chattel, so could anyone. At bottom, the English were not their friends.[73] Although the Wampanoag would continue its alliance with the Pilgrims until Massasoit's death many years later, there had been a fundamental shift in the dynamics of the region.

Drinking and Sabbath Fines

The rising tensions between English and Indians coincided with Stephen Hopkins's growing alienation from the very colony he'd helped to establish, perhaps a sign that he believed that everything he'd worked for was starting to unravel.[74] He'd wanted to live in harmony with the Native Americans in the splendor of the New World. He'd wanted his family to share this life with him. But the crowds of English that had come after the *Mayflower* appeared to be spoiling any hope for this future. In a sense, Plymouth's success—in which Hopkins had played so vital a role—precipitated his personal descent.

The June 1636 fight with Tisdale was the first of several incidents where Hopkins found himself on the wrong side of Plymouth's laws. By 1637, Hopkins had obtained a license to run a tavern out of his house.[75] In October of that year he was brought before the colonial court for allowing "men to drink in his house upon the Lord's Day" before religious services had ended, according to colony records. Not only did Hopkins permit drinking on the Sabbath, but he also allowed people to drink more than was necessary "for ordinary refreshing." To top it off, he let his customers "play at shovel board," another Sabbath violation in the eyes of the Separatists, who unlike the Anglicans frowned upon sport and game playing on Sundays.[76] Hopkins was fined two pounds.[77]

In January 1638 Hopkins was again brought into court for drinking-related accusations. This time, he allowed "excessive drinking in his house," according to colony records. One of his patrons got so drunk he was cited for laying "under the table [and] vomiting in a beastly manner." The man was fined. Hopkins, however, was acquitted after the testimony of five people was heard by the court, which indicates that the heavy drinking may have occurred before the visit to Hopkins's home.[78]

In June of the same year Kenelm and John Winslow visited Hopkins's house-tavern and subsequently brought him to court, accusing Hopkins of two offenses, according to colony records: first, selling beer for two pence a quart when it wasn't worth a single pence; and second, "selling wine at such excessive rates" that it caused "the oppressing and impoverishing of the colony." Significantly, the two men had served on the jury that convicted Hopkins of battering John Tisdale. Brothers of Edward Winslow, they both were newcomers who eventually developed personal ties to the Bay Colony. While Hopkins might have been charging all his customers "excessive rates" at the time, perhaps he intentionally slighted those two in particular for their role in the Tisdale case.

In September 1638 Hopkins was again charged for three more instances of selling "wine, beer, strong waters, and nutmegs at excessive rates," according to colony records. For the five aggregate offenses, he was obligated to pay five pounds, a not-insubstantial fine.[79]

The Dorothy Temple Affair

On February 4, 1639, Hopkins found himself again brought before the General Court. The Hopkins household employed at the time an unmarried indentured servant whose name was Dorothy Temple.[80] Temple, who was about nineteen years old, likely helped care for the Hopkins's younger children, who in age ran from Elizabeth, then about four years old, to Caleb, who was then about sixteen.

Hopkins's older children, through his first marriage, were adults—Constance about thirty-three years old and married and Giles about thirty-one. Though the exact date of the death of Hopkins's second wife, Elizabeth, is unknown, it is believed that she died sometime in the early 1640s, just a year or two before Hopkins himself died in 1644, so she, too, would probably have been living in the Hopkins's household during Temple's time with the family.[81] At the time of the court date, Temple was under contract for two more years, after which she'd be free and left to her own devices.[82]

The trouble started when Temple gave birth to a child. Hopkins wanted to kick the young mother and infant out of the home, refusing to honor the rest of the term of her indenture.[83] As Hopkins knew from his own experience in Virginia, contracts of indenture were a very important source of labor for American settlements. As such, colonial governments expected the terms of indentures to be rigidly observed by both parties. Just as a servant wouldn't be released from the obligation to perform the services they promised, a master wouldn't be released of the obligation to house, feed, and clothe the servant during the period of the contract. Of course, colonies were not immune to the whims of its inhabitants and to changes in circumstances and so had occasion to deal with parties seeking to end a contractual relationship, but when they did, courts almost always enforced scrupulous compliance with the terms of the indenture.[84]

Plymouth's General Court at the time included then governor Thomas Prence and assistants William Bradford, Edward Winslow, and John Alden. The court ordered that for the remaining two years of Temple's contract, Hopkins was, according to colonial records, to "keep her and her child, or provide that she may be kept with food and [clothing] during said term." If Hopkins refused, the colony would provide for Temple and her child and bill Hopkins for the costs.[85]

Hopkins rejected the court's decision. He adamantly refused to honor his contractual obligation to support Dorothy Temple and her child.

The governor and his assistants were not pleased. They ordered Hopkins to be put in jail for contempt of court. Hopkins would be held "until he shall either receive his servant, Dorothy Temple, or else provide for her elsewhere at his own charge during the term she has yet to serve him," according to colony records.[86] Hopkins, who'd sat on the General Court himself only a few years before, now sat in the colony's jail. Whether he felt humiliated or humbled is unknown. Did his fellow colonists ridicule him? Did they chastise him for turning out a young woman in need? Did he care? What is known is that he was incarcerated for four days.

On February 8 the court reconvened and released Hopkins, for he'd found a solution involving the colony's jail keeper, John Holmes.[87] Hopkins agreed to pay Holmes three pounds and "other consideration." In return, Holmes would take Temple and her child into his home—he was married and had one young child—for the final two years of her indenture.[88]

The incident raises many questions, the most important being why Stephen Hopkins turned out this young mother and refused to honor his obligations under the indenture. Given his own experience as an indentured servant, it would be reasonable to assume that he had some amount of sympathy for Temple. He treated his other servants well, for instance coming to the aid of Edward Doty and Edward Leister in the wake of their duel and successfully petitioning for the reduction in their painful sentences.[89] He seemed well disposed toward women, had a warm relationship with Elizabeth, and loved his daughters.[90] While the total term of Temple's indenture is not known, she likely had been in the Hopkins household for several years before the dispute arose in February 1639. Why the sudden change? History has only preserved the few sparse facts from the General Court's records, but several possible explanations arise.

One possibility is that Hopkins was morally outraged that Temple got pregnant out of wedlock. The seventh commandment, after all, prohibited adultery. For years, Hopkins had reminded Jamestown parishioners of this rule as he read from the liturgy during his time as Reverend Buck's clerk. Perhaps he was practicing what he'd preached and wanted to use the young mother as an example for all to see. Perhaps this was a lesson he was trying to drive home, too, for his own daughters. Not only had Temple violated a commandment; she'd also violated the law, which forbade intimacy out of wedlock.[91] Perhaps as a former assistant to the governor, Hopkins strove for the social high ground. The argument, of course, might have greater weight had not Hopkins himself run afoul several times in recent years of both the moral and secular laws pertaining to drinking and keeping the Sabbath. The theory is further weakened by other instances in which Hopkins acted without passing judgment. For example, only a few years later, he volunteered to care for a teenage boy named Jonathan Hatch who was a recurring disciplinary problem for the colony. Among the several difficulties the boy had been involved in was an incident where his sister, according to colonial records, was cited for "lying in the same bed" with him. While the exact nature of the alleged encounter was not documented, some level of licentiousness was certainly implied. Nevertheless, only a month after the episode, Hopkins took Hatch into his home, which he thereafter shared with Hopkins's four young daughters, the eldest of which was about the same age as Hatch's sister.[92] Such a move would seem to indicate that Hopkins did not readily assume a higher morality than other colonists.

Perhaps, then, Hopkins acted against Temple for financial reasons. Feeding, clothing, and supporting a newborn who could not contribute to the household was a new burden for which Hopkins had not contracted. Was Hopkins being tightfisted? He'd been previously fined for overcharging clients for beer and wine in his tavern, so maybe greed motivated him in the Temple affair. It is a possibility, although Hopkins was a fairly affluent man. For example, in a 1633 tax levy, only four other people out of eighty-nine total paid more in taxes than did Hopkins.[93] Not only was he able to raise sufficient corn and cattle to feed his family, but he'd had enough time and resources to run a tavern out of his house.[94] Of course, the accumulation of wealth doesn't diminish the possibility of a miserly personality, but in Hopkins's case the evidence would point against avarice, for when he took in the wayward Jonathan Hatch only a few years later, he did so without asking for or receiving any compensation.[95]

The most likely explanation for why Stephen Hopkins demanded that Dorothy Temple leave his household was the identity of her son's father. His name was Arthur Peach, and he'd recently been executed for murdering a Native American. Peach had sailed in 1635 to Virginia. By 1637, he was in New England. Peach was like John Tisdale in at least one respect: he didn't like Indians, and he'd fought for the Bay Colony in the Pequot War, receiving praise for his "good service," according to William Bradford.[96] The following year—when he had the relationship with Dorothy Temple—he was living in Plymouth in the employ of Edward Winslow.[97]

Apparently, Peach's spending habits outpaced his earning ability, and being "out of means and loth to work," in the words of Bradford, he decided to flee Plymouth for the Dutch settlement in Manhattan. Of course, impregnating Temple also may have played a role in his decision, for Peach would face not only criminal punishment under colonial law but also the ongoing financial obligation to his child and Temple. Peach convinced three others under indenture to run away with him.[98] The group of four traveled southwest from Plymouth, making for Narragansett Bay in modern-day Rhode Island. On the way, they met a Narragansett.[99] Peach and the others lured the man into a trap and planned to attacked him. When the others balked, Peach boasted that he'd kill the native himself, just as he'd done to so "many of them," according to Bradford, during the recent Pequot War. Peach stabbed the man and stole all his valuables.[100]

As word spread of the murder, a panic grew among the native people, for the Pequot had predicted that their defeat would be followed by a sweeping slaughter of all other New England tribes. The Narragansett came to believe that Peach's act was the first phase in what would become a general massacre. They were all about to be hunted down and murdered.[101]

In September 1638 Peach and two of his three accomplices were tried by a jury of twelve Plymouth men, a group that included John Holmes, the man who ultimately took over Hopkins's contract with Dorothy Temple. The suspects were found guilty and executed.[102] It was the second execution in the history of Plymouth Colony, the first being that of John Billington in 1630.[103] That three Englishmen were hanged for the death of one Indian was thought by some to be too severe, but it might have been a vindication to Stephen Hopkins to see that justice could be done for both English immigrant and American native equally; that is, that even the most severe form of justice would not be withheld when native people were the victims.[104]

Learning that his maidservant had sinned and broken the law with Arthur Peach was very likely too much for Hopkins to endure. Peach had murdered an innocent man in cold blood, and he'd bragged about killing many others. Not only that, but the incident had set the entire countryside on edge with tension. They'd just suffered through a horrible conflict with the Pequot. Any accidental confrontation or misunderstanding between English and American could spark a new conflagration. Stephen Hopkins most likely viewed Dorothy Temple as guilty by association. He might have been wrong to blame his servant for the conduct of her lover, who was a reprehensible man, but this background seems to be the most plausible reason why Hopkins turned the young woman out of his house.[105]

Hopkins's Growing Disenchantment

Hopkins would soon be at odds with the colony again. In December 1639 he was back in court for two alleged offenses. Someone accused him of selling "a looking glass" for nearly twice as much as a similar mirror could be bought at the Massachusetts Bay Colony. The court made no decision in the matter, indicating that it would wait for more information to be presented, and the matter appeared to have been subsequently dismissed.

In the second offense charged that month, Hopkins was accused of selling "strong water without license." Hopkins confessed to the second infraction, which indicated that he must have by this point lost his license from the colonial government to run a tavern, and was fined three pounds.[106]

As his legal troubles mounted, Hopkins started selling off his lands situated near Plymouth, perhaps an early indication of deepening estrangement with the colony. In July 1637 he sold a wharf he'd constructed and its associated buildings and land near the mouth of the Eel River, the place where Squanto had long ago gathered eels for the hungry settlers when he was likely living with Hopkins.[107]

In August 1638 Hopkins was granted permission by the governor's assistants—a group which that year included both William Bradford and Myles Standish—to build a house among the native people in Mattachiest, in modern-day Barnstable, Cape Cod, for the purpose of wintering his cattle.[108] At the time, Hopkins was the only colonist to establish a residence this far onto the cape.[109] Whereas men like Edward Winslow had moved northward, settling in places closer to their more powerful neighbors of the Bay Colony, Hopkins went the other way, desiring instead to move closer to native communities.

Bradford and Standish seemed to have known of Hopkins's disillusionment, for as part of their agreement to let him build a place on Cape Cod they insisted, according to colonial records, that he not "withdraw . . . from the town of Plymouth."[110] In November 1638 Hopkins sold six acres just south of Town Brook.[111] In June 1642 he acquired a house and farmland in Yarmouth, Cape Cod,[112] making it quite probable that he was at that time considering moving away from Plymouth despite the limitation the General Court had tried to impose in 1638.[113]

Hopkins's time at the vanguard was over. His day had come and gone. He'd brought his family to America to try to make a better life. He'd marched desolate shores looking for the right spot to locate their settlement. He'd suffered with his fellow *Mayflower* passengers through the first winter, helping the sick, comforting the dying, and burying the dead. He'd stepped to the forefront and sought out the Indians who lived in this part of New England. When mistrust on both sides was at its peak, he'd volunteered to take Samoset into his home, with his wife and young children, and through conversation and companionship, worked with Samoset to turn the tide from apprehension to harmony. Massasoit had sat on Hopkins's carpet to commemorate what would become a lasting peace treaty between the Wampanoag and the English. Hopkins had walked through the wilderness to visit Massasoit in order to affirm the treaty, even sharing the same bed with the Wampanoag sachem and his wife.

Hopkins believed that the two peoples could peacefully share the vastness of America. But the prosperity of the settlement that he helped create became a harbinger of the doom of Hopkins's vision. English Puritans flooded New England, and what once was plentiful and open native hunting land became crowded with expanding settlements. English need and greed butted against Indian inheritance. Conflict was inevitable. And in Stephen Hopkins's mind, it was regrettable.

10 | AN END AMONG FRIENDS

We are such stuff
As dreams are made on, and our little life
Is rounded with a sleep.
—*The Tempest*, act 4, scene 1

BY JUNE 1642, WHEN STEPHEN HOPKINS acquired the Yarmouth land, his health was starting to get the better of him. He never moved, instead remaining in Plymouth, living in the house he'd built so many years before. On June 6, 1644, Hopkins sat down to complete his last will and testament. He'd turned sixty-three a few months before. Nearly twenty-four of those years, he'd spent in New England. He'd not live to see the coming harvest. His *Mayflower* shipmates William Bradford and Myles Standish were with him to witness his will.

Bradford, Standish, and Hopkins

When viewed through the lens of conventional history, it was an odd assembly. Two great men were visiting an obscure curiosity. In the traditions that have developed about the *Mayflower* and Plymouth Rock and the lives of the "Pilgrim Fathers," Bradford and Standish are well known to all but the most casually informed. Hopkins, however, has primarily been consigned to anecdotes and footnotes. Major thoroughfares in both Provincetown and Plymouth today proudly display names such as Standish and Bradford. One short dead-end road in Plymouth carries the name Hopkins.

None stood more eminent among the original settlers at Plymouth than William Bradford. He was instrumental in shepherding the colony through its formative years, and stayed at the forefront of their society and government for decades until his death. Five months after they landed in North America in the late fall of 1620, the Pilgrims' first governor suddenly died. Bradford was chosen by his peers to replace the man and was reelected governor thirty times over the next thirty-five years. In *Of Plymouth Plantation*, he wrote the definitive history of the fledgling colony, and the book would, over the centuries that followed, have an indelible impact on American politics, folklore, and mythos. If anyone could be considered the father of the Pilgrim Fathers, it would have to be William Bradford.

Even so, Captain Myles Standish is likely an even better-known figure in Pilgrim tradition, thanks largely to Henry Wadsworth Longfellow, who in 1858 published his famous poem, *The Courtship of Miles Standish*. Not only did Standish serve as the military director for the Pilgrims' colony and lead many of the early exploratory forays, but he also spent most of his years as an elected official in the colonial government. He helped found one of Plymouth Colony's extensions, the settlement at Duxbury, as the number of English immigrants grew and they started to spread out along the coastline of Massachusetts. History has honored him with statues and monuments, and the Commonwealth of Massachusetts has named a state forest after him. The Myles Standish Monument, fittingly located in Duxbury, stands at 116 feet and is the third tallest shrine in the United States dedicated to an individual, surpassed only by two structures, both of which celebrate George Washington, one in Baltimore and the second and most famous, of course, located on the National Mall in Washington, DC.

Stephen Hopkins, on the other hand, has been understood as somewhat of a rogue. Throughout his life, he showed a passionate strain of independence. There is no record that Hopkins ever formally joined the Separatist church in Plymouth, which means that he likely remained an Anglican to the end in a colony that subverted the authority of the Church of England.[1] Hopkins was forever an outsider and oftentimes suffered for it. Shakespeare may have used William Strachey's account of Hopkins's one-man mutiny on Bermuda to create the ludicrous character Stephano in *The Tempest*.[2] Historians have blamed him for the *Mayflower* dispute that prompted the creation of the Mayflower Compact.[3] Even his fellow Pilgrims found him to be a sometimes violent, debauching libertine, as shown in the string of legal difficulties he'd encountered in recent years.[4]

Despite the obvious differences in their social statures, Bradford and Standish heeded Hopkins's call in 1644 to witness his will. The somber meeting was meaningful, for the act of witnessing a will was a tradition with roots reaching back in England to practices before the Norman Conquest and beyond even England's shores, to the Roman Empire and further still, to the city-state of classical Athens and even earlier, to the eras described in the Old Testament.[5] Settling one's estate with a will is important today, and it was in the days of the colony at Plymouth. In that age, it was considered the most solemn act in a person's life and, as such, was managed with great deliberation and prudence.[6]

Although the law required a will to be witnessed by men of the appropriate age in order to be legitimate, there were plenty of other witnesses available in the colony, which by 1644 had grown from the few dozen survivors of the deadly first winter to approximately two thousand people.[7] And there were plenty of reasons why someone of the standing of Bradford or Standish might politely decline his invitation. Yet there they both were on that day in June.

Standish's Promise

Especially worthy of note is the burden that Standish undertook to satisfy Hopkins's request, for he lived a significant distance from the other two. Hopkins declared in his will that he was feeling weak, and he died sometime shortly after completing the instrument, which meant that he probably drafted it in his home in Plymouth.[8] Like Hopkins, Bradford lived in Plymouth. Standish, however, had moved in 1631 to the new settlement at Duxbury. It would have taken Standish several hours to travel the rough-hewn paths through the coastal forests from Duxbury to reach Plymouth and Hopkins's house. Standish was at the time about sixty years old, an advanced age for that era, and he would not have lightly undertaken such a journey, one that as supervisor of Hopkins's will he would have to repeat many times over the next decade on Hopkins's behalf. There had to be a good reason.

While it is possible that Bradford and Standish agreed to help Hopkins solely out of respect for his contributions to the colony, a more likely explanation is such an appreciation was combined with a bond of friendship that had grown between the men over the course of their many years together. The three had worked closely together under difficult and often dangerous circumstances, enduring a crucible in which relationships were likely either forged into friendship or dissolved into enmity. Their presence suggests the former.

Appointing Standish as a supervisor of his will, a role designed to help the will's executor settle the estate, was significant. Hopkins named his son, Caleb, as the executor,[9] and while the exact birth date of Caleb Hopkins is unknown, in June 1644 he was likely not yet twenty-one years old, which meant he wasn't yet of the age of majority necessary to pay the estate's creditors and collect from its debtors, as well as other critical duties.[10] Given Caleb's youth, the bulk of his duties fell therefore to Standish.[11]

For the Pilgrims, the role of supervisor appeared to be an important probate duty and was given to close friends. Myles Standish acknowledged as much ten years later, in 1655, when he drafted his own will. He appointed his second wife and a young son as executor and appointed two men as supervisors. In his will, Standish described the two supervisors as "his loving friends" who would "be helpful to my poor wife and children by their Christian counsel and advice."[12]

William Bradford followed the same protocol. Like Standish, he appointed, in 1657, his wife to be executor of his own will, and like Standish, he appointed three friends as supervisors to assist his wife. Bradford referred to the three men as "my well-beloved Christian friends" who would dispose of his "estate according to the promises [in the will], confiding much in their faithfulness." He entrusted them with seeing that his wife was taken care of and also put into their care several handwritten manuscripts, which presumably included the seminal history of the colony they established, *Of Plymouth Plantation*.[13]

Standish's commitment to act as the supervisor for Hopkins's estate loaded him with open-ended responsibility, for among his many responsibilities was to work with young Caleb to "advise, devise, and dispose by the best ways and means they can for the disposing in marriage or otherwise for the best advancement of the estate of" four daughters who still lived at home with Stephen in 1644.[14] Deborah was twenty, Damaris sixteen, Ruth fourteen, and Elizabeth only twelve and in poor health.[15] Standish would work for more than a decade—up to the time of his own death—looking out for them.

At the time he consented to become supervisor, Standish was still busy with administrative duties for the colony and likely still held some role in advising on military affairs. He was charged with surveying highways. He was the colony's treasurer from that year to 1649. He stood on several different government committees that set out boundaries between towns as the colony grew and spread inland and stretched farther up and down the coast. And, of course, he still had to care for his farmland and livestock, which could be a full-time occupation in itself. Then there was his family, to whom he no doubt devoted substantial time. Besides his wife, he had five or six children, the youngest three of whom were only nine, eleven, and thirteen years old when Hopkins died.

Despite all these official and familial obligations, Standish labored for years on behalf of Stephen Hopkins to fulfill his commitment as supervisor to Hopkins's will, a burden that required countless trips back and forth between Duxbury and Plymouth. First, he and Caleb divided all of Stephen Hopkins's estate not specifically transferred in his will equally between Deborah, Damaris, Ruth, and Elizabeth. Caleb became the owner of Hopkins's Plymouth home, and Deborah, Damaris, and Ruth stayed with him, as by the terms of the will they all were provided access to the house until they were married.

Elizabeth, however, was apparently too young and too heavily afflicted with health issues to remain under Caleb's care, forcing Standish to help Caleb find a local couple who could take her in and raise her, according to the agreement document in colonial records, "as [their] child until the time of her marriage or until she be nineteen years of age." The search took until the very end of December 1644, when Standish crafted a detailed agreement on Elizabeth's behalf. The couple promised not to work Elizabeth too hard—as all able children were required to in that era of subsistence living—"in consideration of the weakness of the child and her inability to perform such service as may acquit [the couple's cost of] bringing her up and that she not be too much oppressed now in her childhood with hard labor."[16]

In November of that year, while the search on Elizabeth's behalf was still underway, Standish—without any help from Caleb—worked on a complex livestock exchange for Elizabeth's sister, Ruth. Stephen Hopkins had bequeathed a cow named Red Cole to Ruth. Cows were very important livestock in Plymouth, and red cows were known for high milk production.[17] Standish gave a half portion of the ownership rights to Ruth's cow, enabling the purchaser to access one-half of Red Cole's milk production, in exchange for a future right to either two heifers or two steers, which were to be paid to Standish for Ruth's benefit within three years.[18] Standish struck a very shrewd transaction for his friend's daughter, for Ruth, at age fourteen, would be living with her brother and Deborah and Damaris in Stephen Hopkins's house for at least another three years. Between the sisters they had the full rights to two other cows.[19] Ruth wouldn't miss the milk and would gain the benefit of two additional heifers or steers before she'd even turn eighteen.[20] It is also another indication of the lengths Standish went to in order to live up to the trust Stephen Hopkins had placed in him.

Sometime after his father's death, Caleb became a sailor, a calling which took him to distant places and naturally forced him to be away from the colony for long periods. In 1647, presumably during one of Caleb's absences, Standish oversaw the completion of the contract concerning Red Cole on behalf of Ruth, now seventeen years old, when he took possession of the two steers that were promised two and a half years before.[21] By 1651 Caleb was dead, having suffered an accident or illness on the Caribbean island of Barbados, some two thousand miles from Plymouth.[22] There is no record of how Caleb's estate was settled, but presumably Myles Standish was involved, for it has been suggested that at least some of the land that Caleb came to own was turned over to his sister, Elizabeth, who would have been about nineteen at the time.

By this time, Ruth was also dead.[23] Deborah and Damaris were each married and out of the house Stephen Hopkins had built in Plymouth. With Caleb and Ruth no longer alive and Elizabeth living elsewhere, for she was now grown and no longer under the care of the couple who'd in 1644 agreed to raise her, the building stood empty and fell into disrepair.[24] Standish wouldn't stand for it, and in 1652 he arranged to have the colony restore the house. In exchange for the expenditure, the colony would use the structure to store powder and shot and to hold public meetings, but with the exception that the home would revert to the control of any of Hopkins's surviving heirs if they desired to make use of it again.[25]

Standish continued to look after Elizabeth, who never married and apparently suffered ongoing health issues, perhaps including a mental disability or disorder. As late as 1656, the year he died, Standish was bringing a lawsuit on her behalf.[26] By 1659, Elizabeth had disappeared from Plymouth and was presumed to be dead.[27] Even his own death didn't erase the commitment Myles Standish undertook on behalf of Stephen Hopkins, for his wife, Barbara, was involved in the division of Elizabeth's estate.[28]

A Peculiar Item in Hopkins's Estate Inventory

Thus, it was likely an abiding bond that impelled the two Pilgrim heroes to join Stephen Hopkins at his house in June 1644, where they offered him comfort in his final days and helped him with the concluding act of his life. Some of the details of that gathering emerge from colonial records, including the inventory of his estate. Stephen Hopkins lived in a relatively large house. In recent years, when it had been used as a part-time tavern, it had hosted numbers of up to fifteen people or more, and it had enough room for five beds.[29] He didn't entertain much anymore, not after the legal troubles he'd run into, and old age had drained him of the energy. So the home was quiet now—quieter, at least. Though his son, Caleb, and four daughters were still living with Stephen at the time, they were all likely away now, so that their father could focus and organize his thoughts on how he would distribute everything.

A large table sat in the middle of the main room, probably near a hearth, a few chairs and stools scattered around it. Clay-based daub the color of sand coated the walls. Heavy curtains hung from the thick beams of the low ceiling to give the various sleeping areas a semblance of privacy. Some of the curtains were likely drawn; others were left open, revealing large wooden chests situated close to the beds. In an era long before the advent of walk-in closets, the chests were used to store clothes and coats. The ceiling rafters closest to each of the walls were set with hooks. In the bedroom areas and near the front door, coats and hats and cloaks were draped from the metal hooks. Around the hearth and eating area hung a variety of household articles: dull gray skillets; cups and smaller iron kettles; a length of rusting chain; drying herbs; yellowed stalks of corn; a string of onions. Cups and plates and other household wares were stacked on narrow shelves that lined the walls closest to the fireplace. A couple of the shelves were lined with precious books, as well as with Hopkins's financial papers, on which he tracked his debts and debtors. Large kettles and tubs were stacked in out-of-the-way corners.[30]

It was a fairly typical Plymouth household, although it did contain one rather unique item: a pale green rug. It would have showed years of hard use, spots here and there where the threadwork had worn thin, faded stains and scuff marks. Before her death, his wife, Elizabeth, might have periodically urged Stephen to replace it, but Hopkins always had a stubborn streak. The rug was probably special to him. It was special to the entire colony of Plymouth. On this rug, some twenty-four years earlier, the Pilgrims had negotiated their first treaty with the Wampanoag, the local confederation of native tribes. On this rug, the first governor of the colony sat with Massasoit. Without Massasoit's assistance, the English settlers would never have survived that first, critical year.[31] Without their Native American allies, who showed them the proper way to plant and fertilize what would become the colony's staple crop, there would have been no festival to celebrate Plymouth's first harvest. The First Thanksgiving would have never happened. Instead of corn and deer and laughter, there would have been mounded graves and mourning. And without Hopkins's hand in those first tense meetings with the natives, there wouldn't have been a treaty.

In his house, Hopkins had entertained and lodged Samoset and Squanto, two emissaries from Massasoit. On this green rug, perhaps lounging on cushions, Hopkins and his Native American guests sat over several days and evenings, likely talking about the countryside and the seasons and the alliance that the English wanted to develop with the Wampanoag. The conversation and good company helped strengthen slender bonds, and a rapport developed between these men from such different backgrounds. Convinced by Hopkins's hospitality, Samoset then likely persuaded the great Massasoit to enter into the momentous accord.

A Solemn Ritual

Whether Bradford and Standish commented upon the rug when they met with Hopkins to finalize his will is unknown. They probably met at Hopkins's house in the afternoon or early evening of June 6. Early summer in New England is on average rather pleasant, and Hopkins likely left the door to his house open, letting precious sunlight and any swirling breezes into the dark interior. Anything light-colored, like white bedsheets or blankets, would have stood out pale in the near gloom. Sporadic sounds from neighboring houses would have filtered in, a spoon against an iron pot, the laughter of a child, the low noises of a normal day. A fire likely smoldered in the hearth where all the meals were prepared, its embers glowing orange and red through the charred remains of the logs.

Even during the daytime, Hopkins would have had a candle on the table for additional light to help with the exacting business of writing, and its flame would have fluttered, reacting to the breaths of wind that came through the open door. The candle was probably made of tallow, rendered from animal fat, which meant that its light would have been smoky and its scent a little foul. With the declining eyesight of a sixty-three-year-old man, Hopkins would probably have sat forward on his chair, holding his head close to his last will and testament so that he could see his work, squinting to keep the letters in focus. Standish and Bradford would probably have been sitting nearby, waiting patiently.

Carving out a living at the edge of the world meant a life filled with hard labor. Hopkins's hands were therefore probably knotted and stiff from years of rough use. He likely used a quill, which meant that as he wrote the nib lost ink and the lettering became fainter and fainter. This would have forced Hopkins to pause frequently and reach for a small inkwell to replenish the quill. As he drew toward the end, Hopkins might have paused to reread the last few sentences. His body was worn down. His time was nearing its end. According to the instructions he'd just written, they'd lay him next to Elizabeth. He'd buried two children in this land, which was so far away from England. Then his wife. And now it was his turn.

He dipped the quill a final time and continued: "By me Stephen Hopkins."[32]

After he signed his name, Hopkins would have turned to face his two companions, the quill still in his hand. It was time for their contributions to this solemn ritual. Myles Standish signed first, followed by Bradford, who approached, took the quill from the military man, dipped it again, and signed.

The formalities completed, Hopkins might have pushed himself out of the chair, so he could stand next to Standish and Bradford. If age and weakness caused his chin to sink of its own accord toward his chest, he would have made an effort to lift it. He would have straightened his shoulders and back, urging himself to his tallest posture so that he could look squarely into the eyes of his old shipmates. Together they'd been through countless perils. They'd made countless decisions that directly influenced their colony. Together they'd survived, built a new life on a foreign shore far from the comforts and predictability of the developed societies of Europe. Plymouth's success had opened a path into the New World followed by thousands of others. The Massachusetts Bay Colony now flourished to the north. And to the south, the River Colony kept growing along the banks of the great river that the Mohegans called Quinetucket, that the English called Connecticut.

Plymouth's success also affected their first neighbors, the Native Americans: the Wampanoag, the Massachusett, the Nipmuck and Quinnipiac, and Mohegan and Narragansett. And, of course, the Pequot. After such a promising start with them, it seemed to be all turning wrong, and Hopkins probably worried about the world that his sons and daughters and their children would create.

Three Shipmates Say Good-bye

We can well imagine that the gathering might have concluded like this:

His eyes watering—from the strain of scribbling by candlelight, no doubt, he assured himself—Hopkins nodded his deep appreciation to Captain Standish. No words were necessary. In agreeing to supervise the ordering of Hopkins's affairs for his young children, Standish had undertaken a promise that carried with it a most profound responsibility. The two men clasped hands, and Hopkins felt Standish's emotions in the strength of the grip, which he returned as best he could. The gesture was repeated with Bradford.

After a final nod of appreciation, Hopkins watched them head out the door. Through the opening, he could see down the sloping road toward the ocean. Plymouth was situated on high ground—dry ground, not the marsh-sodden stuff he'd known in Virginia. Above the thatched rooftops of the houses lining the street, the skies were turning dark, clouds thickening with the decline of the day. Perhaps they'd see rain overnight. Out in the distance was the bay. And beyond that, lost in a haze that hung over the water, was the hook of Cape Cod, where the *Mayflower* had first dropped anchor in the frigid month of November so many years before.

Both Bradford and Standish would go on to live and work as leaders of the colony for more than a decade after their gathering, but Stephen Hopkins's time quickly drew to a close after he and his friends signed the document that settled his worldly affairs. He probably looked back upon the Pequot War as the final turning point in his life. He hadn't wanted that war. He hadn't wanted any war. Not with the native people. Friendship is what he'd always wanted, what he'd always worked toward. He'd been the one in the spring of 1621 to leave his musket behind when he and Standish first approached the Wampanoag warriors on Watson's Hill. It was fitting, then, that in July 1644 when Myles Standish walked through Hopkins's house to make an inventory of the dead man's estate, he found no weapons.[33]

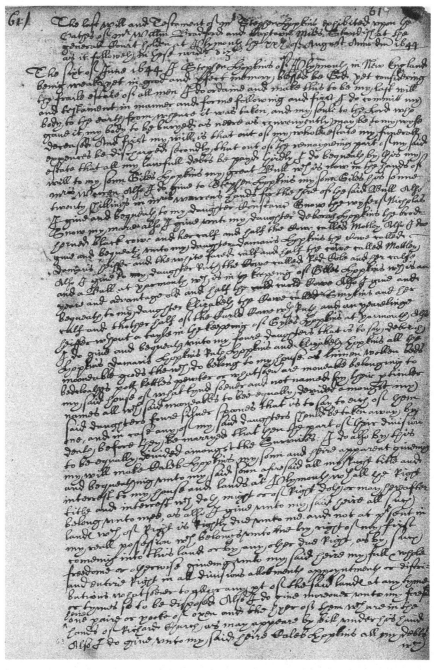

The last will and testament of Stephen Hopkins (1644). Note the variable spelling of Hopkins's first name, which may either reflect a transcription error when the document was recopied by a scrivener or simply be an example of the wonderfully loose standards of spelling in the seventeenth century.

Courtesy of Massachusetts Archives

not are now oweing vnto me or at the day of my death may be oweing
vnto mee either by booke bill or bills or any other way wittsoll, And
vnto mee ffurthermore my will is that my daughters aforesaid
shall haue free recourse to my house in Plymouth, present any occations
there to abide and remayne for such tyme as any of them shall thinke
meete and convenient while single persons And for the faithfull
performance of this my will if doe make and ordayne my aforesaid
sonn and seruit Caleb Hopkins my true and lawfull Executor
ffurther I doe by this my will appoynt and make my said sonn and
Captaine Miles Standish joyntly Supervisors of this my will
according to the true meaning of the same that is to say that
my Executor & supervisor shall make the seuerall diuisions porte
& porteons legacies or whatsoeuer doth appertaine to the fullfilling
of this my will It is also my will that my Executor & Supervisor
shall aduise deuise, and dispose by the best meanes the
raine for the disposeing in marriage or otherwise for the best
aduancement of the estate of the forenamed Deborah Damaris Ruth
and Elizabeth Hopkins Thus trusting in the Lord my will shalbe
truly performed according to the true meaning of the same
I committ the whole disposeing hereof to the Lord that hee
may direct you herein June 6 1644

By me Steven Hopkins

Witness hereof
Myles Standish
William Bradford

EPILOGUE
HOPKINS'S LEGACY:
"FRIEND OF INDIANS"

And by that destiny to perform an act
Whereof what's past is prologue, what to come
In yours and my discharge.

> —*The Tempest*, act 2, scene 1

IF A PERSON IS JUDGED UPON their actions and conduct and decisions, how should Stephen Hopkins be judged? His life reveals a rather complex character. He was a man of many depths. He showed an independence of thought throughout his life. He was intelligent and knowledgeable, a man who read. He could be indignant to the point of recklessness. He could be repentant. He was stubborn when he felt wronged, even at the expense of innocent bystanders, as he showed in the Dorothy Temple affair.

He was adventurous. He was curious and willing to learn about a culture and language that was utterly alien to him. He was courageous. He was charismatic. He was gracious, as when he asked Samoset into his home. He was loyal to people he respected, like Myles Standish and William Bradford, and enjoyed commensurate loyalty returned to him. Perhaps he died wondering if he'd made a difference.

Hopkins's Legacy

Hopkins's influence lasted well beyond his death in 1644. There are an estimated thirty-five million people today who are descended from the passengers of the *Mayflower*. Of these, many hundreds of thousands can claim Stephen

Hopkins as a forebear, which in and of itself could be considered quite a legacy. Among these descendants number many who figured prominently in American history and its culture. Robert Treat Paine was one of the signers of the Declaration of Independence. Alonzo Cushing was a Union soldier who died at the age of twenty-two during the Battle of Gettysburg while fending off Pickett's famous charge.[1] Levi Parsons Morton, Charles Dawes, and Dan Quayle all served as vice presidents of the United States. Painter Norman Rockwell, playwright Tennessee Williams, novelist Thomas Pynchon, actors Richard Gere and Ethan Hawke, and politician Sarah Palin can all trace their ancestry back to Hopkins.[2]

Jonathan Hatch

Although the imprint of his descendants can be seen throughout the history of America, perhaps the best understanding of the legacy that Stephen Hopkins wanted to leave behind can be viewed through the life of a young man who in 1644 would have stood alongside Myles Standish and William Bradford and the other Plymouth mourners as Hopkins's body was lowered into its grave. Hopkins sired a fairly large family in Plymouth, but in his declining years, he also fostered Jonathan Hatch. Hatch was about seventeen years old when Stephen Hopkins died and had lived a tumultuous life in that brief stretch of time.

Hatch had sailed as a boy in 1633 from England with his parents and settled at Dorchester, which was a community in the Massachusetts Bay Colony located south of Boston. He was only twelve or thirteen years old in about 1637 when his father apprenticed him to Richard Davenport, a soldier living in Salem, a town some twenty-five miles north of Dorchester.[3] Davenport ran a penal camp for the Bay Colony.[4]

The fact that Hatch's parents sent a twelve-year-old to such a man as Davenport suggests a troubled household or a troubled youth. While Hatch was in Salem, his father moved with the rest of the family to Cape Cod.[5] Now his parents lived in a different colony entirely, and they were separated by nearly a hundred miles, a world away for a boy in that era. Young Hatch was utterly alone in a strange town in a still-strange land. Davenport was a Puritan firebrand who held strong, negative views about Indians, against whom he'd fought in the Pequot War, where he'd been seriously wounded.[6] Davenport likely impressed his opinions about the natives upon those under his supervision, as his son Nathaniel was killed in December 1675 leading a company of militia alongside Josiah Winslow—son of Edward Winslow—against the Narragansett during King Philip's War.[7]

The conditions of Hatch's apprenticeship in the penal compound were likely arduous. After two years, Hatch ran away, but not before he absorbed some of Davenport's animosity toward Native Americans. The boy was caught in Boston. Arrested in September 1640 as a fugitive from service, he was sentenced to a severe whipping and was, according to colonial records, "committed for a slave" back to Davenport's prison.[8] It was a typical, if harsh, punishment for vagrancy at the time. Hatch immediately ran away again, this time reaching Plymouth Colony, most likely in search of his family. Trouble followed him.

Shortly after he arrived in Plymouth, in October 1640, he was arrested for vagrancy and theft. He was whipped.[9] Two months later, Hatch was sued by another settler for slander because he accused a man of "attempting to lie with an Indian woman," according to Plymouth Colony records.[10] As Davenport had taught him, native people were fit only for disdain. The denunciation of lying with one was likely one of the cruelest insults the boy could think of.

In March 1642 Hatch was arrested again for vagrancy.[11] Again, he was whipped. By this time, though, the Plymouth General Court had discovered that Hatch had run away from Davenport. After being whipped, Hatch was condemned to be returned to the Bay Colony to serve the remainder of his sentence as a slave to Davenport as required under that colony's law.

In the wake of the decision, however, a legal controversy arose. At the time, William Bradford was governor of the colony. Myles Standish was one of the assistants to the governor. The legal issue was a matter of jurisdiction. The Bay Colony's laws might have required that the fugitive Hatch be returned to Davenport, but the boy was now in Plymouth Colony. Was Plymouth required to honor the laws of its northern neighbor?[12]

After considering the matter with his assistants, Bradford decided that, in Plymouth, the Bay Colony's laws had no force or effect. Therefore, Plymouth had no obligation to return the boy to the hard military man.[13] The choice left the Plymouth leaders with a new dilemma, though. What were they to do with this juvenile delinquent?

In April 1642 Bradford resolved to send Hatch into the home of Stephen Hopkins, formally asking his old *Mayflower* shipmate, according to colony records, to take "special care" of the boy.[14] That Hopkins was part of the solution is further evidence suggesting that he and Bradford maintained an ongoing relationship, despite Bradford's leading role in colonial government and Hopkins's fall from social prominence into relative ignominy. It also suggests that even as his own connection to Plymouth Colony was suffering, the sixty-one-year-old Hopkins was willing to serve as a mentor to its future generations.

Hatch After Hopkins

Jonathan Hatch lived with Stephen Hopkins for only a brief time, as the elderly man died only two years after Bradford sent him into Hopkins's home, but their relationship had a profound and lasting impact. After Hopkins's death, Hatch's life took on a very different shape. He no longer committed petty crimes. He moved to Cape Cod, where two of Hopkins's adult children lived, and there married the granddaughter of one of Stephen Hopkins's closest friends.[15] Hatch became a responsible member of the colony and was selected by none other than Myles Standish himself to help lay out the first public roadway on the cape, one that would be used for more than two centuries.[16]

Significantly, Hatch also overcame his prejudice against Indians. Animus turned to affinity, and he became their devoted friend. On Cape Cod he blurred boundaries between the two peoples, establishing, for example, a homestead miles away from his nearest English neighbor but quite close to a local Wampanoag village. Hatch befriended the tribe's leader, and like Stephen Hopkins, he took the time and effort to learn their language. Trading with these and other Wampanoag became his chief means of providing for his family.[17] By putting himself in their midst and far from any of his fellow Englishmen, he was dependent on the strength of his relationship with the native people, an arrangement that worked to everyone's benefit.[18]

A Different Kind of Disobedience

As it was for the man who briefly fostered him, the strength of Jonathan Hatch's attitude toward Indians would ultimately bring him into conflict with colonial authority. In 1652 he was charged with supplying a gun, powder, and shot to a native, a serious violation of a law enacted to limit native access to weapons, which the English feared might at some point be turned against them—the very motivation that drove John Tisdale to help confiscate weapons from the Wampanoag before the outbreak of King Philip's War.[19]

In 1658 Hatch was again brought to court, this time because he failed to turn in a Wampanoag friend who'd threatened to shoot Plymouth's governor.[20] In 1670 he was fined, according to colonial records, for "selling liquors to the Indians," something that the paternalistic colonial leaders found to be morally repugnant.[21] Hatch continued trading with his Wampanoag friends despite laws intended to restrict such commerce, and later in life he even helped natives who got caught up in King Philip's War.

King Philip's War

In 1675 King Philip's War finally shattered the long peace between the Wampanoag and the Pilgrims that Stephen Hopkins helped forge.[22] Massasoit's son, Metacomet, waged war against Edward Winslow's son, Josiah, who was then governor of Plymouth Colony. The conflict began in the southeastern corner of New England, where John Tisdale was among the first who died, but soon spread and prompted English fears that the native people from Massachusetts to Virginia would soon join in open revolt. Those fears were stoked during the first year of the conflict when the momentum swung in favor of the Wampanoag.

Metacomet's early successes and colonial diplomatic blunders enticed more native nations to join the outbreak, and battles flared up as far north as New Hampshire and Maine. Some native tribes remained allied with the English, however, and the colonies eventually mobilized more resources in response to initial setbacks. Plymouth colonist Benjamin Church became a prominent leader of the English forces. Under his management, the tide started to turn. The English eventually captured Metacomet's wife and son, and one of Church's native scouts shot and killed the Wampanoag sachem.[23]

The war's toll was tremendous. Four to seven thousand Native Americans died. Two thousand more fled New England. Another one thousand were sold into slavery. One-tenth of the region's entire English adult male population died in combat.[24] The economies of both communities suffered. Countless native crops, livestock, and villages were devastated. Colonial crops and thousands of cattle were destroyed, with the total economic loss being estimated at around £100,000. At least a dozen English towns were so thoroughly shattered that they were abandoned, some not to be rebuilt for many years. The English wouldn't recover their lost material wealth and population for decades. The Wampanoag and their allies never did.[25]

The English's treatment of natives during and after war demonstrated a prevailing bigotry that remained engrained for centuries to come. For example, John Quincy Adams—sixth president of the United States and admirer of the Mayflower Compact—was at one time a staunch proponent of Euro-American domination of the native population. While he'd been devoted to the cause of slave emancipation for many years, animus seemed to power his early views of Native Americans, whom he once denounced as mere "hordes of savages."[26]

It wasn't until after Adams was serving as a US congressional representative from the Plymouth District of Massachusetts, after he'd served as president from 1825 to 1829, that his views toward Indians started evolving.[27] He ultimately came to see their cause in the same vein as the cause of antislavery, and by 1841 he would lament about the country's Native American policy in an entry in his diary: "It is among the most heinous sins of this nation, for which I believe God will one day bring them judgment—but at His own time and by His own means."[28]

Though Adams personally moved away from an attitude similar to men such as John Tisdale and Richard Davenport, who were biased against Indians, into one more compatible with that of Stephen Hopkins, the nation did not and continued to subjugate and abuse Native Americans, uprooting entire populations and pushing them from their homelands.

A Small Reunion

The policies that John Quincy Adams regretted in 1841 started to take shape at the conclusion of the Pequot War and were expanded in the wake of King Philip's War. Josiah Winslow seemed to view Indians with intolerance. Like the Bay Colony did after the Pequot War, Josiah Winslow's Plymouth government in 1676—during the height of the war—promulgated several laws regarding Indian combatants and their families. First, in July, Winslow's council of war issued a decree that one-half the number of any enemy natives captured by Plymouth militia volunteers became their property.[29] The rest became property of the colony.[30] Captive women and children were to be assigned to English homes as domestic servants. Then, in November, Winslow's government decided that all adult male captives had to be sold out of the colony.[31] No male captive above the age of fourteen could remain.[32] Any ringleaders were to be summarily tried and executed. The rest were to be sold into slavery.[33]

Under the law, about one thousand natives were eventually transported to sugar plantations in the Caribbean.[34]

Not everyone endorsed the policies of Josiah Winslow's government. For example, despite his high-profile role in fighting the Wampanoag and their allies, Benjamin Church was very much opposed to their post-conflict enslavement. While Church would later himself hold African slaves, he adamantly opposed the subjection of the Indians whom he'd fought, finding Plymouth's policy "so hateful" that he felt compelled to object to it, even though his stance turned many of his English friends against him.[35]

Jonathan Hatch appeared to share Church's view. Although he'd only been about forty-nine years old at the start of King Philip's War, Hatch chose not to fight for Josiah Winslow, likely motivated to stay on the sideline because of his long friendship with the Wampanoag on Cape Cod. In 1679, a year after the war ended, Hatch conspired with Church to free three captives before they could be shipped off to the Caribbean.

Church had taken many prisoners during the action he saw in the war, and as a result of Winslow's laws Church became the holder of several Wampanoag. Hatch paid Church for three of them—a man, his wife, and their son. Because of the new laws harshly limiting Indian independence, Hatch brought the woman to the Plymouth General Court and petitioned for the release of the entire family. Choosing to have only the woman accompany him to court seemed to have been a calculated choice by Hatch to create the most favorable—that is, the least threatening—impression upon Governor Winslow and the other members of the court. Hatch claimed that he had a contract with the woman's two brothers, who were willing to pay to free her and her husband and child. According to colonial records, he asserted that the brothers had already paid him "three pounds silver" and had agreed to pay three more pounds when the family was released.[36] The fact that three pounds silver had supposedly been exchanged, with the promise of more, strongly suggests that Hatch had fabricated the entire agreement, for at the time a colonial law restricted Indians' ability to hold money out of the fear that they would use it to buy liquor.[37]

Whether any silver actually changed hands, or if it did, how it came into the hands of the woman's brothers, the record does not state, but given Hatch's friendly history with Indians, it's probable that the "payment" terms were favorable to all involved. The court honored Hatch's "contract" and released the husband and wife from slavery. The couple's son presented a special case, however. Given a colony law that required minor Native Americans to remain in English custody until the age of twenty-four, the court ordered Hatch to keep the boy until he reached that age, at which point he, too, would "be released forever," according to colonial records.[38] Surely, Hatch made accommodations that kept the family intact.

Sadly, the episode helped only one small family, three people out of a thousand who were sold into hellish slavery. King Philip's War and its aftermath represented the antithesis of what Stephen Hopkins had hoped to create when he first invited Samoset and then Squanto into his home, introducing them to his wife and young children, sharing food and sharing stories, but perhaps he would have taken heart in the small measures that his one-time ward was able to achieve in the face of the disastrous changes in the overall relationship between immigrant and native. Hopkins had taken in a wayward youth with a bigoted attitude and helped set the boy's life upon an entirely different trajectory. It was a fitting legacy for the man who'd helped overcome mutual suspicion between immigrant and native and assured the survival of Plymouth Colony.

Jonathan Hatch died in 1710 at the age of eighty-four and was buried in Falmouth, Cape Cod. The inscription on the original gravestone marking his life has long since weathered away. An updated headstone installed in 1991 carries a simple inscription: "Settler of Falmouth. Friend of Indians." Stephen Hopkins would have been proud.

ACKNOWLEDGMENTS

MY SINCERE THANKS GO TO JAMES FITZGERALD, my agent, who took me on when this book was little more than an idea, and to Yuval Taylor at Chicago Review Press, who took a chance on the idea and helped shape it into this book. Without the two of them, none of the preceding would have been possible. I'd also like to thank Jerome Pohlen and the staff at Chicago Review Press, who shepherded the project to its completion.

Alden T. Vaughan, affiliate professor at Clark University and professor emeritus of history at Columbia University, read the manuscript, and I am indebted to him for his invaluable comments, input, and advice. His contributions have made the book much better.

I am very grateful to my wife, Diane, who spent many hours reading drafts and listening to ideas, and to my daughters, Abby and Charlotte, who like their mother suffered through countless conversations about the people and events of some four hundred years ago. My mother, Judy, and father, David, likewise read and provided invaluable advice on drafts of the manuscript, which I deeply appreciate. They also instilled in me a love of books and history, which I even more deeply appreciate.

I am indebted to Jayne and Rick Suhler, who also read and provided excellent input on the manuscript and took the time to discuss all aspects of the writing and publishing process. I am also thankful to Julie Winner and Joel Mack, each of whom provided encouragement and advice and support.

I thank David Hogan for the many hours of encouragement, aid, and guidance on this book, as well as on the business of writing itself. David Levy's help has been essential, and I am thankful for it. I also express my gratitude to Richard Roseborough, Ole Oleson, and Michael Jones, each of whom has contributed to this project.

NOTES

Introduction

1. Margaret Hodges, *Hopkins of the Mayflower* (New York: Farrar, Straus and Giroux, 1972), 118; Roger A. Stritmatter and Lynne Kositsky, *On the Date, Sources and Design of Shakespeare's "The Tempest"* (Jefferson, NC: McFarland, 2013), 33.

1. Hopkins and the *Sea Venture*

1. Lorri Glover and Daniel Blake Smith, *The Shipwreck That Saved Jamestown* (New York: Henry Holt and Company, 2008), 69.
2. Glover and Smith, *Shipwreck That Saved Jamestown*, 1; Wesley Craven, *The Southern Colonies in the Seventeenth Century* (Baton Rouge: Louisiana State University Press, 1949), 93.
3. Glover and Smith, *Shipwreck That Saved Jamestown*, 73–74, 78.
4. Caleb Johnson, *Here Shall I Die Ashore* (Bloomington, IN: Xlibris, 2007), 15.
5. Keith Wrightson, *English Society: 1580–1680* (New Brunswick, NJ: Rutgers University Press, 1982), 25; see also William Harrison, *The Description of England* (Washington, DC: Folger Shakespeare Library, 1994), 117–119.
6. Johnson, *Here Shall I Die*, 17, 19; Percy MacQuoid, "The Plate of Winchester College," *Burlington Magazine for Connoisseurs* 2, no. 5 (July 1903): 149.
7. Evidence of Hopkins's literacy includes the inventory of his estate made in 1644, which listed among his effects "diverse books." See George Bowman, ed., *The Mayflower Descendant*, vol. 2 (Boston: Massachusetts Society of Mayflower Descendants, 1900), 14–17.
8. Richard Greaves, *Society and Religion in Elizabethan England* (Minneapolis: University of Minnesota Press, 1981), 334; Adam Fox, *Oral and Literate Culture in England, 1500–1700* (Oxford: Oxford University Press, 2000), 406–409; Heidi Brayman Hackel, *Reading Material in Early Modern England: Print, Gender, and Literacy* (Cambridge: Cambridge University Press, 2005), 55–57.
9. Michael Hattaway, ed., *A New Companion to English Renaissance Literature and Culture* (Chichester, UK: Wiley-Blackwell, 2010), 1:33.
10. Hattaway, *New Companion*, 33.
11. Harrison, *Description of England*, 76.

12. Ian Green, *Humanism and Protestantism in Early Modern English Education* (New York: Routledge, 2016), 84. For the location of the Hopkins's household, see Johnson, *Here Shall I Die*, 167n115.

13. Arthur Leach, *A History of Winchester College* (New York: Charles Scribner's Sons, 1899), 1–2; see also John N. Miner, *The Grammar Schools of Medieval England* (Montreal: McGill-Queen's University Press, 1990), 19, 124–125.

14. Leach, *History*, 90–91.

15. Thomas Kirby, *Winchester Scholars* (London: Henry Frowde, 1898), xii. The rules for admission favored those of modest means as well as residents of Winchester, both of which describe Hopkins.

16. Kirby, *Winchester Scholars*, xii.

17. Leach, *History*, 315–316; see also Ian Green, *Humanism and Protestantism in Early Modern English Education* (London: Routledge, 2016), 255–256.

18. Reginald M. Gleneross, "Virginia Gleanings in England," *Virginia Magazine of History and Biography* 29 (1921): 38; see also Leslie Stephen and Sidney Lee, eds., *Dictionary of National Biography*, vol. 24, *Hailes–Harriott* (New York: Macmillan, 1890), 412.

19. In his will, John Harmar left a not-insubstantial sum to "the poor of the city of Winchester." Gleneross, "Virginia Gleanings," 36–39.

20. N. J. G. Pounds, *A History of the English Parish: The Culture of Religion from Augustine to Victoria* (Cambridge: Cambridge University Press, 2004), 187–190: "The clerk had to be literate, capable of reading parts of the liturgy as well as singing." See also J. Wickham Legg, ed., *The Clerk's Book of 1549* (London: Harrison and Sons, St. Martin's Lane, 1903), xviii; Rev. John Henry Blunt, *The Reformation of the Church of England* (New York: Pott and Amery, 1870), 497n4; J. H. Bernard, *The Psalter in Latin and English* (London: A. R. Mowbray, 1911), xv.

21. Legg, *Clerk's Book*, xxi, xxv.

22. William Strachey, "A True Reportory," in *Captain John Smith: Writings*, ed. James Horn (New York: Literary Classics of America, 2007), 1002.

23. As recounted at the end of the chapter, when marooned on Bermuda and condemned to die, Hopkins switched from logic to emotion to ask for his life. His pleas were persuasive, for he brought so many of the aristocrats in the expedition to his side that they were able to successfully change the mind of the governor. See Strachey, "True Reportory," 1003.

24. Peter Mack, *Elizabethan Rhetoric: Theory and Practice* (Cambridge: Cambridge University Press, 2004), 47.

25. Mack, *Elizabethan Rhetoric*, 47.

26. Johnson, *Here Shall I Die*, 21, 23.

27. Mack, *Elizabethan Rhetoric*, 50.

28. Johnson, *Here Shall I Die*, 27.

29. See Simon Neal, "Investigation into the Origins of Mary and Elizabeth, the Wives of Stephen Hopkins," *Mayflower Quarterly* 78, no. 2 (June 2012): 138; Johnson, *Here Shall I Die*, 27; John Duthy, *Sketches of Hampshire* (London: Longman, 1839), 340.

30. Johnson, *Here Shall I Die*, 27.

31. Neal, "Investigation into the Origins," 138.

32. Glover and Smith, *Shipwreck That Saved Jamestown*, 38, 41; see also Exodus 3:7-8, King James Version.

33. Francis Coleman, *Virginia Reader: A Treasury of Writings from the First Voyages to the Present* (London: Octagon Books, 1972), 67; Glover and Smith, *Shipwreck That Saved Jamestown*, 42.

34. Glover and Smith, *Shipwreck That Saved Jamestown*, 47-48; see also Frank Grizzard, Jr. and D. Boyd Smith, *Jamestown Colony: A Political, Social, and Cultural History* (Santa Barbara: ABC-CLIO, 2007), xxvii-xxviii: "In the original company and in the two relief compliments, the First and Second Supply of 1608, there were 294 persons.... Misreading the environment's hostility, the company sent men untrained, wrongly trained, or unneeded to a wilderness colony. Only the craftsmen and artisans brought with them skills of immediate use and an understanding of productivity related to individual efforts."

35. Glover and Smith, *Shipwreck That Saved Jamestown*, 53-54.

36. Glover and Smith, 62-63, 66.

37. Grizzard and Smith, *Jamestown Colony*, 91; Charles Campbell, *History of the Colony and Ancient Dominion of Virginia* (Philadelphia: J. B. Lippincott, 1860), 52. Hunt worked to reconcile the hostile differences between competing factions among the aristocrats on the governing council and even once helped to diffuse a mutiny. Campbell, *History of the Colony*, 43.

38. Campbell, 95; Grizzard and Smith, *Jamestown Colony*, 32-33.

39. Campbell, *History of the Colony*, 95; Grizzard and Smith, *Jamestown Colony*, 32-33. Buck had studied at both Oxford University and Cambridge University.

40. Legg, *Clerk's Book*, xxv; Pounds, *History of the English*, 188.

41. David Norton, *A Textual History of the King James Bible* (Cambridge: Cambridge University Press, 2005), 5-6; Blackford Condit, *The History of the English Bible* (New York: A. S. Barnes, 1882), 328.

42. Condit, *History of the English*, 328-329; Leach, *History*, 320.

43. The Authorized Version of the Bible—as it was officially called—was first published in 1611 in London by the King's Printer. See Sir Winston Churchill, *Churchill's History of the English-Speaking Peoples* (Barnes & Noble, 1995), 159-160; Condit, *History of the English*, 329-330; Norton, *Textual History*, 1.

44. Harmar likely held a keen interest in Jamestown; in fact, one of his nephews in 1622 sailed to Virginia and spent the rest of his life in Jamestown colony, becoming a "prominent planter" and member of its legislative body. See *Virginia Magazine of History and Biography* 3 (1896): 274.

45. Glover and Smith, *Shipwreck That Saved Jamestown*, 54.

46. Churchill, *Churchill's History*, 163; R. B. Outhwaite, *Dearth, Public Policy and Social Disturbance in England, 1550-1800* (Cambridge, UK: Press Syndicate of the University of Cambridge, 1991), 1-3; Jack A. Goldstone, "Urbanization and Inflation: Lessons from the

English Price Revolution of the Sixteenth and Seventeenth Centuries," *American Journal of Sociology* 89, no. 5, (March 1984), 1122–1123, and see table I on 1123; H. M. Hyndman, *The Historical Basis for Socialism in England* (London: Kegan, Paul, Trench, 1883), 39.

47. Grizzard and Smith, *Jamestown Colony*, xxxiv. See also Alexander Brown, *The First Republic in America* (Boston: Houghton, Mifflin, 1898), 79: "A single share was £12 10s., to yield a dividend at the end of seven years. All who went to Virginia were to be registered in a book, 'that it may always appear what people have gone to the plantation, at what time they went, and how their persons were valued,' every extraordinary man, as divines, etc., having an extra value."

48. Colonial clergy earned more than domestic counterparts. While information about what the typical parish priest might have earned in the early seventeenth century is difficult to ascertain, evidence can be derived that would put it in the range of about £100 a year, perhaps a little more. See Katherine French, Gary Gibbs, and Beat Kumin, eds., *The Parish in English Life 1400–1600* (Manchester, UK: Manchester University Press, 1997), 166; see also Stanford Lehmberg, *Cathedrals Under Siege: Cathedrals in English Society, 1600–1700* (University Park: Pennsylvania State University Press, 1996), 48, where it is reported that in the mid-seventeenth century a preacher in eastern England received a salary of £160 per year. Based on Campbell, *History of the Colony*, 52, the pay of Buck's predecessor at Jamestown "appears to have been £500 a year," making the premium that the London Company likely committed to Buck to be about four to five times the normal salary he might have expected by remaining in England. A similar multiplier might have been used to induce Stephen Hopkins to be Reverend Buck's clerk. According to French, Gibbs, and Kumin's *Parish in English Life*, 166, the typical pay for a parish clerk in the first decade of the seventeenth century was about £5. The same level of premium would have yielded Hopkins around £20 to £25 per year.

49. Johnson, *Here Shall I Die*, 23.

50. Dominic Shellard and Siobhan Keenan, eds., *Shakespeare's Cultural Capital: His Economic Impact from the Sixteenth to the Twenty-First Century* (London: Palgrave Macmillan, 2016), 14.

51. Shellard and Keenan, *Shakespeare's Cultural Capital*, 14.

52. Grizzard and Smith, *Jamestown Colony*, xl. The Second Virginia Charter of May 23, 1609, specifically bound employees of the London Company, which received the royal charter, "for a space of seven years." See Grizzard and Smith, *Jamestown Colony*, 299.

53. It is unknown whether Hopkins was able to transmit to his wife, Mary, any of his wages during his time in Jamestown. The estate inventory taken at Mary Hopkins's death in May 1613, which would have included all of Stephen Hopkins's assets in England as well as those passed down to Mary from her mother-in-law who'd previously died, revealed a total value of about twenty-five pounds. See Johnson, *Here Shall I Die*, 150.

54. Glover and Smith, *Shipwreck That Saved Jamestown*, 73–74; see also Kieran Doherty, *Sea Venture: Shipwreck, Survival, and the Salvation of the First English Colony in the New World* (New York: St. Martin's Press, 2007), 2.

55. Sir Sidney Lee, *A Life of William Shakespeare* (New York: Macmillan, 1916), 306; Doherty, *Sea Venture*, 2. At one point Strachey was attending performances at Blackfriars, "sometimes once, twice, and thrice in a week." Jonathan Hart, *The Poetics of Otherness: War, Trauma, and Literature* (New York: Palgrave Macmillan, 2015), 60.

56. Doherty, *Sea Venture*, 3.

57. Strachey married Frances Forster in 1595. They had a child who would have been around thirteen when Strachey sailed on the *Sea Venture*. See Culliford, *William Strachey*, 7, 33.

58. Glover and Smith, *Shipwreck That Saved Jamestown*, 77-78.

59. Strachey, "True Reportory," 979-980.

60. Glover and Smith, *Shipwreck That Saved Jamestown*, 91.

61. Strachey, "True Reportory," 980.

62. Strachey, 981.

63. Strachey, 982-983.

64. Strachey, 983.

65. Strachey, 985-986.

66. Strachey, 986.

67. John Smith, *Travels and Works of Captain John Smith*, ed. Edward Arber, vol. 2 (Edinburgh: John Grant, 1910), 633; see also Glover and Smith, *Shipwreck That Saved Jamestown*, 124-125.

68. Smith, *Travels and Works*, 2:637.

69. Strachey, "True Reportory," 986-987.

70. Nathaniel Philbrick, *Mayflower* (New York: Penguin Group, 2006), 25; George F. Willison, *Saints and Strangers* (Orleans, MA: Parnassus Imprints, 1945), 465n1.

71. *The Complete Works of William Shakespeare*, Harvard Edition, ed. Rev. Henry Hudson (Boston: Ginn & Heath, 1880), 7:25-26, 26n60; Shakespeare, *The Tempest*, ed. Grace Tiffany (Boston: Wadsworth, Cengage Learning, 2012), 83n229: "still vex'd Bermoothes: always stormy Bermuda islands." See also Maurice Hunt, "Shakespeare's 'Still-Vexed' *Tempest*," *Style* 39, no. 3 (2005): 299.

72. Glover and Smith, *Shipwreck That Saved Jamestown*, 130; Strachey, "True Reportory," 1002.

73. Glover and Smith, *Shipwreck That Saved Jamestown*, 131-132.

74. Glover and Smith, 133.

75. Susan Kingsbury, ed., *The Records of the Virginia Company of London*, vol. 3 (Washington, DC: US Government Printing Office, 1933), 12; Craven, *Southern Colonies*, 64-65.

76. Glover and Smith, *Shipwreck That Saved Jamestown*, 130, 133-134; Strachey, "True Reportory," 1002.

77. Gates belonged to Gray's Inn, one of the few Inns of Court in London that sanctioned the practice of law. For a list of London establishments for learning and practicing law, see Harrison, *Description of England*, 80.

78. Grizzard and Smith, *Jamestown Colony*, 298.

79. See, e.g., William Falconer, *The New Universal Dictionary of the Marine* (Cambridge, UK: Cambridge University Press, 2011), 97. For an analogue in the colonial setting, see James

Stanier Clark and John McArthur, eds., *The Naval Chronicle*, vol. 27, *January–June 1812* (Cambridge: Cambridge University Press, 2010), 7: "The 7th of February, 1788, was a memorable day which established a regular form of government on the coast of New South Wales [in Australia]. For obvious reasons, all possible solemnity was given to the proceedings necessary on this occasion. On a space previously cleared, the whole colony was assembled; the military drawn up and under arms . . . and near the person of the governor those who were to hold the principal officers under him. The royal commission was then read. . . . By this instrument, Arthur Phillip was constituted and appointed captain-general and governor-in-chief in and over the territory."

80. See, e.g., rules 4–10 in Kingsbury, *Records*, 3:13–15.

81. Strachey, "True Reportory," 1009.

82. James Horn, *A Land as God Made It: Jamestown and the Birth of America* (New York: Basic Books, 2005), 163.

83. Strachey, "True Reportory," 997–998.

84. Glover and Smith, *Shipwreck That Saved Jamestown*, 127.

85. Doherty, *Sea Venture*, 53–54; Thomas Clayton, *Rambles and Reflections: From Biscay to the Black Sea and from Aetna to the North Cape with Glimpses at Asia, Africa, America, and the Islands of the Sea* (Chester, PA: Press of the Delaware Country Republican, 1892), 364–365.

86. Hobson Woodward, *A Brave Vessel: The True Tale of the Castaways Who Rescued Jamestown and Inspired Shakespeare's "The Tempest"* (New York: Viking Penguin, 2009), chap. 1, loc. 240, Kindle; Alden T. Vaughan, "Namontack's Itinerant Life and Mysterious Death: Sources and Speculations," *Virginia Magazine of History and Biography* 126, no. 2 (April 2018): 179, 180; see also Smith, *Travels and Works*, 2:638–639.

87. The Powhatan Confederacy spoke a dialect of Algonquian, as did all natives living from the Chesapeake Bay to the Gulf of St. Lawrence, including those of the Wampanoag Confederacy, which was the dominant nation in the area where the Pilgrims established Plymouth Colony.

88. Woodward, *Brave Vessel*, chap. 7, locs. 1233, 1245.

89. As recounted in "Journey to Pokanoket" in chapter 8, Hopkins's facility with the Algonquian tongue was displayed in the summer of 1621 when he and another Pilgrim traveled to Pokanoket to reinforce a treaty with the Wampanoag Confederacy. At one point, the two Englishmen were without their primary translator, yet they were still able to conduct conversations on rather abstract topics such as discourtesy, thievery, sin, and the punishment of God. See Henry Dexter, ed., *Mourt's Relation* (Boston: John Kimball Wiggin, 1865), 111. Dexter's edition, referenced throughout this book, has been described by modern scholars as a "monumental effort [that] has aided a generation of scholars" and has been praised as a "faithful reproduction of the original, letter for letter." Dwight B. Heath, ed., *Mourt's Relation: A Journal of the Pilgrims at Plymouth* (Bedford, MA: Applewood Books, 1963), xvin6. Another example of Hopkins's knowledge of Algonquian can be seen in the event from December 1621 or January 1622 recounted in chapter 9, when, without the help of native interpreters, Hopkins was able to understand the Narragansett messenger's explanation of the snakeskin-wrapped arrows. See also Vaughan, "Namontack's Itinerant Life," 196:

"English and Algonquian interpreters struggled for several decades to translate a mostly oral language into an alphabet-based language, and vice versa, in the absence in the early years of bilingual texts."

90. Strachey, "True Reportory," 999.

91. Strachey, 1008.

92. Strachey, 1008–1009; see also Campbell, *History of the Colony*, 95.

93. Woodward, *Brave Vessel*, chap. 7, locs. 1258–1270, Kindle; Vaughan, "Namontack's Itinerant Life," 187; Smith, *Travels and Works*, 2:638–639.

94. Glover and Smith, *Shipwreck That Saved Jamestown*, 140.

95. Doherty, *Sea Venture*, 76.

96. Smith, *Travels and Works*, 2:638.

97. Doherty, *Sea Venture*, 1.

98. Strachey, "True Reportory," 1000–1001, 1014.

99. Glover and Smith, *Shipwreck That Saved Jamestown*, 138.

100. Campbell, *History of the Colony*, 96.

101. Strachey, "True Reportory," 1000.

102. Strachey, 1001.

103. Glover and Smith, *Shipwreck That Saved Jamestown*, 150.

104. Strachey, "True Reportory," 1001–1002.

105. See rule 8, Kingsbury, *Records*, 3:15.

106. Strachey, "True Reportory," 1007.

107. Strachey, 1002.

108. Strachey, 1002.

109. Strachey, 1002.

110. Strachey, 1003.

111. Strachey, 1003.

112. Because Hopkins raised religious grounds as part of his argument, some historians seem to have used this to lump him in with the Puritan September rebels, who had primarily wielded religious arguments. This treatment is incorrect. First, Hopkins was not associated with the September mutiny. Second, though Strachey recorded that Hopkins relied on scripture (albeit "falsely quoted," according to Strachey), the chronicler never, either explicitly or through implication, tied Hopkins to Puritanism at all, whereas the September leader was suspected of being a Brownist—a radical Puritan strain linked to the Separatists. See Glover and Smith, *Shipwreck That Saved Jamestown*, 162. Third, the September leader held such strong views that he had to be "compelled" to take part in "the common Liturgy and form of Prayer," whereas Hopkins throughout the duration of their stay on Bermuda *actually led* the congregation through those very elements of the formal Anglican Church service. Strachey, "True Reportory," 1001. The leadership in Virginia were supporters of the Church of England, especially during its earlier years, when Stephen Hopkins resided there. Although it appears that in practice the colony's antagonism against Anglican dissent softened over time, its belligerent reputation remained intact, which is why more than ten years later the

Separatists in Leiden were wary of settling too close to the Jamestown settlements. William Bradford, *History of Plymouth Plantation 1620-1647*, vol. 1 (Boston: Houghton Mifflin Company, 1912), 65. That Hopkins didn't stray from the Church of England is further borne out by the fact that he later violated the Separatists' Sabbath Day laws, and it appears as though he never formally joined the Separatist church that the Pilgrims established in Plymouth Colony. Nathaniel Shurtleff, ed., *Records of the Colony of New Plymouth in New England*, vol. 1 (Boston: William White, 1855), 68; Hodges, *Hopkins of the Mayflower*, 230.

113. Strachey, "True Reportory," 1003.

114. Strachey, 1004–1005.

115. Given that at the time, a parish clerk was indeed considered akin to a domestic servant, it would be reasonable to conclude that Hopkins was thus employed by Reverend Buck. Legg, *Clerk's Book*, xxv. What's more, in the years following Hopkins's ultimate departure from Jamestown, Buck twice wrote to the London Company to request that they send him "some servants . . . to be a helper to me in my business," and "apparently relied on indentured servants to improve" land that he owned in the colony. See Kingsbury, *Records*, 3:443–444, 460–461; Grizzard and Smith, *Jamestown Colony*, 33.

116. Buck's wife and two daughters sailed with him on the third supply mission. Grizzard and Smith, *Jamestown Colony*, 33.

117. For example, while on board a ship, a captain would regularly invite his officers and other dignitaries for dinner, with each of them being served by either personal servants or ship boys, who would stand behind the men at the table, waiting to refresh their master's cup or attend to any other needs. See Glover and Smith, *Shipwreck That Saved Jamestown*, 82. As chaplain for the colony, a position of importance, Reverend Buck would likely have been included in such affairs during their time at sea, along with Somers, Newport, and Gates. As there is no record that the *Sea Venture* carried any ship boys, Hopkins would have likely served in that capacity. The custom was likely continued on Bermuda. Doherty, *Sea Venture*, 76n4.

118. Even if Hopkins were not waiting on his master during such a conversation, it would seem reasonable that Buck might mention to his clerk such an important request from the governor, for Hopkins played an integral role in the conduct of all the religious ceremonies.

119. Campbell, *History of the Colony*, 96–97.

2. Hopkins at Jamestown

1. Horn, *Land as God Made*, 169–171; Campbell, *History of the Colony*, 80.

2. George Percy, "A Trewe Relacyon," in *Captain John Smith*, 1100. See also Campbell, *History of the Colony*, 93; Horn, *Land as God Made*, 176–177; Rachel B. Herrmann, "The 'tragicall historie': Cannibalism and Abundance in Colonial Jamestown," *William and Mary Quarterly* 68, no. (January 2011): 47–49.

3. Jamestown had been built as a small triangular-shaped fort. It was spread over about an acre and was enclosed by a fence, a palisade made by fixing wooden planks and posts into the ground. Three watchtowers commanded each of the three angles of the triangle enclosure. Inside were a church, storehouses, and the settlers' dwellings. Glover and Smith, *Shipwreck*

That Saved Jamestown, 175. The houses were arranged on streets that ran parallel to each of the fort's outer walls. Inside the space left in the middle of the compound was a marketplace, a storehouse, a guardhouse, and the church. Brown, *First Republic*, 129.

4. Campbell, *History of the Colony*, 97–98.

5. Horn, *Land as God Made*, 179; Campbell, *History of the Colony*, 98.

6. Horn, *Land as God Made*, 136; John Fiske, *Old Virginia and Her Neighbours*, vol. 1 (Boston and New York: Houghton, Mifflin, 1897), 146–147. Like Thomas Gates, De La Warr had fought in the Low Countries against Spain and was also a veteran of the brutal campaigns in Ireland. Grizzard and Smith, *Jamestown Colony*, 229–230. He superseded Gates as governor.

7. Campbell, *History of the Colony*, 101; Horn, *Land as God Made*, 180–181.

8. Brown, *First Republic*, 127.

9. Campbell, *History of the Colony*, 98.

10. Brown, *First Republic*, 129.

11. Brown, 129.

12. Campbell, *History of the Colony*, 101; Horn, *Land as God Made*, 183.

13. Horn, *Land as God Made*, 183; Legg, *Clerk's Book*, xvii–xviii, xx–xxi, xxv.

14. Campbell, *History of the Colony*, 102.

15. Legg, *Clerk's Book*, xxv–xxvii, xxx–xxxii; Pounds, *History of the English*, 188.

16. Grizzard and Smith, *Jamestown Colony*, 33.

17. The prior chaplain for the colony, Robert Hunt, "[u]pon any alarm . . . was ready for defense as any" in the colony. Campbell, *History of the Colony*, 51. Buck and Hopkins would have continued in that tradition.

18. Brown, *The First Republic*, 134; Horn, *Land as God Made*, 189–190.

19. Grizzard and Smith, *Jamestown Colony*, xxv, xxxvi–xxxvii.

20. Strachey, "True Reportory," 1026.

21. Brown, *First Republic*, 129; John Rolfe, *A True Relation of the State of Virginia left by Sir Thomas Dale, Knight, in May 1616* (New Haven: Yale University Press, 1951), 39.

22. Grizzard and Smith, *Jamestown Colony*, xxviii, xxxvi, 174.

23. Grizzard and Smith, *Jamestown Colony*, xxx–xxxi.

24. Brown, *First Republic*, 135–138; Horn, *Land as God Made*, 184–192.

25. Brown, *First Republic*, 151, 155, 208; Horn, *Land as God Made*, 193–200.

26. See chapter 6.

27. Alexander Brown, *The Genesis of the United States* (Boston: Houghton, Mifflin, 1890), 1:498–499.

28. Vaughan, "Namontack's Itinerant Life," 190–191.

29. Brown, *First Republic*, 158; Horn, *Land as God Made*, 207–211.

30. Grizzard and Smith, *Jamestown Colony*, 167–169; Brown, *First Republic*, 173–175. Pocahontas also converted to Christianity. Brown, *First Republic*, 175, 203.

31. Ralph Hamor, *A True Discourse of the Present State of Virginia* (Richmond: Virginia State Library, 1957), 61–68.

32. Brown, *First Republic*, 203–205.

33. Grizzard and Smith, *Jamestown Colony*, 167–169.
34. See, e.g., W. Noel Sainsbury, ed., *Calendar of State Papers, Colonial Series, 1574–1660* (London: Longman, Green, Longman & Roberts, 1860), 18; Samuel Purchas, *Purchas His Pilgrimes*, vol. 19 (Glasgow: James MacLehose and Sons, 1906), 118.
35. Grizzard and Smith, *Jamestown Colony*, 171.
36. See chapter 8.
37. Edward D. Neill, "Virginia Governors Under the London Company," in *Macalester College Contributions: Department of History, Literature, and Political Science* (St. Paul, MN: Pioneer Press, 1889), 9; Conway Robinson, *Abstract of the Proceedings of the Virginia Company of London, 1619–1624*, vol. 1 (Richmond, VA: Virginia Historical Society, 1888), 187; see also Horn, *Land as God Made*, 196–197.
38. Grizzard and Smith, *Jamestown Colony*, xxvii: "Governmental confusion continued, stemming directly from factionalism on the Virginia council, a weak presidency, and the absence of vital elements of the English social structure. From what little is known about how settlers were recruited, it appears likely that the principal investors recruited their own colonists and placed their clients on the council. This ensured factionalism."
39. See chapter 4.
40. Hamor, *True Discourse*, 14, 55.
41. See chapter 8.
42. Hamor, *True Discourse*, 16; Virginia Bernard, *A Tale of Two Colonies: What Really Happened in Virginia and Bermuda?* (Columbia: University of Missouri Press, 2011), 167.
43. Hamor, *True Discourse*, xvii. Of course, Rolfe knew and appreciated Reverend Buck and thus likely maintained a relationship with Hopkins. They had all shared experiences aboard the *Sea Venture* and on Bermuda that likely forged ties. It would be natural to assume, therefore, that Hamor and Hopkins, if not fast friends, were well acquainted and perhaps on good terms with each other. See R. S. Thomas, *The Religious Element in the Settlement at Jamestown* (Petersburg, VA: Franklin Press, 1898), 27.
44. There is a slight possibility that the Pilgrims independently learned of the red coat gift, for Hamor mentioned the detail in passing in a book he wrote on behalf of the London Company, but the chances would have been slim and the evidence weighs against it, as only a few hundred impressions were likely sold and the Separatists were living among the Dutch in Leiden at the time. See Charles Rivington, *The Records of the Worshipful Company of Stationers* (London: Nichols and Sons, 1883), 2; Lyman Patterson, *Copyright in Historical Perspective* (Nashville: Vanderbilt University Press, 1968), 4–5; "A Bibliography of Colonial Virginia," in *Fifth Annual Report of the Library Board of the Virginia State Library* (Richmond, VA: Davis Bottom, Superintendent of Public Printing, 1908), 36; Charles Rivington, *The Records of the Worshipful Company of Stationers* (London: Nichols and Sons, 1883), 5. Edward Arber, *A Transcript of the Registers of the Company of Stationers of London 1554–1640*, vol. 3 (London: Privately Printed, 1876), 44, 153b, 265; Lena Cowen Orlin, *Material London ca. 1600* (Philadelphia: University of Pennsylvania Press, 2000), 331; Scott Christianson, *100 Documents that Changed the World* (New York: Universe

Publishing, 2015), 67; Hamor, *True Discourse*, viii; Bradford, *History of Plymouth Plantation*, 1:66n1. William Brewster, a church elder and leader of the Leiden community, did possess a copy of John Smith's *A Description of New England*, which was published in 1616, and it appears as though the would-be colonists aboard the *Mayflower* principally relied on this as their source for information about the New World, for Smith himself "bitterly related how [the Separatists] had insisted that his 'books and maps were better cheap to teach them than myself.'" Philbrick, *Mayflower*, 59.

45. Hamor, *True Discourse*, 37–39.

46. See chapter 8.

47. Under the terms of the royal charter then governing the colony in Virginia, every person going to the colony would serve in Jamestown for a term of seven years. In exchange for his service, the colonist would receive a share of the London Company and be entitled to share in Company dividends. Grizzard and Smith, *Jamestown Colony*, xl, xxxiv, 299. There is no record that Hopkins left the colony before the expiration of his term of indenture. Because of the constant shortage of manpower, it is very doubtful that Governor Dale released him sooner. See Sainsbury, *Calendar of State Papers*, 13–17; John Rolfe, *A True Relation of the State of Virginia left by Sir Thomas Dale, Knight, in May 1616* (New Haven: Yale University Press, 1951), 39. The spring of 1616, when Dale himself shipped aboard the *Treasurer* with John Rolfe and Pocahontas, coincided with the natural expiration of Hopkins's seven-year term. Sainsbury, *Calendar of State Papers*, 17.

48. Johnson, *Here Shall I Die*, 58.

49. Neal, "Investigation into the Origins," 126.

50. Purchas, *Purchas His Pilgrimes*, 19:118; Edward Neill, *History of the Virginia Company* (New York: Joel Munsell, 82 State Street, 1869); see also Sainsbury, *Calendar of State Papers*, 18.

51. Sainsbury, *Calendar of State Papers*, 18.

52. Johnson, *Here Shall I Die*, 61.

53. E. K. Chambers, *William Shakespeare: A Study of Facts and Problems*, vol. 1 (Oxford: Clarendon Press, 1930), 250, 491. As he'd been replaced as governor, Thomas Gates in July 1610 left Jamestown to return to England. He brought with him William Strachey's *True Reportory* that chronicled the *Sea Venture*'s voyage and their time on Bermuda. Brown, *First Republic*, 133–134. It is believed that because of the many associations he shared with Strachey and the Company, Shakespeare obtained access to the private letter shortly after its arrival in London in 1610, a period that would coincide with the writing of *The Tempest*. Paul Raffield, *The Art of Law in Shakespeare* (Portland, OR: Hart Publishing, 2017), 195–196; S. G. Culliford, *William Strachey 1572-1621* (Charlottesville: University Press of Virginia), 492.

54. Chambers, *William Shakespeare*, 491–492.

55. *A New Variorum Edition of Shakespeare: "The Tempest,"* ed. Horace Furnes, vol. 9 (Philadelphia: J. B. Lippincott, 1892), 313; A. J. Rowse, *Shakespeare the Man*, rev. ed. (London: Macmillan Press, 1988), 225; Culliford, *William Strachey*, 492.

3. The Pilgrim Expedition

1. Walter Besant, *The History of London* (London: Longmans, Green, 1893), 154; Peter Marshall, *Heretics and Believers: A History of the English Reformation* (New Haven: Yale University Press, 2017), 389–412; Churchill, *Churchill's History*, 138–144; Mike Ashley, *The Mammoth Book of British Kings and Queens* (New York: Carroll & Graf, 1998), 633, 637, 640; David Hackett Fischer, *Albion's Seed: Four British Folkways in America* (New York: Oxford University Press, 1989), 23.

2. Ashley, *Mammoth Book*, 641–642.

3. John Marshall, *John Locke, Toleration and Early Enlightenment Culture* (Cambridge: Cambridge University Press, 2006), 228.

4. Ashley, *Mammoth Book*, 645.

5. Ashley, 645.

6. Churchill, *Churchill's History*, 152.

7. Churchill, 153–154.

8. Fischer, *Albion's Seed*, 23: "The Puritans believed that evil was a palpable presence in the world, and that the universe was a scene of cosmic struggle between darkness and light. They lived in an age of atrocities without equal until the twentieth century."

9. Willison, *Saints and Strangers*, 26.

10. Churchill, *Churchill's History*, 146, 148.

11. Jeremy Bangs, *Strangers and Pilgrims, Travellers and Sojourners: Leiden and the Foundations of Plymouth Plantation* (Plymouth: General Society of Mayflower Descendants, 2009), 206–207.

12. Churchill, *Churchill's History*, 155.

13. Ashley, *Mammoth Book*, 646–647.

14. Churchill, *Churchill's History*, 158–159.

15. A. Guggenberger, *A General History of the Christian Era*, vol. 2 (St. Louis: B. Herder, 1901), 355; Alan Stewart, *The Cradle King: A Life of James VI & I* (London: Pimlico, 2004), 193–194.

16. Willison, *Saints and Strangers*, 48.

17. Samuel R. Gardiner, *History of England from the Accession of James I to the Outbreak of the Civil War*, vol. 1, *1603—1642* (London: Longmans, Green, 1884), 96, 222–223; Leo F. Solt, *Church and State in Early Modern England, 1509–1640* (Oxford: Oxford University Press, 1990), 149.

18. Gardiner, *History of England*, 1:96–97; Solt, *Church and State*, 149.

19. Guggenberger, *General History*, 2:356.

20. Churchill, *Churchill's History*, 159.

21. Guggenberger, *General History*, 2:356; James Sharpe, *Remember, Remember: A Cultural History of Guy Fawkes Day* (Cambridge, MA: Harvard University Press, 2005), 74–77.

22. Guggenberger, *General History*, 2: 357; Solt, *Church and State in Early Modern England*, 149.

23. Guggenberger, *General History*, 2:357–358; see also Michael Questier, *Dynastic Politics and the British Reformations, 1558-1630* (Oxford: Oxford University Press, 2019), 342.

24. Churchill, *Churchill's History*, 143.

25. Peter Wilson, *Europe's Tragedy: A New History of the Thirty Years War* (London: Penguin, 2010), 787.

26. Peter Wilson, *The Thirty Years War: Europe's Tragedy* (Cambridge, MA: Belknap Press, 2009), 10, 789, 795.

27. Bradford, *History of Plymouth Plantation*, 1:24–25.

28. Henry Dexter and Morton Dexter, *The England and Holland of the Pilgrims* (Boston: Houghton, Mifflin, 1906), 403–406; Bradford, *History of Plymouth Plantation*, 1:22.

29. Willison, *Saints and Strangers*, 33. See also Fischer, *Albion's Seed*, 69: "The Puritans were encouraged by their ministers to think of themselves as 'the saints,' and to believe that grace descended to their children."

30. The edition cited herein, which is interspersed with footnote commentary, was retitled *History of Plymouth Plantation 1620–1647*, edited by Worthington C. Ford and published in two volumes in 1912 by Houghton Mifflin for the Massachusetts Historical Society. The text from Bradford's original *Of Plymouth Plantation* is identical in the retitled edition. For evidence of the importance of this edition, see L. H. Butterfield, "Worthington Chauncey Ford, Editor," *Proceedings of the Massachusetts Historical Society* 3, vol. 83 (1971): 69; see also editor Samuel E. Morison's introduction to the 1952 Knopf publication of Bradford's *Of Plymouth Plantation 1620–1647* (New York: Alfred A. Knopf, 1952), viii, acknowledging that Ford's 1912 edition "is a monument of scholarship, providing abundant notes and illustrations; every scholar should be grateful to it, and I am indebted to Mr. Ford for many of my notes."

31. Bradford, *History of Plymouth Plantation*, 1:27, 36–37, and 36n1.

32. Bradford, 1: 39, 40–41, 45.

33. Bradford, 1:53.

34. Bradford, 1:55.

35. Bradford, 1:54–55.

36. Bradford, 1:56–57.

37. Bradford, 1:57. The sources for these tales of horror at the hands of the native people might have come from Dutch or French traders who'd spent time along the eastern coast of America, or from the Spanish who'd been battling and subjugating natives in Central and South America for over a century, or from Englishmen's travails at Jamestown.

38. Bradford, *History of Plymouth Plantation*, 1:59–60.

39. Bradford, 1:41–42, 41n2, 75, 88–89.

40. Charles Francis Adams, *Three Episodes of Massachusetts History*, vol. 1 (Boston: Houghton, Mifflin, 1892), 45–46; see also Philbrick, *Mayflower*, 20.

41. Charles Levermore, *Forerunners and Competitors of the Pilgrims and Puritans*, vol. 1 (Brooklyn: New England Society, 1912), 1.

42. Azel Ames, *The May-Flower and Her Log* (Boston and New York: Houghton, Mifflin, 1907), 6–7.

43. Bradford, *History of Plymouth Plantation*, 1:89n1, 94–95.

44. Willison, *Saints and Strangers*, 101.

45. Bradford, *History of Plymouth Plantation*, 1:101n1.

46. Bradford, 1:104n3.

47. Bradford, 1:103n3 continued from previous pages; Philbrick, *Mayflower*, 21.

48. Adams, *Three Episodes*, 1:46–47.

49. Philbrick, *Mayflower*, 21.

50. Bradford, *History of Plymouth Plantation*, 1:112.

51. Philbrick, *Mayflower*, 21.

52. Bradford, *History of Plymouth Plantation*, 1:108.

53. Willison, *Saints and Strangers*, 129–130.

54. See, e.g., Glover and Smith, *Shipwreck That Saved Jamestown*, 71; Johnson, *Here Shall I Die*, 63; Doherty, *Sea Venture*, 81.

55. There is also no record that he ever formally joined the church that the Saints established in Plymouth Colony. Hodges, *Hopkins of the Mayflower*, 230.

56. Johnson, *Here Shall I Die*, 65, 158.

57. From among the Saints, Edward Fuller was responsible for one servant. John Carver brought six servants. Isaac Allerton brought one. Edward Winslow was responsible for three. William Brewster brought two. William White brought two people. From among the Strangers, William Mullins was responsible for one servant. Stephen Hopkins brought two men. Christopher Martin was responsible for one servant.

58. Philbrick, *Mayflower*, 19.

59. Philbrick, 6–7. Two of the *Mayflower*'s crew members, pilot and mate Robert Coppin and pilot John Clarke, had sailed before to America but stayed with the colonists only until the *Mayflower* departed. See Philbrick, *Mayflower*, 24. One of the *Mayflower*'s sailors, William Trevor, was hired to stay with the colony for one year and left after he served his term. He had previously worked on a ship that sailed to the New England coast in 1619. See Charles Edward Banks, *The English Ancestry and Homes of the Pilgrim Fathers* (Baltimore: Genealogical Publishing, 1962), 90. Trevor apparently did not rank highly in the regard of Robert Cushman, one of the leaders of the Separatists who helped organize the expedition on the *Mayflower*. See Bradford, *History of Plymouth Plantation*, 1:270.

60. Stanley Johnson, "John Donne and the Virginia Company," *English Literary History* 14, no. 2 (June 1947):127–128, 130. Donne's interest in the New World would continue for a long time after the *Sea Venture* left port, lasting at least until 1622 when, after the Powhatan Confederacy attacked and killed hundreds of English colonists at Jamestown, he delivered a famous sermon to the London Company justifying the colonial enterprise under the guises of both divine and secular law. See Kasey Evens, *Colonial Virtue: The Mobility of Temperance in Renaissance England* (Toronto: University of Toronto Press, 2012), 130.

61. Doherty, *Sea Venture*, 2.

62. Daniel Starza Smith, *John Donne and the Conway Papers: Patronage and Manuscript Circulation in the Early Seventeenth Century* (Oxford: Oxford University Press, 2014), 187–188.

63. George Sampson, *The Concise Cambridge History of English Literature*, 3rd ed. (Cambridge: Cambridge University Press, 1970), 152.

64. Smith, *John Donne and the Conway Papers*, 187–188; Jennifer Speake, ed., *Literature of Travel and Exploration*, vol. 2 (New York: Fitzroy Dearborn, 2003), 983–984. Contemporaneous correspondence indicates that in 1616 Purchas might have chaired the Mermaid Club, and he certainly remained closely in touch with everything related to Virginia and its colony at Jamestown.

65. Purchas, *Purchas His Pilgrimes*, 19:5–72. Hopkins's mutiny is described in pages 30–32. See also Speake, *Literature of Travel*, 2:984; Culliford, *William Strachey*, 151.

66. *Dictionary of National Biography*, ed. Leslie Stephens, vol. 13 *Craik—Damer* (New York: Macmillan, 1888), 37; P. J. Wallis, "The Library of William Crashawe," *Transactions of the Cambridge Biographical Society* 2, no. 3 (1956): 215.

67. Alexander Whitaker, *Good Newes from Virginia* (London: William Welby, 1613), A4v–B3v.

68. William Crashaw, *A Sermon Preached in London Before the Right Honorable Lord Lavvarre* (London: William Welby, 1610), D3v.

69. Crashaw, *Sermon Preached in London*, C3r–C3v.

70. Bradford, *History of Plymouth Plantation*, 1:37n1.

71. Philbrick, *Mayflower*, 115.

72. Nathaniel Morton, *New England's Memorial* (Boston: Congregational Board of Publication, 1855), 170.

73. Eugene Aubrey Stratton, *Plymouth Colony: Its History & People 1620–1691* (Ancestry Publishing, 1986), 357; see also Bangs, *Strangers and Pilgrims*, 178: "The Pilgrims' minister in Leiden, John Robinson, was evidently well acquainted with Standish."

74. Bradford, *History of Plymouth Plantation*, 1:102–103, 304.

75. Bradford, 1:28.

76. Bradford, 1: 97–98, 98n2, 121; Ames, *May-Flower*, 11.

77. Bradford, 1:126.

78. Bradford, 1:117.

79. Philbrick, *Mayflower*, 22.

80. Bradford, *History of Plymouth Plantation*, 1:103.

81. Bradford, 1:109–110, 126–127.

82. Bradford, 1:129.

83. Bradford, 1:136–140; Philbrick, *Mayflower*, 28.

84. Bradford, *History of Plymouth Plantation*, 1:145n6.

85. Bradford, 1:138.

86. Bradford, 1:140.

87. The *Mayflower* had sixty-five passengers who embarked in London. Its final total was 102, which meant that thirty-seven were Saints. Considering that twenty Saints remained behind when the *Speedwell* abandoned its voyage meant that fifty-seven Saints sailed for the New World.

88. Bradford, *History of Plymouth Plantation*, 1:120.

89. Philbrick, *Mayflower*, 29.

90. Bradford, *History of Plymouth Plantation*, 1:142.

91. Bradford, 1:135–136, 142n4, 142–144.

92. Bradford, 1:145n6; see also Banks, *The English Ancestry*, 18: "The officers and crew consisted of a captain, four mates, four quartermasters, surgeon, carpenter, cooper, cooks, boatswains, gunners and about thirty-six men before the mast, making a total of fifty, bringing the number of persons aboard the ship during the voyage to about one hundred and fifty."

93. Bradford, *History of Plymouth Plantation*, 1:149.

94. Strachey, "True Reportory," 1019–1020. The Powhatan had exploited the division between sailor and settler and openly traded with the mariners while denying any commerce with the colonists.

95. Bradford, *History of Plymouth Plantation*, 1:149.

96. Bradford, 1:149.

97. Philbrick, *Mayflower*, 23.

98. Bradford, *History of Plymouth Plantation*, 1:147.

99. Philbrick, *Mayflower*, 23–24.

100. Bradford, *History of Plymouth Plantation*, 1:147.

101. Bradford, 1:148n1, continuing from previous page.

102. Glover and Smith, *Shipwreck That Saved Jamestown*, 83–84.

103. Glover and Smith, 84–85.

104. Glover and Smith, 87–88.

105. See, e.g., Glover and Smith, *Shipwreck That Saved Jamestown*, 86.

106. Justin Winsor, *Elder William Brewster of the Mayflower: His Books and Autographs* (Cambridge, MA: John Wilson and Son, 1887), 39.

107. Philbrick, *Mayflower*, 30.

108. Philbrick, 29.

109. Bradford, *History of Plymouth Plantation*, 1:150.

110. Bradford, 1:150.

111. Banks, *The English Ancestry*, 17, 19–20.

112. Bradford, *History of Plymouth Plantation*, 1:150.

113. Bradford, 1:150–151. The exact purpose for shipping the great screw was not recorded, but some historians have speculated that it might have been a jackscrew—a mechanical device for lifting heavy timber to be used in building houses—while others have insisted that the screw was part of a printing press that they'd used to print religious tracts in the Netherlands. Philbrick, *Mayflower*, 365. Either of these devices would have been sufficient to perform the task reported by Bradford, and its use revealed the resourcefulness typical in mariners of that age, who often were confronted by midocean challenges where life and death hung in the balance.

114. When a crashing wave hits a ship square on its beam, or side, the wave will capsize the boat if the wave is higher than the width of the beam. The *Mayflower* was about twenty feet wide at its widest point, and its side works rode about six feet above the water line, which meant that if a twenty-six foot high wave crashed across the side of the *Mayflower*, it would capsize and all would be lost. See Bradford, *History of Plymouth Plantation*, 1, 143, 147–148. The

gale strength winds that the *Mayflower* was encountering were blowing anywhere between thirty to sixty miles per hour. While the distance over which the wind is blowing and the length of time it blows must be factored as well as its speed, winds blowing at forty-five miles an hour might generate waves with heights of twenty-eight or more feet, which would have put the *Mayflower* in grave danger. At a minimum, wallowing without steerage in such seas could work loose the masts from their anchor points, the socket deep in the hull in which the mast is set. Even standing rigging might not secure a mast against the irregular heaving of a ship without steerage. The loss of a mast—even one of three—could have been catastrophic, for without masts to carry sails, a ship would be left helpless in midocean, drifting aimlessly on any currents that might catch it until food and drinkable water were consumed and its passengers and crew died one by one.

115. Bradford, *History of Plymouth Plantation*, 1:147, 151.

116. Philbrick, *Mayflower*, 31.

117. Bradford, *History of Plymouth Plantation*, 1:151.

118. Bradford, 1:151.

119. William Bradford, *History of Plymouth Plantation 1620-1647*, vol. 2 (Boston: Houghton Mifflin, 1912), 400.

120. Bradford, *History of Plymouth Plantation*, 1:151.

121. Philbrick, *Mayflower*, 33; Bradford, *History of Plymouth Plantation*, 1:151-152.

4. The Mayflower Compact

1. Philbrick, *Mayflower*, 33; Bradford, *History of Plymouth Plantation*, 1:152, 158n.

2. Bradford, *History of Plymouth Plantation*, 1:152n4.

3. Fredrick Freeman, *The History of Cape Cod*, vol. 1 (Boston: Geo. C. Rand & Avery, 1858), 27.

4. Henry David Thoreau, *Cape Cod* (Boston: Houghton, Mifflin, 1893), 2-3.

5. See chapter 5.

6. Philbrick, *Mayflower*, 3-4.

7. Bradford, *History of Plymouth Plantation*, 1:152.

8. Philbrick, *Mayflower*, 36.

9. Philbrick, 37.

10. Bradford, *History of Plymouth Plantation*, 1:152.

11. Paul Schneider, *The Enduring Shore: A History of Cape Cod, Martha's Vineyard, and Nantucket* (New York: Owl Books, 2000), 197; Theodore Burbank, *Cape Cod Shipwrecks* (Salty Pilgrim Press, 2013), chap 1, loc. 45, Kindle.

12. Philbrick, *Mayflower*, 37.

13. Burbank, *Cape Cod Shipwrecks*, 4; Philbrick, *Mayflower*, 37-38; Paul S. Krantz, Jr., *Riding the Wild Ocean* (Charleston: History Press, 2018), 11-12. In 1602, Bartholomew Gosnold called the area "Tucker's Terror" and the southern point of Monomoy Island "Point Care," although neither Christopher Jones nor his crew would have known about the experience, as it wasn't published until 1625. Levermore, *Forerunners and Competitors*, 1:43, 46. In 1606 the French explorer Samuel Champlain tried to pass through from the open sea to

Nantucket Sound in a shallow-drafted pinnace that could swim in only four feet of water. He survived only "by the grace of God" and declared the passage to be "a very dangerous place." Like the descriptions from Gosnold, however, Champlain's exploits were unknown to the English until 1632, well after the voyage of the *Mayflower*. W. L. Grant, *Voyages of Samuel de Champlain: 1604–1618* (New York: Charles Scribner's Sons, 1907), 71n1, 93–94.

14. Dexter, *Mourt's Relation*, 3.

15. Bradford, *History of Plymouth Plantation*, 1:134–135.

16. William Blackstone, *Commentaries on the Laws of England in Two Volumes*, vol. 1 (Philadelphia: J. B. Lippincott, 1893), 467: "**These artificial persons are called bodies politic, bodies corporate** (corpora corporata) **or corporations**: of which there is a great variety subsisting, for the advancement of religion, of learning, and of commerce; in order to preserve entire and forever those rights and immunities, which, if they were granted only to those of which the body corporate is composed, would upon their death be utterly lost and extinct."

17. Blackstone, *Commentaries*, 1:471: "But, with us in England, the king's consent is absolutely necessary to the erection of any corporation, either impliedly or expressly given. . . . The methods by which the king's consent is expressly given are either by act of parliament or charter." See also on page 473: "All the other methods, therefore, whereby corporations exist, by common law, by prescription, and by act of parliament, are of the most part reducible to this of the king's letters-patent or charter of incorporation."

18. Susan Kingsbury, ed., *The Records of the Virginia Company of London*, vol. 1 (Washington, DC: US Government Printing Office, 1906), 22: "As a result of this movement the letters patent of 1609 were issued, transforming the undertakers into a body politic. In this case also the documents are especially characteristic of the organization. Whereas the Crown was formerly the source of all power, beginning with 1609 the council of the company, acting as a standing committee for the adventurers rather than in the name of the King, exercised the controlling authority."

19. In its patent to Smyth of Nibley the London Company gave the patentees "grants of incorporation by some usual or fit name or title, with liberty to them and their successors from time to time to frame and make orders, ordinances, and constitutions for the rule of government . . . [as long as they] be not repugnant to the laws of England or to the form of government by the said Treasurer, Council, and company to be established." Kingsbury, *Records*, 3:133. While Pastor Robinson in his letter, probably written in the latter part of July 1620 (Dexter, *Mourt's Relation*, xli note d), might have perfectly foreseen the *Mayflower's* November landfall outside the scope of the London Company's patent, thus anticipating the need for the formation of a new political body governed by mutual consent, it is more likely that by "body politic" he was referring to the corporate entity already formed by operation of their patent. That the Pilgrims became a corporate entity as a consequence of their patent was highlighted by Robinson's use of the present perfect tense "are become," which indicates that the formation of the "body politic" had already been created. "Are become" is the Early Modern English equivalent of "have become."

20. Brian Herzogenrath, *An American Body Politic: A Deleuzian Approach* (Hanover, NH: University Press of New England, 2010), 55–56; see also Kingsbury, *Records*, 3:133; and discussion in the "Draftsmen at the Table" section of chapter 4. One of the features of a corporate entity, according to William Blackstone, a prominent eighteenth-century English jurist, was the ability to "establish rules and orders for the regulation of the whole, which are a sort of municipal laws of this little republic; or rules and statutes may be prescribed to it at its creation, which are then in the place of natural laws." Blackstone, *Commentaries*, 1:467–468. Though no copy of the Pilgrims' 1620 patent survives, it is believed that the grant was similar in form to what is known as the "Smyth of Nibley" patent, which allowed the patentees to create a temporary government under certain circumstances. See Samuel Eliot Morison, "The Plymouth Colony and Virginia," *Virginia Magazine of History and Biography* 62, no. 2 (1954):150, 152–153; Kingsbury, *Records*, 3:133. Just as the government for the Smyth of Nibley colony was in the end to be instituted by the London Company, so, too, was that for the Pilgrims. Kingsbury, *Records*, 3: 133; Samuel Eliot Morison, "The Mayflower's Destination, and the Pilgrim Fathers' Patents," in *Publications of the Colonial Society of Massachusetts*, ed. Walter Muir Whitehill, vol. 38, *Transactions 1947–1951* (Boston: Colonial Society of Massachusetts, 1959), 389.

21. Bradford, *History of Plymouth Plantation*, 1:65.

22. Morison, "Plymouth Colony and Virginia," 154–155.

23. Bradford, *History of Plymouth Plantation*, 1:135–136.

24. Bradford, 1:135–136, 136n1, 192, 192n1; Ames, *May-Flower*, 158; 162–163, 163n2.

25. Bradford, *History of Plymouth Plantation*, 1:190.

26. Bradford, 1:190. See also Dexter, *Mourt's Relation*, 5: "This day before we came to harbor [at Provincetown], [we] observ[ed that] some [were] not well affected to unity and concord, but gave some appearance of faction."

27. Dexter, *Mourt's Relation*, 9n27, continued from previous page.

28. Grizzard and Smith, *Jamestown Colony*, xxvi, 259.

29. Dexter, *Mourt's Relation*, xvi–xviii.

30. Dexter, 5–6.

31. Bradford, *History of Plymouth Plantation*, 1:189–190.

32. Bradford, 1:191.

33. Bradford, 1:189.

34. Of course, this experiment in self-government played out within the confines of England's colonial patenting system. The Pilgrims ultimately obtained a valid patent for their New England colony and as late as 1636 referred to the "corporation" created by virtue of that patent. See David Pulsifer, ed., *Records of the Colony of New Plymouth in New England*, vol. 11, *Laws 1623–1682* (Boston: William White, 1861), 6–7.

35. Bradford, *History of Plymouth Plantation*, 1:76.

36. Philbrick, *Mayflower*, 25.

37. In a letter Robert Cushman railed against Martin's capabilities as governor: "Have not the philosophers and all wise men observed that, even in settled commonwealths, violent

governors bring either themselves, or [the] people, or both, to ruin; how much more in the raising of commonwealths, when the mortar is yet scarce tempered that should bind the walls." Bradford, *History of Plymouth Plantation*, 1:145. Note how Cushman's reference reinforces Blackstone's commentary that a governance of a corporation acts akin to that of a municipality. See Blackstone, *Commentaries*, 1: 467–468, cited in chapter 4.

38. Strachey, "True Reportory," 1002.

39. See, e.g., Philbrick, *Mayflower*, 39; Hodges, *Hopkins of the Mayflower*, 184; Ames, *May-Flower*, 254n4.

40. Dexter, *Mourt's Relation*, 8–9. There is no list of the men who were first to leave the *Mayflower* and explore the immediate vicinities of Cape Cod. However, Stephen Hopkins was most certainly one of them. First, the number of men who went on November 11 was nearly the same as those who went on November 13, for which Hopkins was named as one of three special advisers to Myles Standish. Second, those who went on November 11 were "well armed," as were the men who went on November 13. According to William Bradford, swords, muskets, and armor were in short supply when the *Mayflower* left England. Bradford, *History of Plymouth Plantation*, 1:129. As such, those who possessed arms likely participated in both excursions. And third, those who went on November 11 returned with red cedar for firewood, a variety that was specifically noted for its sweet aroma. As discussed later in chapter 6, red cedar would have been unknown to the men who'd been only in England, for that species was native to the New World and wasn't introduced into England until 1664. See Charles Sprague Sargent, *Silva of North America* vol. 10 (Boston: Houghton, Mifflin, 1896), 95. Of course, Hopkins would have been well acquainted with the species, as he labored felling cedar trees in Bermuda that were used to construct the two ships that transported the castaways to Jamestown.

41. Dexter, *Mourt's Relation*, 13–14.

42. Bradford, *History of Plymouth Plantation*, 1:190.

43. Stratton, *Plymouth Colony*, 179.

44. Among the Saints, Isaac Allerton had retained John Hooke as a servant; William Brewster had Richard and Mary More; John Carver had John Howland, William Latham, Desire Minter, Jasper More, Roger Wilder, and a woman known only as Dorothy, who was a maidservant; William White had William Holbeck and Edward Thompson; and Edward Winslow was responsible for Ellen More, George Soule, and Elias Story. Among the Strangers, Stephen Hopkins had retained Edward Doty and Edward Leister; Christopher Martin had John Langemore and Solomon Prowe; and William Mullins was responsible for Robert Carter. Dexter, *Mourt's Relation*, 7–8, 7n27; see also Stratton, *Plymouth Colony*, 179.

45. George Ernest Bowman, *The Mayflower Compact and Its Signers* (Boston: Massachusetts Society of Mayflower Descendants, 1920), 18.

46. See Dexter, *Mourt's Relation*, 7n27.

47. Thomas Prince, *A Chronological History of New England*, vol. 1 (Boston: Kneeland & Green, 1736), 105.

48. Stratton, *Plymouth Colony*, 284, 317.

49. Stratton, 311, 335.

50. Dexter, *Mourt's Relation*, 9n27 continued from previous page.

51. Bradford, *History of Plymouth Plantation*, 1:190–191.

52. The Pilgrims had contracted with several of the *Mayflower*'s sailors for their services for a period of one year: John Alden, John Allerton, Thomas English, William Trevore, and a man whose name was recorded only as Ely. Of these Alden, Allerton, and English signed the Compact. See Dexter, *Mourt's Relation*, 7n27. Alden, who was a cooper, decided to stay after the term of his contract and became noted in the colony, serving as assistant to the governor and treasurer, among other positions. Stratton, *Plymouth Colony*, 232–233. Allerton and English both might have been affiliated with the Saints from their days in Leiden; both died the first winter in the New World. Stratton, *Plymouth Colony*, 234, 289. Trevore and Ely, who like Allerton and English might have had links to the Saints, either demurred, were ill at the time, or perhaps stated their intent to leave immediately after the one year term of their contract had expired. See Dexter, *Mourt's Relation*, 7n27.

53. For information on the other Strangers, see Stratton, *Plymouth Colony*, 245, 253, 255, 264, 295, 323, 331, 343, 367.

54. Stratton, *Plymouth Colony*, 245.

55. For example, after only an hour of their twenty-four-hour punishment for dueling, Hopkins intervened on behalf of both Doty and Leister; upon his appeal, they were released from the remainder of their punishment. Prince, *Chronological History*, 1:105. The incident suggests that Hopkins might have cared somewhat for Doty and Leister, not only because of their value to his household but also as individuals—as young men who like Hopkins himself had indentured themselves in a bid to make a better place for themselves in the world.

56. Strachey, "True Reportory," 1014; see also Henry Llewellyn Williams et al., *The Two Americas: Their Complete History, from the Earliest Discoveries to the Present Day* (New York: Will C. Sadler, 1881), 33: "But the want of provision was not the only deficiency; there [also] was a total want of principal and order."

57. Horn, *Land as God Made*, 171; Salma Hale, *History of the United States from Their First Settlement as Colonies to the Close of the Campaign of 1814* (Aberdeen: George Clark and Son, 1848), 22; Williams et al., *Two Americas*, 33.

58. Campbell, *History of the Colony*, 97–98.

59. Morison, "Plymouth Colony and Virginia," 152.

60. That the colonists chose John Carver over Martin after the creation of the Mayflower Compact supports this view. See Bradford, *History of Plymouth Plantation*, 1:192.

61. Robert Ashton, ed., *The Works of John Robinson, Pastor of the Pilgrim Fathers*, vol. 2 (London: John Snow, 1851), 132.

62. Bradford, *History of Plymouth Plantation*, 1:20–22.

63. Bradford, 1:20n3.

64. Perry Miller, *Errand into the Wilderness* (Cambridge, MA: Belknap Press, 2000), 21n14, 22. Robinson had been closely in contact with another group of Puritans who, though

they disagreed with the Separatists about the need to formally separate themselves from the Church of England, believed in the congregational approach to organizing worship; that is, the power of churches to govern themselves independent of the Anglican hierarchy. Robinson was strongly influenced by them and agreed with them on the major principles.

65. Robert Ashton, ed., *The Works of John Robinson, Pastor of the Pilgrim Fathers*, vol. 3 (London: Doctrinal Tract and Book Society, 1851), 43.

66. Ashton, *Works of John Robinson*, 2:225.; see also Prince, *Chronological History*, 1:92: "These [Church] Officers, being chosen and ordained, have no lordly, arbitrary or imposing power, but can only rule and minister with the consent of the brethren."

67. Bradford, *History of Plymouth Plantation*, 1:20–22.

68. Champlin Burrage, *The Church Covenant Idea: Its Origin and Its Development* (Philadelphia: American Baptist Publication Society, 1904), 50.

69. See, e.g., Kieran Doherty, *William Bradford: Rock of Plymouth* (Brookfield, CT: Twenty-First Century Books, 1999), 20–25; Benjamin Hanbury, *Historical Memorials Relating to the Independents or Congregationalists, from Their Rise to the Restoration of the Monarchy*, vol. 1 (London: Congregational Union of England and Wales, 1839), 279–280: "The saints being thus gathered as a people that shall dwell by themselves, and not reckoned among the nations, because they are chosen out of the world, and separated from the same, and being building as a city compact together in itself, and growing up in Christ the chief cornerstone, unto an holy temple in the Lord, are made the habitation of God by the Spirit, and do dwell alone in safety in a land of wheat and wine."

70. Prince, *Chronological History*, 1: vi-viii.

71. Prince, 1:88; see also Howard Millar Chapin, *Hypocrisie Unmasked by Edward Winslow 1646* (Providence: Club for Colonial Reprints, 1916), 98: "[It's] true, we profess and desire to practice a separation from the world, and the works of the world, which are works of the flesh."

72. Andrew Robinson, ed., *Encyclopedia of U.S. History*, vol. 1, *Colonial Beginnings Through Revolution, 1500 to 1783* (Washington, DC: CQ Press, 2010), 215.

73. Bradford, *History of Plymouth Plantation*, 1:134n4, continuing from prior page; see also Thomas Goddard Wright, *Literary Culture in Early New England, 1620–1730* (New Haven: Yale University Press, 1920), 15.

74. Doherty, *William Bradford*, 52–53; Jacob Baily Moore, *Lives of the Governors of New Plymouth and Massachusetts Bay* (New York: Gates & Stedman, Publishers, 1848), 54. Bradford would be elected the second governor of the colony in April 1621, when Carver died suddenly.

75. Among the books of William Brewster recorded when he died in 1644 were works by Francis Bacon, Peter Martire Vermigli, Seneca, and Aristotle, as well as *The Prince* by Niccolo Machiavelli and *The Commonwealth of England* by Sir Thomas Smith. See George Bowman, ed., *The Mayflower Descendant*, vol. 3 (Boston: Massachusetts Society of Mayflower Descendants, 1901), 19–27. Among the books of William Bradford recorded when he

died in 1657 was *Six Books of the Commonwealth* by Jean Bodin. See Bowman, *Mayflower Descendant*, 2:232-233.

76. Bradford, *History of Plymouth Plantation*, 1:192, 192n1.

77. See Dexter, *Mourt's Relation*, 43-45, identifying Standish in a group with other Separatists and distinct from the Strangers: "So ten of our men were appointed who were of themselves willing to undertake it, to wit, Captain Standish, Master Carver, William Bradford, Edward Winslow, John Tilley, Edward Tilley, John Howland, and three of London, Richard Warren, Stephen Hopkins and Edward Doty . . . ." See also Bangs, *Strangers and Pilgrims*, 178-179, noting that Standish became personally acquainted in Leiden with the Separatists' pastor, John Robinson.

78. Ames, *May-Flower*, 29.

79. Strachey, "True Reportory," 1002.

80. See, e.g., *Vindiciae contra tyrannos*, a tract published in 1579 in the aftermath of the St. Bartholomew's Day massacre of Protestant Huguenots in France. Its anonymous author argued that kings are ultimately accountable to the people, thus making government an agency accountable to its citizens.

81. Bradford, *History of Plymouth Plantation*, 1:192, see also note 1, indicating Carver may have served as governor of the *Speedwell* during its short tenure.

82. Bradford, 1:75, 192.

83. See Thomas Hobbes, *Leviathan* (London: Andrew Crooke, 1651); John Locke, *Two Treatises of Government* (London: Awnsham and John Churchill, 1698). In 1625, five years after the creation of the Compact, Dutch jurisprudential thinker Hugo Grotius published *De jure belli ac pacis*, which outlined the social contract theory and served as a foundation for the later work of Hobbes and Locke. See Deborah Baumgold, "Pacifying Politics: Resistance, Violence, and Accountability in Seventeenth-Century Contract Theory," *Political Theory* 21, no. 1 (February 1993): 6-8.

84. See Mark Vishniak, "Justification of Power in Democracy," *Political Science Quarterly* 60, no. 3 (September 1945): 356; for a discussion of other contributions that Plymouth Colony made to the development of American law, see also George Haskins, "The Legal Heritage of Plymouth Colony," in David Flaherty, ed., *Essays in the History of Early American Law* (Chapel Hill: University of North Carolina Press, 1969), 122, 130.

85. Scott Christianson, *100 Documents that Changed the World* (New York: Universe Publishing, 2015), 62-67.

86. Andrew W. Robertson, ed., *Encylopedia of U.S. Political History*, vol. 1 (Washington, DC: CQ Press, 2010), 216.

87. See, e.g., Jay Milbrandt, *They Came for Freedom: The Forgotten, Epic Adventure of the Pilgrims* (Nashville: Nelson Books, 2017), xviii; Moore, *Lives of the Governors*, 24, see note. In 2016 the governor of Massachusetts issued an executive order that honored "the establishment of New England's oldest municipality, settled by those seeking religious freedom and memorializing their commitment to democracy in what would be a precursor to the Constitution of the United States, the Mayflower Compact." See Mass. Exec. Order No. 570 (September

20, 2016), https://www.mass.gov/executive-orders/no-570-reaffirming-and-expanding-the -plymouth-massachusetts-400th-anniversary.

88. Harry Alonzo Cushing, *The Writings of Samuel Adams*, vol. 1 (New York, London: G. P. Putnam's Sons, 1904), 71–73.

89. David McCullough, *John Adams* (New York: Simon & Schuster, 2001), 253–254.

90. George Haynes et al., *Proceedings of the American Antiquarian Society*, vol. 30 (Worcester, MA: American Antiquarian Society, 1921), 288n1; Ronald M. Peters, Jr., *The Massachusetts Constitution of 1780: A Social Compact* (Amherst: University of Massachusetts Press, 1978), 21.

91. Vishniak, "Justification of Power," 358n11, citing Benjamin Perley Poore, *The Federal and State Constitutions, Colonial Charters, and other Organic Laws of the United States* (Washington, 1878), part I, 956–957.

92. J. Jefferson Looney, ed., *The Papers of Thomas Jefferson, Retirement Series*, vol. 1, *4 March 1809 to 15 November 1809* (Princeton: Princeton University Press, 2004), 58–59.

93. Looney, *Papers of Thomas Jefferson,* 102; *The Writings of Thomas Jefferson*, ed. H. A. Washington, vol. 8 (Washington, DC: Taylor & Maury, 1854), 166.

94. Abraham Lincoln's 1863 Gettysburg Address. See Frederick W. Osborn, *American Patriotic Selections: Famous State Papers of Washington, Jefferson, and Lincoln* (New York: Effingham Maynard, 1890), 59; Gabor S. Boritt, *Lincoln and the Economics of the American Dream* (Chicago: University of Illinois Press, 1994), 282; see also Haynes et al., *Proceedings*, 30:278.

5. Mutual Suspicion

1. Dexter, *Mourt's Relation*, 9.

2. Thomas Hobbes, *Leviathan* (New York: Barnes & Noble Books, 2004), 94–95.

3. Hobbes, *Leviathan*, 91–92.

4. Walter Besant, *The History of London* (London: Longmans, Green, 1893), 151; Glover and Smith, *Shipwreck That Saved Jamestown*, 14; Francis Sheppard, *London: A History* (Oxford: Oxford University Press, 1998), 126.

5. Besant, *History of London*, 151, 181–182; Sheppard, *London: A History*, 128.

6. Besant, *History of London*, 182, 186; Roy Porter, *London: A Social History* (Cambridge, MA: Harvard University Press, 1994), 82–84.

7. Besant, *History of London*, 183; Sheppard, *London: A History*, 193.

8. Besant, *History of London*, 183–184; see also Sheppard, *London: A History*, 190.

9. Besant, *History of London*, 184, 186; Porter, *London: A Social History*, 82–84.

10. Levermore, *Forerunners and Competitors*, 1:10–11.

11. Ashley, *Mammoth Book*, 646.

12. S. J. Connolly, *Contested Island: Ireland 1460–1630* (Oxford: Oxford University Press, 2007), 253–254.

13. Connolly, *Contested Island*, 254; see also Philip Wilson, "The Flight of the Earls," *The Nineteenth Century and After, A Monthly Review* 55 (1904): 481, where an eyewitness described the destruction: "Tyrone . . . had been reduced to a desert, and in the neighboring counties

also . . . [were] found everywhere men dead of famine . . . . [Along one road between two towns], a distance of about twenty miles, there lay a thousand dead, and that . . . there were above three thousand starved in Tyrone." Witnesses described horrid suffering, which included cases of cannibalism and even a case where three children under ten survived by "eating their dead mother, upon whose flesh they had fed twenty days past."

14. M. Perceval-Maxwell, *The Scottish Migration to Ulster in the Reign of James 1* (Belfast: Ulster Historical Foundation, 1973), 17–19.

15. Perceval-Maxwell, *Scottish Migration*, 17–19.

16. Jonathan Bardon, *The Plantation of Ulster: War and Conflict in Ireland* (Dublin: Gill & Macmillan, 2011), chap. 2, loc. 879, Kindle.

17. Ashley, *Mammoth Book*, 649.

18. Peter and Fiona Somerset Fry, *A History of Ireland* (New York: Barnes & Noble Books, 1988), 137.

19. Bardon, *Plantation of Ulster*, chapter 10, locs. 2511, 4203–4217; Ashley, *Mammoth Book*, 649.

20. Levermore, *Forerunners and Competitors*, 1:11.

21. Alan Taylor, *American Colonies* (New York: Penguin Books, 2001), 122–123.

22. Bardon, *Plantation of Ulster*, preface, loc. 38.

23. Many of the early English explorers and immigrants viewed the Native Americans much as they did the natives of Ireland. See Taylor, *American Colonies*, 123; Richard Hakluyt, *Voyages in Search of the North-West Passage* (London: Casseell, 1886), 109; John Pinkerton, ed., *A General Collection of the Best and Most Interesting Voyages in All Parts of the World*, vol. 12 (London: Longman, Hurst, Rees, Orme, and Brown, 1812), 557; Somerset Fry, *History of Ireland*, 127; Levermore, *Forerunners and Competitors*, 1:44, 64; Dexter, *Mourt's Relation*, 87. The Englishmen who campaigned in Ireland brutalized the Irish more than did those who sailed and settled in America, at least in the early decades of colonization in New England.

24. Taylor, *American Colonies*, 119.

25. Levermore, *Forerunners and Competitors*, 1:12.

26. Taylor, *American Colonies*, 51. Rival European countries even created a notorious "Black Legend" that assigned particularly brutal and destructive tactics to the Spanish in all of the Americas.

27. Taylor, 122; Robert Johnson, *Nova Britannia: Offering Most Excellent Fruits by Planting in Virginia* (London: Samuel Macham, 1609), 13–14.

28. In both Ireland and America, the English adhered to the axiom that "might makes right," a view that was held for over two hundred years and even endorsed by the US Supreme Court in Johnson v. McIntosh, 21 US (8 Wheat.) 543 (1823), where the court discussed the doctrine of discovery and the right of conquest as applied to the English and European subjugation of the Native Americans. See also Harry S. Stout, *American Aristocrats: A Family, a Fortune, and the Making of American Capitalism* (New York: Basic Books, 2017), 52.

29. The most violent conflicts in America's early colonial history were vastly less costly in terms of lives lost than those in Ulster during the Nine Years' War. For example, in the Pequot War that took place from 1636 to 1638 between the Pequot and an alliance of English colonies

and Native Americans who allied themselves with the English, about seven hundred Pequot were killed or taken into captivity. *Journal of John Winthrop*, ed. James Savage, Richard S. Dunn, and Laetitia Yeandle (Cambridge, MA: Harvard University Press, 1996), 228. In the larger conflict known as King Philip's War that lasted from 1675 to 1678 between a Native American alliance and English colonists, a clash which some consider to be among the deadliest wars in American history, an estimated seventy-two hundred Native Americans and up to three thousand English settlers were killed. James Drake, *King Philip's War: Civil War in New England 1675–1676* (Amherst: University of Massachusetts Press, 1999), 1, 4. During the Nine Years' War in Ireland, as many as twenty-five thousand Irish perished, either from starvation, disease, or battle, as did over forty thousand English soldiers. Perceval-Maxwell, *Scottish Migration to Ulster*, 17–19; Bardon, *Plantation of Ulster*, chap. 2, loc. 879.

30. Open conflict leading to subjugation was not a European invention, of course, and Native Americans were not immune to the lure of domination and capturing slaves through force. See, e.g., Andrés Reséndez, *The Other Slavery: The Uncovered Story of Indian Enslavement in America* (Boston: Houghton Mifflin, 2016), 3; Harald Prins and Bunny McBride, *Asticou's Island Domain: Wabanaki Peoples at Mount Desert Island 1500–2000, Acadia National Park Ethnographic Overview and Assessment* (Boston: Northeast Region Ethnography Program National Park Service, 2007), 1:2, 17–18; Reuben G. Thwaites, ed., *The Jesuit Relations and Allied Documents: Travel and Explorations of the Jesuit Missionaries in New France, 1610–1791*, 3:89–91; Smith, *Travels and Works*, 2:720; Daniel Gookin, *Historical Collections of the Indians in New England* (New York: Arno Press, 1972), 22.

31. Bradford, *History of Plymouth Plantation*, 1:155–156.

32. At least some of the English promoters of colonization understood that such conduct undermined their goals. See James Phinney Baxter, ed., *Sir Ferdinando Gorges and His Province of Main*, vol. 2 (Boston: Prince Society, 1890), 20.

33. Gookin, *Historical Collections*, 7–9; Prins and McBride, *Asticou's Island Domain*, 1:1–2.

34. See, e.g., Charles Banks, *The History of Martha's Vineyard*, vol. 1 (Boston: George H. Dean, 1911), 68; Roger Williams, *Collections of the Rhode Island Historical Society*, vol. 1 (Providence: John Miller, 1827), 18.

35. Prins and McBride, *Asticou's Island Domain*, 1:17.

36. Neal Salisbury, *Manitou and Providence: Indians, Europeans, and the Making of New England, 1500–1643* (New York: Oxford University Press, 1982), 41.

37. Salisbury, *Manitou and Providence*, 41.

38. Prins and McBride, *Asticou's Island Domain*, 1:17.

39. Salisbury, *Manitou and Providence*, 41–42.

40. Arthur Phillips, *The Phillips History of Fall River* (New York: Dover Press, 1944), 14; see also Samuel C. Drake, *Biography and History of the Indians of North America* (Boston: Antiquarian Institute, 1837), 18.

41. Bradford, *History of Plymouth Plantation*, 1:210; Virginia Baker, *Massasoit's Town Sowams in Pokanoket, Its History, Legends and Traditions* (Miami: HardPress Publishing, 1904), 6. See also Lucien Carr, "Notes on the Crania of New England Indians," in *Anniversary Memoirs*

of the Boston Society of Natural History (Boston: Boston Society of Natural History, 1880), 3; Rebecca Fraser, *The Mayflower: The Families, the Voyage, and the Founding of America* (New York: St. Martin's Press, 2017), 67–68; Philbrick, *Mayflower*, 48.

42. Salisbury, *Manitou and Providence*, 42.

43. Phillips, *Phillips History*, 14.

44. Salisbury, *Manitou and Providence*, 69.

45. Salisbury, 105; Herbert Sylvester, *Indian Wars of New England*, vol. 1 (Cleveland: Arthur H. Clark, 1910), 132–134.

46. Sylvester, *Indian Wars of New England*, 1:173–174.

47. Schneider, *Enduring Shore*, 9–10.

48. Levermore, *Forerunners and Competitors*, 1:32–33, 45.

49. Levermore, 1:37–38, 47–48, 53.

50. Levermore, 1:60.

51. Levermore, 1:62.

52. Levermore, 1:63.

53. Levermore, 1:63–64.

54. Levermore, 1: 66–67.

55. Henry Burrage, ed., *Rosier's Relation of Waymouth's Voyage to the Coast of Maine, 1605* (Portland, ME: Stephen Berry Press, 1887), 82, 86, 109–111.

56. Burrage, *Rosier's Relation*, 112–113, 117–118, 121–122.

57. Burrage, 127–129.

58. Burrage, 129.

59. See, e.g., Somerset Fry, *History of Ireland*, 128, where several Irish "lads had been lured onto a ship carrying cargo of wine and encouraged to sample it. They drank too much and found themselves locked into their cabin and the ship underway; they were being taken as hostages . . . and spent the next three years half-starved and in chains . . . [along] with about thirty other teenagers and children, some as young as ten."

60. If the English sailor who'd investigated the Abenaki encampment was not lying about the number of Abenaki warriors at the encampment, that they were armed and waiting and trying to maneuver the Englishmen into a narrow creek from which escape would be difficult, then it seems as though both the locals and the explorers had undertaken an elaborate dance of fraud and pretense, each side trying to manipulate the other in order to gain advantage and exact some kind of nefarious toll.

61. Burrage, *Rosier's Relation*, 131.

62. Burrage, 150.

63. Burrage, 39–40.

64. Burrage, 51.

65. Schneider, *Enduring Shore*, 44.

66. Charles C. Mann, *1491: New Revelations of the Americas Before Columbus* (New York: Vintage Books, 2011), 54; B. F. De Costa, "Plymouth Before the Pilgrims," *Magazine of American History* 8, no. 2 (1882): 813.

67. Schneider, *Enduring Shore*, 45–46.

68. Schneider, 46–47; see also J. Franklin Jameson, ed., *Voyages of Samuel de Champlain 1604–1618* (New York: Charles Scribner's Sons, 1907), 99.

69. Schneider, *Enduring Shore*, 47.

70. Schneider, 43.

71. John Smith, "The Generall Historie of Virginia, New-England, and the Summer Isles," in *Captain John Smith*, 589; Schneider, *Enduring Shore*, 43–44.

72. Smith, "Generall Historie of Virginia," 593.

73. Banks, *History of Martha's Vineyard*, 1:69.

74. Smith, "Generall Historie of Virginia," 593.

75. Banks, *History of Martha's Vineyard*, 1:70; see also Prince, *Chronological History*, 1:185, expressing that the Nauset were particularly "incensed against the English."

76. Thomas Weston, *History of the Town of Middleboro, Massachusetts 1669–1905* (Boston: Houghton, Mifflin), 1n2. Other members of the Wampanoag Confederation were the Pocaset at Rehoboth, Swansea, and Tiverton, the Saconet at Little Comptom, the Nemasket at Middleboro, the Agawan at Wareham, the Manomet at Sandwich, the Sakatucket at Mashpee, the Mattakee as Barnstable, the Nobsquasset at Yarmouth, the Monamoy at Chatham, and the natives on Martha's Vineyard and Nantucket.

77. See, e.g., Smith, *Travels and Works*, 2:698.

78. Smith, *Travels and Works*, 2:697–699; James A. Clifton, ed., *Invented Indian: Cultural Fictions & Government Policies* (New Brunswick, NJ: Transaction Publishers, 2007), 73.

79. James Phinney Baxter, ed., *Sir Ferdinando Gorges and His Province of Maine*, vol. 1 (Boston: The Prince Society, 1890), 209–210.

80. Smith, *Travels and Works*, 2:699.

81. Schneider, *Enduring Shore*, 66.

82. See, e.g., Drake, *Biography and History*, 8: "It is said that it was chiefly owing to [Hunt's] perfidy that the Indians of New England were become so hostile to the voyagers." One contemporary feared of "a war now new begun between the inhabitants of those parts and us." Baxter, *Sir Ferdinando Gorges*, 1:211. John Smith echoed the unease in 1615, noting that Hunt's actions "move[d] their hate against our nation." John Smith, "A Description of New England," in *Captain John Smith*, 162.

83. Bradford, *History of Plymouth Plantation*, 1:210.

84. Phinehas Pratt, *A Declaration of the Affairs of the English People That First Inhabited New England* (Boston: T. R. Marvin & Son, 1858), 8.

85. Pratt, *Declaration*, 8–9.

86. Baxter, *Sir Ferdinando Gorges*, 2:29, 212.

87. Purchas, *Purchas His Pilgrimes*, 19:129.

88. Purchas, 19:130.

89. Bradford, *History of Plymouth Plantation*, 1:206–208. "Their desire of revenge was occasioned by an English man, who having many of them on board [his ship], made a great slaughter with their murderers [small cannon used on ships to clear the decks of enemy if

a ship is boarded] and small shot, when as (they say) they offered no injury on their parts. Whether they were English or no, it may be doubted, yet they believe they were [English]."

90. Bradford, 1:208.

91. Purchas, *Purchas His Pilgrimes*, 1:131, 276. See also Alexander Young, *Chronicles of the Pilgrim Fathers of the Colony of Plymouth, from 1602 to 1625* (Boston: Charles C. Little and James Brown, 1844), 190n3; E. J. Chandler, *Ancient Sagadahoc* (San Jose, CA: Authors Choice Press, 2000), 49.

92. See Dexter, *Mourt's Relation*, 84, where Samoset tells the Pilgrims that his homeland is one "day's sail with a great wind," a fact he'd have known only by passage via an English or French sailing vessel, as the canoes of the native people of coastal New England at the time did not have that capability.

93. Purchas, *Purchas His Pilgrimes*, 19:131–132.

94. Purchas, 19:132.

95. The date of Dermer's departure would appear to have been at the very end of June or beginning of July, based upon the date of the last letter he wrote from America before he died. William Bradford had a copy of Dermer's June 30, 1620, letter, and his reference to it is all that is known about its contents. The date of the letter and the fact that it was carried to someone in England implies that Dermer completed it while in Jamestown, which was then still the only viable colony in the New World.

96. Bradford, *History of Plymouth Plantation*, 1:209.

97. Baxter, *Sir Ferdinando Gorges*, 2:29; see also Schneider, *Enduring Shore*, 73.

98. Bradford, *History of Plymouth Plantation*, 1:209–210.

99. Bradford, 1:210. Bradford was explicit when writing of all the reasons why Massasoit and the Wampanoag proceeded very cautiously with regard to the new immigrants from England: "These thing[s] were partly the reason why they [i.e., the Wampanoag] kept aloof and were so long before they came to the English [i.e., the Pilgrims at Plymouth Colony]."

100. Purchas, *Purchas His Pilgrimes*, 19:129.

101. It was a natural cycle, albeit cataclysmic, that had played out time after time in different geographic areas throughout the history of humanity where different peoples came into contact via trade and exploration. See Jared Diamond, *Guns, Germs, and Steel* (New York: W. W. Norton, 1999), 205–206. A smallpox epidemic killed millions of Roman citizens over a period of fifteen years. The bubonic plague pandemic known as the Black Death killed an estimated 30 to 60 percent of Europe's total population over the course of about twenty years—killing between seventy-five and two hundred million people in Europe and Asia combined. What happened centuries before to Rome, Asia, and Europe unfolded in the sixteenth century in New England's coastal societies.

102. Salisbury, *Manitou and Providence*, 103.

103. Purchas, *Purchas His Pilgrimes*, 19:129–130.

104. Thomas Morton, *The New English Canaan* (Boston: Prince Society, 1883), 132–133.

105. S. F. Cook, *The Indian Population of New England in the Seventeenth Century* (Berkeley: University of California Press, 1976), 31.

106. Bradford, *History of Plymouth Plantation*, 1:220; see also Dexter, *Mourt's Relation*, 103, where Edward Winslow and Stephen Hopkins described in their own words the horrors that they witnessed in the summer of 1621 on their journey to Pokanoket to visit Massasoit, where land that had been cleared for farming and signs of former habitation was desolate; see also Young, *Chronicles*, 183n3.

107. Salisbury, *Manitou and Providence*, 105.

108. Phillips, *The Phillips History of Fall River*, 14; Salisbury, *Manitou and Providence*, 105.

109. John Smith, "New England Trials," in *Captain John Smith*, 184: "God had laid this country open for us." See also Gookin, *Historical Collections*, 8; Morton, *New English Canaan*, 132–133; Morton, *New England's Memorial*, 44.

110. Bradford, *History of Plymouth Plantation*, 1:254.

111. Smith, *Travels and Works*, 2:933; see also Pratt, *Declaration*, 8; Morton, *New England's Memorial*, 44.

112. Adams, *New England Canaan*, 6–7.

113. Morton, *New England's Memorial*, 37–38.

114. Salisbury, *Manitou and Providence*, 106: "The fear that they had been rendered spiritually powerless was one response which enabled the [Native American] survivors to understand their plight in familiar terms."

6. Finding Plymouth Rock

1. Dexter, *Mourt's Relation*, 10.

2. As mentioned earlier, red cedar would have been unknown to the Englishmen, for it was only introduced into England in 1664. See Sargent, *Silva of North America*, 10:95.

3. Dexter, *Mourt's Relation*, 11.

4. Dexter, 11.

5. Philbrick, *Mayflower*, 46; Dexter, *Mourt's Relation*, 11–12; Bradford, *History of Plymouth Plantation*, 1:162.

6. Dexter, *Mourt's Relation*, 12.

7. Bradford, *History of Plymouth Plantation*, 1:162.

8. Dexter, *Mourt's Relation*, 5.

9. Prince, *A Chronological History*, 1:73; see also Dexter, *Mourt's Relation*, 27: "We could neither go to, nor come from, the shore but at high water, which was much to our hindrance and hurt, for oftentimes they waded to the middle of the thigh and oft to the knees to go and come from land. Some did it necessarily and some for their own pleasure, but it brought to the most, if not all, coughs and colds, the weather proving suddenly cold and stormy, which afterward turned to scurvy, whereof many died."

10. Bradford, *History of Plymouth Plantation*, 1:162.

11. Dexter, *Mourt's Relation*, 13, 13n37. The armor was called a corselet, a heavy piece of metal covering that protected the chest. Seventeenth-century muskets were cumbersome weapons that weighed about twenty pounds, so heavy that the musketeer often used a stand on

which to rest the barrel because a man couldn't hold the four-foot-long iron barrel steady simply with his hand.

12. Dexter, 13–14.

13. Dexter, 43–45. Hopkins's selection lends support to the possibility that he played a role in mediating the insurrection itself. Until this point, Hopkins had not been not mentioned in the accounts written by the Pilgrims. For him to jump onto the pages at this consequential moment implies that he might have been an active participant in the events immediately preceding it, which were dominated by the formation of the Mayflower Compact.

14. Dexter, *Mourt's Relation*, 10n32.

15. Dexter, 15, 15n44.

16. David Bushnell, "The Treatment of Indians in Plymouth Colony," in *New England Encounters: Indians and Euroamericans 1600–1850*, ed. Alden T. Vaughan (Boston: Northeastern University Press, 1999), 60.

17. Bradford, *History of Plymouth Plantation*, 1:162–164; see also Dexter, *Mourt's Relation*, 15: "they marched after [the Nauset] into the woods lest other of the *Indians* should lie in ambush."

18. Bradford, *History of Plymouth Plantation*, 1:162–164.

19. See, e.g., Dexter, *Mourt's Relation*, 111, which shows that Hopkins was able to engage in conversations with the natives that lived in the Massachusetts area that included rather abstract topics such as discourtesy, thievery, sin, and the punishment of God. See also chapter 1, note 89.

20. Dexter, *Mourt's Relation*, 15n46.

21. Bradford, *History of Plymouth Plantation*, 1:164.

22. Dexter, *Mourt's Relation*, 16.

23. Dexter, 17.

24. Dexter, 17–18.

25. Dexter, 18–19.

26. Dexter, 19, 19n63.

27. Dexter, 19–20.

28. Dexter, 20–21.

29. Bradford, *History of Plymouth Plantation*, 1:165.

30. Dexter, *Mourt's Relation*, 21–22.

31. Dexter, 22.

32. Dexter, 22.

33. Dexter, 22.

34. Dexter, 23–24. Matchlock muskets, which predated flintlock muskets, relied on a slow-burning match cord to ignite the charge of the firearm. Pulling the trigger caused an arm holding the burning tip of the match cord to swing down upon the firing pan, which would have been loaded with a small amount of gunpowder. Once ignited, the charge in the firing pan would kindle the larger charge of gunpowder loaded into the bottom of the

gun's barrel, which in turn would explode, sending the lead ball racing down and out the barrel at high velocity.

35. Dexter, *Mourt's Relation*, 24–25.

36. Dexter, 27.

37. Dexter, 27–28.

38. That Stephen Hopkins participated in the Second Exploration is implied by a discussion that took place on November 30 over a grave that the Pilgrims discovered. The remains showed yellow hair and one of those involved in the discussion explained that Native Americans had black hair. Such a universal characterization would be known only to someone who'd spent substantial time America, as Hopkins alone among the Pilgrims had.

39. Dexter, *Mourt's Relation*, 28–29.

40. Dexter, 29–30.

41. Dexter, 30.

42. See Dexter, 31: "We knew not how we should find or meet with any of the Indians, except it be to do us a mischief."

43. Dexter, 30–31.

44. Bradford, *History of Plymouth Plantation*, 1:166.

45. Dexter, *Mourt's Relation*, 32.

46. Contacting the people of Cape Cod to communicate with them and to make "full satisfaction" to them for the corn was aligned with Hopkins's objective of establishing amiable relations.

47. Dexter, *Mourt's Relation*, 38–39.

48. Dexter, 38.

49. Dexter, 40.

50. Dexter, 39–40. The advocates for Agawom overstated the case, for Smith himself was rather equivocal of the harbor, both criticizing it and praising it in the space of a few sentences. Smith, "Description of New England," 148.

51. Dexter, 40.

52. Bradford, *History of Plymouth Plantation*, 1:167n1; Dexter, *Mourt's Relation*, 41.

53. Prince, *Chronological History*, 1:76.

54. Dexter, *Mourt's Relation*, 41–42.

55. Bradford, *History of Plymouth Plantation*, 1:167–168.

56. Dexter, *Mourt's Relation*, 42.

57. Dexter, 45.

58. Dexter, 45n61.

59. Gregory A. Zielinski and Barry D. Keim, *New England Weather, New England Climate* (Hanover: University Press of New England, 2003), 169–170, 173, 178, 181–182.

60. Sebastian Junger, *The Perfect Storm* (New York: W. W. Norton, 2009), 223.

61. Dexter, *Mourt's Relation*, 45–47.

62. Dexter, 46–48.

63. Dexter, 49–50.

64. Bradford, *History of Plymouth Plantation*, 1:170; Dexter, *Mourt's Relation*, 51.

65. Dexter, *Mourt's Relation*, 51.
66. Bradford, *History of Plymouth Plantation*, 1:170; Dexter, *Mourt's Relation*, 51–52.
67. Dexter, *Mourt's Relation*, 52.
68. Dexter, 54–55.
69. Dexter, 53; Bradford, *History of Plymouth Plantation*, 1:171.
70. Dexter, *Mourt's Relation*, 52–53.
71. Strachey, "True Reportory," 1019, 1030.
72. Dexter, *Mourt's Relation*, 53.
73. Bradford, *History of Plymouth Plantation*, 1:171.
74. Dexter, *Mourt's Relation*, 53.
75. Dexter, 53–55.
76. Dexter, 56.
77. Bradford, *History of Plymouth Plantation*, 1:173; Dexter, *Mourt's Relation*, 56.
78. Dexter, *Mourt's Relation*, 56–57.
79. Bradford, *History of Plymouth Plantation*, 1:173–174.
80. Dexter, *Mourt's Relation*, 57–58.
81. Bradford, *History of Plymouth Plantation*, 1:174–176; Dexter, *Mourt's Relation*, 59.
82. Dexter, *Mourt's Relation*, 59.
83. Prince, *Chronological History*, 1:76; Dexter, *Mourt's Relation*, 60n205 continued from prior page.
84. See, e.g., Doherty, *William Bradford: Rock of Plymouth*, 73.
85. Doherty, *William Bradford*, 73.
86. Prince, *A Chronological History*, 1:76.
87. Bradford, *History of Plymouth Plantation*, 1:177.
88. Dexter, *Mourt's Relation*, 60.
89. The one at which the explorers had sheltered is now called Clark's Island for the name of the sailor in the shallop who'd first stepped ashore. Dexter, 58, 58n198. The second island, Saquish Head, is now no longer an island, as time and the powers of wind and sea have raised a neck of land that connects it to the long peninsula protecting the northeastern part of Plymouth Bay. Dexter, 60n209.
90. Dexter, 59, 59n203.
91. Dexter, 61–63.
92. Dexter, 63–64.
93. Dexter, 63–65.
94. Dexter, 64.
95. See John A. Goodwin, *The Pilgrim Republic: An Historical Review of the Colony of New Plymouth* (Boston: Houghton, Mifflin, 1899), 100: "Of course this first site examined would be that which had been approved on December 21st by Governor Carver, Captain Standish, and Masters Bradford, Winslow, Warren, and Hopkins; for the decision of such men would have received the first and fullest consideration."
96. Bradford, *History of Plymouth Plantation*, 1:167–168.

97. Dexter, *Mourt's Relation*, 64.
98. Dexter, 65, and see 65n236.
99. Strachey, "True Reportory," 1026.
100. Dexter, *Mourt's Relation*, 69; Prince, *Chronological History*, 1:80.
101. See, e.g., Willison, *Saints and Strangers*, 1.

7. A Deadly, Discontented Winter

1. John Smith, *Travels and Works of Captain John Smith*, ed. Edward Arber, vol. 1 (Edinburgh: John Grant, 1910), 259; Smith, *Travels and Works*, 2:749, 941.
2. Smith, "Advertisements," in *Captain John Smith*, 794, 796.
3. New England was much colder in the seventeenth and eighteenth centuries than today. See Fischer, *Albion's Seed*, 52.
4. Dexter, *Mourt's Relation*, 65–66.
5. Prince, *Chronological History*, 1:80.
6. Dexter, *Mourt's Relation*, 65.
7. Dexter, 66.
8. Dexter, 65–66.
9. A twenty-five foot trunk of an oak tree with a twenty-four-inch diameter can weigh over five thousand pounds. A similar length trunk of a pine tree with a twelve inch diameter can weigh nearly a thousand pounds.
10. Prince, *A Chronological History*, 1:93.
11. Dexter, *Mourt's Relation*, 66.
12. Matthew 12:1–8, King James Version.
13. Dexter, *Mourt's Relation*, 66.
14. Prince, *Chronological History*, 1:80; Dexter, *Mourt's Relation*, 66n241.
15. Philbrick, *Mayflower*, 81.
16. Dexter, *Mourt's Relation*, 66.
17. Bradford, *History of Plymouth Plantation*, 1:177.
18. Prince, *A Chronological History*, 1:80.
19. Dexter, *Mourt's Relation*, 72.
20. Philbrick, *Mayflower*, 82.
21. Dexter, *Mourt's Relation*, 67.
22. Dexter, 67–68, also see 67n244.
23. Doherty, *William Bradford*, 29.
24. Dexter, *Mourt's Relation*, 72.
25. Dexter, 68.
26. Philbrick, *Mayflower*, 84.
27. Dexter, *Mourt's Relation*, 68–69, and see 69n249.
28. Prince, *Chronological History*, 1:80.
29. Dexter, *Mourt's Relation*, 69, see 69n252; Prince, *Chronological History*, 1:96.
30. Dexter, *Mourt's Relation*, 70.

31. Doherty, *William Bradford*, 114.
32. William Hubbard, *A General History of New England from the Discovery to 1680* (Boston: Charles C. Little and James Brown, 1848), 111; see also Henry Johnson, *The Exploits of Myles Standish* (New York: D. Appleton, 1897), 12–13; Willison, *Saints and Strangers*, 131.
33. Strachey, "True Reportory," 1002.
34. Dexter, *Mourt's Relation*, 70.
35. Dexter, 70.
36. Prince, *A Chronological History*, 1:96.
37. Young, *Chronicles*, 173.
38. Dexter, *Mourt's Relation*, 72. Despite the frost and foul weather, it could have been much worse for the Pilgrims. While the temperature had plummeted below freezing several times during their explorations of Cape Cod and even resulted in blizzard-like conditions during parts of the nor'easter, the winter since then had been fairly mild when compared to the norms for the region. Young, *Chronicles*, 105n1. For example, Plymouth Harbor usually froze from Christmas to March, turning along with its shoreline into "an expense of ice and snow," a fact that would have severely hampered—if not rendered impossible—the ability of the colonists to journey to and from the *Mayflower* at its anchorage so distant from the embarkation point on Plymouth Rock. Young, *Chronicles*, 173n5.
39. Dexter, *Mourt's Relation*, 72–73.
40. Dexter, 73–74.
41. Dexter, 74–76. The shoes of one of them had to be cut off because his feet "were so swelled with cold, and it was a long while after ere he was able to [walk again]."
42. Dexter, 76–78.
43. Prince, *Chronological History*, 1:97–98.
44. Dexter, *Mourt's Relation*, 79.
45. Dexter, 55, 79.
46. Dexter, 79–80.
47. Dexter, 80.
48. Dexter, 80.
49. Dexter, 80–81.
50. Dexter, 81.
51. Dexter, 81.
52. There are at least two reasons for this conclusion. First, he was the soldier and therefore would have had more familiarity and better expertise with the weapon. Second, the weapon was likely Standish's "snaphance" musket, which was of higher quality and better reliability of Hopkins's matchlock musket. See Dexter, 52.
53. Dexter, 81.
54. Dexter, 81.
55. Dexter, 81.
56. Dexter, 81–82, and see 81nn288–289.
57. Dexter, 81.

58. See, e.g., Henri de Tonti, *An Account of Monsieur de la Salle's Last Expedition and Discoveries in North America* (London: J. Tonson, 1698), 8–9: Native Americans "proclaim . . . war by great outcries, or rather dreadful howlings." This strong probability is supported by the fact that at around the same time Massasoit convened an important religious ceremony to try via spiritual compulsion to expel the English.

59. See, e.g., Strachey, "True Reportory," 1019, where the Powhatan sent envoys to the fort at Jamestown under the auspices of potential trade "when indeed they came as but spies to discover our strength."

60. Prince, *Chronological History*, 1:98.

61. Young, *Chronicles*, 181n3.

62. Prince, *Chronological History*, 1:98.

63. Prince, 1:99.

64. Taylor, *American Colonies*, 18.

65. Taylor, 18.

66. Williams, *Collections*, 1:95, 110, 112; Lucianne Lavin, *Connecticut's Indigenous Peoples: What Archeology, History, and Oral Traditions Teach Us About Their Communities and Cultures* (New Haven: Yale University Press, 2013), 282–284.

67. Taylor, *American Colonies*, 18.

68. Bradford, *History of Plymouth Plantation*, 1:211–212.

69. Williams, *Collections*, 1:111.

70. Gookin, *Historical Collections*, p. 14.

71. Williams, *Collections*, 1:111–112.

72. Bradford, *History of Plymouth Plantation*, 1:211–212.

73. Williams, *Collections*, 1:121.

74. Bradford, *History of Plymouth Plantation*, 1:211–212.

75. Hubbard, *A General History*, 60.

76. Bradford, *History of Plymouth Plantation*, 1:193–194, and see 194n1; Bradford, 2:405.

77. Bradford, 1:194–196.

78. Bradford, 1:196, and see 196n2.

79. Pratt, *Declaration*, 17; Philbrick, *Mayflower*, 90; Bowman, *Mayflower Descendant*, 2:76.

80. Pratt, *Declaration*, 7.

81. Goodwin, *The Pilgrim Republic*, 114.

82. Bradford, *History of Plymouth Plantation*, 1:194.

83. Bradford, 1:196–198.

84. Bradford, 1:197.

85. Bradford, 1:192–193.

86. Prince, *Chronological History*, 1:103; Joseph Sawyer, *History of the Pilgrims and Puritans* (New York: Century History, 1922), 2:315.

87. Bradford, *History of Plymouth Plantation*, 1:193.

88. Prince, *Chronological History*, 1:103. In the summer of 1630 John Billington killed his English neighbor, shooting him down in cold blood. He was executed in September of that year.

Philbrick, *Mayflower*, 175. Bradford, *History of Plymouth Plantation*, 1:395 n1. William Bradford's 1625 description of Billington turned out to be prescient: "he is a knave, and so will live and die."

89. Bradford, *History of Plymouth Plantation*, 1:198–199, 208.

90. Bradford, 1:208.

91. Bradford, 1:210.

92. Charles Francis Adams Jr., ed., *The New England Canaan of Thomas Morton* (Boston: Prince Society, 1883), 123, 161, 163–164. When Morton returned to New England in 1625 he started his own settlement on Massachusetts Bay in what is now Quincy, Massachusetts, where he opened trading relations with the local Massachusett people. Adams, *New England Canaan*, 9; Bradford, *History of Plymouth Plantation*, 2:48–49; see also Adams, *New England Canaan*, 17.

93. See Purchas, *Purchas His Pilgrimes*, 19:130, where Dermer recounted that Massasoit answered the Englishman's many questions.

94. In so doing, Massasoit was employing the very same strategy that the Powhatan had done at Jamestown. See Strachey, "True Reportory," 1019. That Massasoit held the Pilgrims as enemies is supported by the context of the situation of March 1621. To this point the Wampanoag had never taken any action that could be considered as welcoming of the Pilgrims or their settlement. In fact, the only recorded acts supported the tone that the Nauset had set on Cape Cod. Massasoit had tried to curse the Pilgrims. He'd set a trap to ambush them. His people stole any English tools that they came across. He perceived them as enemies, who'd perhaps come to take revenge for the deaths of Dermer's men.

95. Hubbard, *General History*, 58.

8. Samoset and the Spring Thaw

1. Dexter, *Mourt's Relation*, 82–84.

2. Dexter, 83.

3. Prince, *A Chronological History*, 1:99.

4. Dexter, *Mourt's Relation*, 84.

5. James Phinney Baxter, *Christopher Levett of York* (Portland, ME: Gorges Society, 1893), 117.

6. Dexter, *Mourt's Relation*, 83–85.

7. Edward Winslow, *Good News from New England* (London: I.D. for William Bladen and John Bellamie, 1624), 60–61.

8. See, e.g., Young, *Chronicles*, 183n2: "It is difficult to conceive how they could converse together so as to be mutually understood." See also Vaughan, "Namontack's Itinerant Life," 196: "English and Algonquian interpreters struggled for several decades to translate a mostly oral language into an alphabet-based language, and vice versa, in the absence in the early years of bilingual texts."

9. Dexter, *Mourt's Relation*, 84, 99–100. The horseman's coat was likely the same red coat that Stephen Hopkins and Edward Winslow later presented to Massasoit when the two

visited the Wampanoag sachem in the summer of 1621, the idea for which gift came from Hopkins's experience at Jamestown.

10. Dexter, *Mourt's Relation*, 85.

11. Prince, *A Chronological History*, 1:103.

12. Dexter, *Mourt's Relation*, 85.

13. Baxter, *Christopher Levett of York*, 117.

14. Dexter, *Mourt's Relation*, 85.

15. The order of the various topics recorded in Bradford's *Of Plymouth Plantation* and in *Mourt's Relation* should be trusted as a guide to the sequence of events, as they are corroborated by Thomas Prince, the early eighteenth-century history noted for his accuracy. When chronicling the history of the Pilgrims he not only used primary sources such as *Mourt's Relation* and *Of Plymouth Plantation* but also had access to and relied upon handwritten notes and volumes by William Bradford that have since been lost. Prince, *Chronological History*, 1:vi–viii. In pages 99–100, Prince specifically notes that the details about the Nauset encounter with the Pilgrims and their prior conflict with Dermer and Hunt all took place on March 17, the morning after he'd appeared in the settlement, which corroborates the sequence in *Mourt's Relation*.

16. Dexter, *Mourt's Relation*, 84.

17. Dexter, 85–86.

18. Dexter, 83–84.

19. Bradford, *History of Plymouth Plantation*, 1:199.

20. Adams, *New England Canaan*, 244.

21. Morton confused the roles of Samoset and Squanto. See, e.g., Adams, *New England Canaan*, 244n2. Some modern historians have given credence to Morton's assertion that Massasoit held a prisoner during the first winter of the Pilgrims. See, e.g., Salisbury, *Manitou and Providence*, 108, maintaining that it was Squanto rather than Samoset who was Massasoit's captive, an assertion that both contradicts Morton's statement that the captive was the first visitor to the Pilgrims, which clearly was Samoset and not Squanto, and runs against the politics of the confederacy that Massasoit maintained. Why would he imprison Squanto, a man from Patuxet who belonged to the Wampanoag Confederacy, yet let roam free Samoset, a man from a distant land and a distant clan and nation?

22. Several factors seem to support Morton's assertion. First, while available evidence points to the fact that Samoset freely chose in 1619 to accompany Squanto back to Patuxet from Maine, by the time he walked into Plymouth and greeted the English settlers, Samoset had been in Massasoit's domain for some eight months. This would have been an extraordinarily long time for a man to be away from his kin, especially a sagamore like Samoset, for tribal leadership particularly relied on personal ability and charisma to maintain stability among the various families and factions. Dexter, *Mourt's Relation*, 84; Salisbury, *Manitou and Providence*, 42. Second, when he approached the English settlers he carried a bow but only two arrows, one of which was headed with an arrow tip, the other of which was simply a feathered shaft. Dexter, *Mourt's Relation*, 84. Such a strange and limited armament

would have been unusual for a man so far away from his own people, with five days of overland travel through the territories of rival clans who might mean him harm. Prins and McBride, *Asticou's Island Domain*, 1:2. Third, he ultimately divulged information of high military value, telling the settlers how many warriors were at the disposal of Massasoit and the Nauset on Cape Cod. Dexter, *Mourt's Relation*, 85–86. If Samoset were *not* a captive of Massasoit, and thus friendly with the Wampanoag sachem, why would he share such sensitive intelligence? It seems more likely that Samoset shared the information in order to try to curry favor with the English.

23. Samoset knew of Thomas Hunt's kidnapping of several Nauset and Patuxet men. See Dexter, *Mourt's Relation*, 86.

24. Dexter, *Mourt's Relation*, 85. Why did Samoset refuse to leave Plymouth? A logical explanation is that he feared English kidnapping less than returning to the control of Massasoit. It was only after the apparent breakthrough with Hopkins that Samoset willingly left the colonists, which might imply that he'd been encouraged by Hopkins's words that the English wanted peace with Massasoit. Samoset probably recognized that with the English as an ally, Massasoit's influence in the region would greatly increase. He therefore likely believed that bringing such an offer from the English to the Wampanoag leader would not only ensure his freedom but also might win himself significant prestige.

25. Dexter, 87.

26. Prins and McBride, *Asticou's Island Domain*, 1:115–116.

27. Levett was associated with the efforts of Sir Ferdinando Gorges to colonize Maine and spurred on, in part, by "the achievement of the brave men who had successfully established themselves at Plymouth." See Baxter, *Christopher Levett of York*, 11–12.

28. Baxter, *Christopher Levett of York*, 104.

29. Baxter, 101–102.

30. Henry Burrage, *The Beginnings of Colonial Maine 1602–1658* (Portland, ME: Marks Printing House, 1914), 172n2. "His name appears in early records as above [i.e., as "Somerset"], and is also written Samoset, Samosett, Sameset, Sammerset, Sammeset, etc."

31. See, Baxter, *Christopher Levett of York*, 112.

32. See, e.g., Hubbard, *A General History*, 58.

33. See, e.g., Salisbury, *Manitou and Providence*, 114.

34. Salisbury, 114. This theory also doesn't adequately explain the timing of Massasoit's approach to the Pilgrims. Why did he chose this point in time for the sudden change in demeanor? The Pilgrims were at their absolute weakest in February and March. Dozens had died. Dozens more were dying. Though the settlers surreptitiously tried to bury their dead, it is likely that Massasoit's observers knew of at least some of the deaths, for it would have been difficult not to notice when the population was halved in such a short period. If Massasoit intended on making the English his allies simply because they could help him against the Narragansett, it would have made most sense for him to immediately embrace them when they arrived, so as to ally with them at their strongest. The extraordinary delay between the Pilgrims' arrival and Samoset's appearance in the settlement supports the other evidence

indicating that Massasoit desired the Pilgrims to leave his land right up until Samoset convinced him otherwise.

35. Bradford, *History of Plymouth Plantation*, 1:211–212

36. Dexter, *Mourt's Relation*, 87–88.

37. Dexter, 88–89.

38. It is possible that, despite all the demonstrations of animosity, Massasoit might have entertained the notion of an alliance with the English, but the evidence of his lack of readiness to pursue such a plan suggests that the option was only one of several strategies he had available to him, which is why he sent Samoset into Plymouth to learn more about their strength and their intentions. It could have been peace. It could have been war. It could have been a continuation of the current standoff. Momentum toward a formal peaceful accord didn't appear to begin until after Samoset's visit.

39. Dexter, *Mourt's Relation*, 88–89.

40. Dexter, 89.

41. Dexter, 89.

42. Bradford, *History of Plymouth Plantation*, 1:200n2 continuing from previous page.

43. Dexter, *Mourt's Relation*, 90.

44. For example, in Winslow's published journal entitled *Good News from New England*, Winslow described an incident in December 1621 or January 1622 when the sachem of the Narragansett sent a messenger to Plymouth bearing a bundle of arrows wrapped in a snakeskin. According to Winslow, Myles Standish gave charge of the messenger to "me and another." Hopkins was the second man. See Winslow, *Good News from New England*, 2–3; Bradford, *History of Plymouth Plantation*, 1:240–244, and particularly 241n1.

45. Two of the sailors from the *Mayflower* were onshore and followed some distance behind the two settlers. They were unarmed and perhaps trailed along merely to catch a closer glimpse of the natives. See Dexter, *Mourt's Relation*, 90.

46. Dexter, 90.

47. Dexter, 90–91.

48. Dexter, 91.

49. Philbrick, *Mayflower*, 96.

50. Dexter, *Mourt's Relation*, 91–92.

51. Dexter, 92–93. *Mourt's Relation* identifies Standish and a "master Williamson" as the two men who met Massasoit at Town Brook. There was no one named Williamson on the *Mayflower*. William Brewster's father was also named William and the use of "Williamson" for "William's son" was used for identification. For example, William Brewster's own son, whose name was Jonathan Brewster, was referred to as "Jonathan Williamson Bruster." See George Bowman, ed., *The Mayflower Descendant*, vol. 6 (Boston: Massachusetts Society of Mayflower Descendants, 1904), 58.

52. Stratton, *Plymouth Colony*, 311, 372.

53. Bradford, *History of Plymouth Plantation*, 1:167; Dexter, *Mourt's Relation*, 43–45.

54. See, e.g., Dexter, *Mourt's Relation*, 92, where Winslow's exchange on Watson's Hill with Massasoit was difficult because "the interpreters did not well express it."

55. Dexter, 93. As discussed in chapter 10, the estate of Stephen Hopkins contained a green rug. A survey of the surviving estate inventories of the *Mayflower* passengers revealed that only William Brewster and William Bradford appeared to have green rugs at that time. For Brewster, see Emma C. Brewster Jones, *The Brewster Genealogy*, vol. 1 (New York: Grafton Press, 1908), lxiii. For Bradford, see Bowman, *Mayflower Descendant*, 2:229. Assuming Brewster's house was even completed, since he was with Standish at Town Brook, it is improbable that his rug would have been used. Brewster had no adult servants with him and his children were young. Although it is likely that William Bradford was lodging with the Brewster family, he was unavailable since he was still bedridden from his prior injury. Thus, Hopkins, who was not otherwise engaged, was the most likely person to have pulled the green rug from his own home, along with a handful of cushions, and brought it to the unfinished home used for the negotiation of the peace treaty.

56. Dexter, *Mourt's Relation*, 93–94.

57. Strachey, "True Reportory," 1031.

58. Dexter, *Mourt's Relation*, 94.

59. Robert A. Williams, Jr., *Linking Arms Together: American Indian Treaty Visions of Law and Peace, 1600–1800* (New York: Routledge, 1999), 47–48; de Tonti, *An Account of Monsieur de la Salle's Last Expedition and Discoveries in North America*, 8–9: Native Americans "proclaim peace with the Calumet [i.e., peace pipe]"; Henry Rowe Schoolcraft, *History of the Indian Tribes of the United States* (Philadelphia: J. B. Lippincott, 1857), 88; see also Williams, *Collections*, 1:62, 75. It was, for example, the only crop that the men tended; all others were cultivated by women. See Williams, *Collections*, 1:35.

60. Dexter, *Mourt's Relation*, 91n317.

61. Dexter, 95–96.

62. Though the record is silent as to who hosted the two Native Americans, Stephen Hopkins was the only Englishman associated with hosting any of the native people at Plymouth during this critical time. Indeed, it had been less than one week since Samoset first walked into the colony. At that time, no Englishman would suffer the presence of the native overnight except for Hopkins. It is highly doubtful that the view of those in any of the other six Pilgrim households had changed in the interim period. While there is a possibility that the two natives slept outside amongst the buildings of Plymouth, that possibility is remote given that the firsthand account of *Mourt's Relation* states that the two men "stay all night **with us**," which implies a closeness of situation. See Dexter, *Mourt's Relation*, 95.

63. Dexter, *Mourt's Relation*, 91: Squanto had lived in London "in Cornhill with master John Slany," a London merchant. The Cornhill area is about half a mile from the area in which Hopkins lived at the time.

64. Prince, *Chronological History*, 1:103.

65. Dexter, *Mourt's Relation*, 96.

66. Bradford, *History of Plymouth Plantation*, 1:210.

67. Prince, *Chronological History*, 1:103–104.
68. Bradford, *History of Plymouth Plantation*, 1:215–216.
69. Prince, *A Chronological History*, 1:104.
70. Prince, 1:114–115; Philbrick, *Mayflower*, 84.
71. Bradford, *History of Plymouth Plantation*, 1:202–203.
72. Bradford, 1:202.
73. Adams, *Three Episodes*, 1:29. Squanto fell ill and died during a mission to trade for corn on Cape Cod, where relations remained problematic at times. Though William Bradford believed Squanto's death was from natural causes, he may have been poisoned in a plot masterminded by Massasoit, with whom Squanto had run afoul as a result of his pursuit of personal gain. See, Philbrick, *Mayflower*, 138.
74. Fraser, *Mayflower*, 90.
75. Bradford, *History of Plymouth Plantation*, 1:216.
76. Prince, *Chronological History*, 1:105.
77. Bradford, *History of Plymouth Plantation*, 1:216.
78. Dexter, *Mourt's Relation*, 98; Bradford, *History of Plymouth Plantation*, 1:219, and see 219n1.
79. Bradford, *History of Plymouth Plantation*, 1:219.
80. Dexter, *Mourt's Relation*, 98.
81. Bradford, *History of Plymouth Plantation*, 1:216–218, and see 216n4.
82. Stratton, *Plymouth Colony*, 311, 373.
83. Prince, *A Chronological History*, 1:106–107.
84. Dexter, *Mourt's Relation*, 104–105.
85. Fraser, *Mayflower*, 79.
86. Gookin, *Historical Collections*, 9–10; Baker, *Massasoit's Town Sowams in Pokanoket*, 4, 7.
87. Dexter, *Mourt's Relation*, 106.
88. Dexter, 99–100.
89. See Chapter 2, supra.
90. Dexter, *Mourt's Relation*, 99–100, 106; Bradford, *History of Plymouth Plantation*, 1:224.
91. Fraser, *Mayflower*, 79–80.
92. Dexter, *Mourt's Relation*, 107.
93. Dexter, 107.
94. Dexter, 107.
95. Dexter, 107.
96. De Tonti, *Account of Monsieur*, 8–9; Schoolcraft, *History of the Indian*, 88; see also Williams, *Collections*, 1:35, 62, 75.
97. Dexter, *Mourt's Relation*, 107–108.
98. Baxter, *Christopher Levett of York*, 117.
99. See, e.g., Burrage, *Rosier's Relation*, 112, 122; Purchas, *Purchas His Pilgrimes*, 19:326; Morton, *New English Canaan*, 16n2.
100. Dexter, *Mourt's Relation*, 107, 109.
101. Winslow, *Good News from New England*, 60–61.

102. Dexter, *Mourt's Relation*, 109-111.
103. Dexter, 110-111.
104. Dexter, 111.
105. Dexter, 111.
106. The possibility becomes probability when Hopkins's two servants—Edward Doty and Edward Leister—are factored in. With two adult males serving the household and tending the family's fields, Hopkins could afford to be absent on such excursions on behalf of the colony as a whole. Very few others in the settlement at this time had that luxury.
107. Bradford, *History of Plymouth Plantation*, 1:230.
108. Dexter, *Mourt's Relation*, 133.
109. Dexter, 133-135.

9. A Melancholy Unraveling

1. Bradford, *History of Plymouth Plantation*, 1:231.
2. Prince, *Chronological History*, 1:114-115.
3. Bradford, *History of Plymouth Plantation*, 1:231n3.
4. Winslow, *Good News*, 2-3; Bradford, *History of Plymouth Plantation*, 1:240-244, 241n1.
5. Prince, *Chronological History*, 1:116-120.
6. Sydney V. James Jr., *Three Visitors to Early Plymouth* (Bedford, MA: Applewood Books, 1963), 6.
7. Benjamin Trumbull, *A Complete History of Connecticut*, vol. 1 (New London, CT: H. D. Utley, 1898), v.
8. Trumbull, *Complete History*, 1:3. And see 47: "The English, on their first settlement at New-Plymouth, entered into such friendly treaties with some of the principal tribes, and conducted themselves with such justice, prudence and magnanimity towards them and the Indians in general, as had the most happy influence to preserve the peace of the country."
9. Philbrick, *Mayflower*, 136, 140.
10. Bradford, *History of Plymouth Plantation*, 1:296n1.
11. Philbrick, *Mayflower*, 162, 175.
12. Philbrick, 161.
13. See, e.g., Philbrick, *Mayflower*; Salisbury, *Manitou and Providence*.
14. Dexter, *Mourt's Relation*, xl.
15. Philbrick, *Mayflower*, 167. One of the reasons that Jamestown had suffered such severe losses during the Starving Time of the winter of 1609-1610 was the way the settlement was grounded upon a communal approach to production, where men were expected to labor in the settlement's fields and in return eat from centrally kept supplies. Purchas, *Purchas His Pilgrimes*, 19:95. In 1616 Thomas Dale scrapped the old system, putting in its place a system where men could retain the product of their labors. Production increased. Brown, *First Republic*, 226-227. The Pilgrims first tried the communal approach to food production, but changed after only two years, instead assigning a parcel of land to each family who would tend the land for their own use. As in Jamestown, the transition was successful.

Bradford was telling in his description of how the decision to change came about; namely, that he—as governor—"gave way" "after much debate" on the subject, and that in making his decision he was guided by "the advice of the chiefest amongst them," a group that no doubt would have included Stephen Hopkins. Bradford, *History of Plymouth Plantation*, 1:300.

16. Shurtleff, *Records of the Colony*, 1:5.

17. Young, *Chronicles*, 127n2 continued from previous page.

18. Shurtleff, *Records of the Colony*, 1:20, 36. Jane Warden (or as the surname was alternatively spelled, Worden) came to New England with a group of colonists assembled in London and led by Francis Stiles that were associated with the Massachusetts Bay Colony. They reached the settlement at Windsor in 1635. Unlike the Puritans who had come from Massachusetts Bay, the Stiles group were all Anglicans, even swearing an oath of conformity to the Church of England before departing London. Richard S. Ross III, *Before Salem: Witch Hunting in the Connecticut River Valley, 1647–1663* (Jefferson, NC: McFarland, 2017), 50; Trumbull, *Complete History*, 49; see also Francis Baylies, *An Historical Perspective of the Colony of New Plymouth* (Boston: Hilliard, Gray, Little, and Wilkins, 1830), 2:250; Bradford, *History of Plymouth Plantation*, 2:391n1.

19. Pulsifer, *Records of the Colony*, 11:8–9, 13.

20. Shurtleff, *Records of the Colony*, 1:41.

21. Edith Tisdale, *Genealogy of Col. Israel Tisdale and His Descendants* (Boston: Metcalf Press, 1909), 19. John Tisdale was not a wastrel. Perhaps because Hopkins was so prominent a personality in Plymouth, after the trial Tisdale immediately moved to Duxbury. Tisdale soon married and eventually had four sons and four daughters. Samuel Hopkins Emery, *History of Taunton, Massachusetts* (Syracuse, NY: D. Mason, 1893), 91. He became an ardent supporter of the colony and sought a martial role. By 1643, Tisdale was part of the militia for Duxbury. In 1645 he was elected constable of Duxbury, a position of "great respectability and honor," and served for several years. Tisdale, *Genealogy*, 19–20. Although Plymouth remained a small colony compared to the massive influx of people that expanded the influence of the Massachusetts Bay Colony, immigrants continued to trickle into Plymouth, which led to expansion. A group of settlers purchased land in 1638 from Massasoit in what is now called Taunton, Massachusetts. The town was situated along the very path that Hopkins and Winslow had traveled with Squanto in the summer of 1621 when they visited Massasoit to affirm the nascent treaty between the Wampanoag and the English. John Tisdale and his family were among the first settlers in Taunton, moving there in about 1650. Emery, *History of Taunton*, 28–29, 91; Tisdale, *Genealogy*, 20.

22. Tisdale, *Genealogy*, 19.

23. Shurtleff, *Records of the Colony*, 1:41–42.

24. William Hubbard, *A Narrative of the Indian Wars in New England* (Worcester, MA: Daniel Greenleaf, 1801), 17.

25. Alden T. Vaughan, "Indian-European Encounters in New England: An Annotated, Contextual Overview," in Vaughan, *New England Encounters*, 10.

26. Trumbull, *Complete History*, 32: "The Indians in general were quick of apprehension, ingenious, and when pleased nothing could exceed their courtesy and friendship. Gravity and eloquence distinguished them in council, address, and bravery in war. They were not more easily provoked than the English, but when once they had received an injury, it was never forgotten."

27. Fraser, *Mayflower*, 138, 141.

28. Ross, *Before Salem*, 49–50; Trumbull, *Complete History*, 50, 52, 53. Dutch colonists from Manhattan erected a trading outpost in Hartford that they called "Good Hope." G. H. Hollister, *The History of Connecticut, from the First Settlement of the Colony to the Adoption of the Present Constitution*, vol. 1 (New Haven, CT: Durrie and Peck, 1855), 18.

29. Fraser, *Mayflower*, 141; Hollister, *History of Connecticut*, 1:18; Ross, *Before Salem*, 50.

30. Fraser, *Mayflower*, 138; Steven T. Katz, "The Pequot War Reconsidered," in Vaughan, *New England Encounters*, 112; George Madison Bodge, *The Soldiers in King Philip's War*, 3rd ed. (Boston, printed for the author, 1906), 6; Trumbull, *Complete History*, 28.

31. Bernard Bailyn, *The Barbarous Years: The Conflict of Civilizations, 1600–1675* (New York: Alfred A. Knopf, 2012), 443; see also Morton, *New England's Memorial*, 120; Bradford, *History of Plymouth Plantation*, 2:233–234. The Pequot asserted that Stone had surprised two Pequot and bound them, demanding that they act as his guides on the Connecticut River. Other Pequot entered the English campsite at night, seeking to free their fellows. Several Englishmen were killed. The rest died when they fled to their pinnace which blew up in an explosion. The Bay Colony demanded that the Pequot deliver to Boston the men who'd killed Captain Stone. Bradford, *History of Plymouth Plantation*, 2:233. The disagreement remained an unresolved hazard to regional peace.

32. As an assistant to the governor, Hopkins would have remained informed about the colony's trading post in Connecticut. He and Jonathan Brewster, who was sending reports of the fluid situation, knew one another quite well. See, e.g., Shurtleff, *Records of the Colony*, 1:14, 31, 54, 61–62, 67. And Hopkins would have learned more about the region from Connecticut settler Jane Warden, the woman he was asked to help in January 1636. From Warden, Brewster, and Governor Winslow, Stephen Hopkins would have been kept abreast of the latest developments.

33. Bailyn, *Barbarous Years*, 10.

34. Bailyn, 443: "Skirmishes with the settlers were commonplace."

35. Tisdale, *Genealogy*, 20.

36. Nathaniel Shurtleff, ed., *Records of the Colony of New Plymouth in New England*, vol. 5 (Boston: William White, 1856), 73–74.

37. Tisdale, *Genealogy*, 20; Emery, *History of Taunton*, 91; Philip Ranlet, "Another Look at the Causes of King Philip's War," in Vaughan, *New England Encounters*, 148. In 1662, Massasoit's son Metacom—also known as King Philip—became chief sachem of the Wampanoag. Over the next ten years, relations began to sour, and by 1671 Wampanoag hostility toward the English, who'd continued to spread onto Wampanoag lands over the years, was near the incendiary point. The two sides tried to negotiate a new peace accord, but a dispute

quickly arose about the meaning of one of the terms. The English insisted that Metacom had agreed to have the Wampanoag to surrender all their firearms. Metacom insisted that he'd agreed to give up only the guns he and his men carried to the negotiations. Plymouth determined to confiscate all weapons, by force if necessary. Philip Ranlet, "Another Look at the Causes of King Philip's War," in Vaughan, *New England Encounters*, 138, 142, 143. John Tisdale was one of the leaders of the militia groups that threatened to march from village to village to seize weapons. The groups were based out of Tisdale's farm in Taunton, an English settlement located some twenty-four miles inland from Plymouth. Shurtleff, *Records of the Colony*, 5:73–74. While the attempt to disarm the Wampanoag didn't cause the subsequent conflict, it was the first of several missteps by the English as they "began blundering their way into a bloody war." Ranlet, "Another Look," 143.

38. See Bradford, *History of Plymouth Plantation*, 2:248, for William Bradford's assessment of the character of John Billington: "He and some of his had been often punished for miscarriages before, being one of the profanest families amongst [us]. They came from London, and I know not by what friends shuffled into [our] company."

39. Allyn Bailey Forbes, ed., *Winthrop Papers*, vol. 3, *1631-1637* (Boston: Massachusetts Historical Society, 1943), 270–271.

40. Fraser, *Mayflower*, 142–143.

41. Fraser, 143; Forbes, *Winthrop Papers*, 3:270; Hollister, *History of Connecticut*, 1:35.

42. Fraser, *Mayflower*, 143.

43. Katz, "Pequot War Reconsidered," in Vaughan, *New England Encounters*, 113; Bradford, *History of Plymouth Plantation*, 2:234–235.

44. Stratton, *Plymouth Colony*, 334.

45. Fraser, *Mayflower*, 143; Bradford, *History of Plymouth Plantation*, 2:234n3.

46. Hollister, *History of Connecticut*, 1:45–46. Oldham's head was split in half and his trunk and limbs brutally mangled.

47. Bradford, *History of Plymouth Plantation*, 2:235–236.

48. Fraser, *Mayflower*, 144.

49. John Winthrop, *The History of New England from 1630 to 1649*, ed. James Savage, vol. 1 (Boston: Phelps and Farnham, 1825), 192–196, 196n1.

50. Bradford, *History of Plymouth Plantation*, 2:242; Fraser, *Mayflower*, 144.

51. Winthrop, *History of New England*, 1:199, 218; Fraser, *Mayflower*, 144–145.

52. Fraser, *Mayflower*, 147.

53. Winthrop, *History of New England*, 218.

54. Shurtleff, *Records of the Colony*, 1: 60–61.

55. Fraser, *Mayflower*, 143, 148–149.

56. Bradford, *History of Plymouth Plantation*, 2:250.

57. Bradford, 2:247–248, and see 248n1.

58. Trumbull, *Complete History of Connecticut*, 1:22–25, 37.

59. Shurtleff, *Records of the Colony*, 1:60–61. Neither Edward Winslow nor his brothers John and Kenelm volunteered.

60. Bradford, *History of Plymouth Plantation*, 2:247–248.

61. Bradford, 2:258.

62. Fraser, *Mayflower*, 150.

63. Bradford, *History of Plymouth Plantation*, 2:256, and see 256n1.

64. Philbrick, *Mayflower*, 253.

65. Philbrick, 167, 175; Fraser, *Mayflower*, 141–142. By 1692, Plymouth Colony was absorbed and became part of the Massachusetts Bay Colony. Fraser, *Mayflower*, 295.

66. Winslow, *Good News from New England*, 28–31.

67. Fraser, *Mayflower*, 145.

68. *Collections of the Massachusetts Historical Society*, series 4, vol. 6 (Boston: Massachusetts Historical Society, 1863), 165–168.

69. *Collections of the Massachusetts Historical Society*, series 3, vol. 1 (Boston: Charles C. Little and James Brown, 1846), 27; Katherine Howlett Hayes, *Slavery Before Race: Europeans, Africans, and Indians at Long Island's Sylvester Manor Plantation, 1651–1884* (New York: New York University Press, 2013), 52.

70. *Collections of the Massachusetts*, series 3, 1:27

71. Fraser, *Mayflower*, 153–154, 184; *Collections of the Massachusetts*, series 4, 6:162n1; Bradford, *History of Plymouth Plantation*, 2:391–394.

72. Stratton, *Plymouth Colony*, 373; Bradford, *History of Plymouth Plantation*, 2:391–394; Sidney Lee, ed., *Dictionary of National Biography*, vol. 21, *Whichcord—Zuylestein* (New York: Macmillan, 1909), 672–674.

73. Fraser, *Mayflower*, 142, 150.

74. Johnson, *Here Shall I Die*, 134.

75. Johnson, 132; Pulsifer, *Records of the Colony*, 11:17.

76. Shurtleff, *Records of the Colony*, 1:68. The fact that Hopkins was not at the Separatists' services supports the theory that he never formally joined their church. See Hodges, *Hopkins of the Mayflower*, 230. The Church of England encouraged sports and games after Sunday services. See Alexis McCrossen, *Holy Day, Holiday: The American Sunday* (Ithaca, NY: Cornell University Press, 200), 10; Willison, *Saints and Strangers*, 46–47, and see n1.

77. Shurtleff, *Records of the Colony*, 1:68.

78. Shurtleff, 1:75.

79. Shurtleff, 1:42, 87, 97; Stratton, *Plymouth Colony*, 84, 156, 378.

80. Stratton, 183.

81. Johnson, *Here Shall I Die*, 133, 156.

82. Shurtleff, *Records of the Colony*, 1:111.

83. Shurtleff, 1:111.

84. Stratton, *Plymouth Colony*, 183.

85. Shurtleff, *Records of the Colony*, 1:111.

86. Shurtleff, 1:112.

87. Stratton, *Plymouth Colony*, 306.

88. Shurtleff, *Records of the Colony*, 1:113.

89. Prince, *Chronological History of New England*, 1:105.

90. See Johnson, *Here Shall I Die*, 251, where in his last will and testament, Stephen Hopkins desires to be buried next to Elizabeth's grave, as well as provides extensively for his daughters.

91. Richard Archer, *Fissures in the Rock: New England in the Seventeenth Century* (Hanover: University Press of New England, 2001), 102.

92. Shurtleff, *Records of the Colony*, 1:35–36.

93. Shurtleff, 1:9–11.

94. See, e.g., Shurtleff, *Records of the Colony*, 1:87, 93.

95. Nathaniel Shurtleff, ed., *Records of the Colony of New Plymouth in New England*, vol. 2 (Boston: William White, 1855), 38.

96. Bradford, *History of Plymouth Plantation*, 2:264.

97. Goodwin, *The Pilgrim Republic*, 406.

98. Bradford, *History of Plymouth Plantation*, 2:264.

99. Goodwin, *The Pilgrim Republic*, 406.

100. Bradford, *History of Plymouth Plantation*, 2:264–266.

101. Goodwin, *The Pilgrim Republic*, 406-407.

102. Shurtleff, *Records of the Colony*, 1:96–97.

103. Bradford, *History of Plymouth Plantation*, 2:268.

104. Morton, *New England's Memorial*, 139; Freeman, *History of Cape Cod*, 1:131–132.

105. Not only did Dorothy Temple have to raise her son without his father, but she also had to pay a legal penalty for her crime of adultery. In June 1639 the General Court found her guilty "for uncleanliness and bringing forth a male bastard." Her punishment was to be "whipped twice." She fainted after the first blow, and the second half of the penalty was abrogated. Shurtleff, *Records of the Colony*, 1:127. Curiously, the man who would have done the whipping was her new master, John Holmes. See Stratton, *Plymouth Colony*, 306.

106. Shurtleff, *Records of the Colony*, 1:137.

107. Pulsifer, *Records of the Colony*, 11:21. That Hopkins acquired land along the very river associated with Squanto serves as further evidence of his connection to the Patuxet man.

108. Shurtleff, *Records of the Colony*, 1:90, 93. It was at Mattachiest where Hopkins and the Pilgrim party in June 1621 first stopped on their journey to retrieve the lost Billington boy. Young, *Chronicles*, 214–216.

109. Frederick Freeman, *The History of Cape Cod: The Annals of Barnstable County*, vol. 1 (Boston: George C. Rand & Avery, 1858), 135.

110. Shurtleff, *Records of the Colony*, 1:93.

111. Pulsifer, *Records of the Colony*, 11:39.

112. Pulsifer, 11:83–84.

113. Johnson, *Here Shall I Die*, 134–135.

10. An End Among Friends

1. Hodges, *Hopkins of the Mayflower*, 230.

2. As noted in the introduction and chapter 2, William Shakespeare may have loosely based his character Stephano on Stephen Hopkins, who was described in William Strachey's account of the 1609 shipwreck of the *Sea Venture*. See, e.g., Stritmatter and Kositsky, *On the Date*, 33.

3. See, e.g., Philbrick, *Mayflower*, 39–40; Sawyer, *History of the Pilgrims*, 2:2.

4. Shurtleff, *Records of the Colony*, 1:42, 75, 68, 111–113. Hopkins's delinquency is discussed in more detail in chapter 9.

5. See Blackstone, *Commentaries on the Laws*, 1:488–490.

6. William Assheton, *Theological Discourse of Last Wills and Testaments* (London: Brab. Aylmer, 1696).

7. Stratton, *Plymouth Colony*, 70.

8. Bowman, *Mayflower Descendant*, 2:12–14.

9. Bowman, 2:12–14.

10. Other duties included making and submitting to the court a detailed inventory of the assets in the probate estate and entering into contracts on behalf of underage heirs or disposing of property to ensure that the wishes of the testator are fulfilled to the extent possible.

11. Contemporaneous evidence indicates that the Plymouth settlers considered the role of supervisor to be commensurate to that of the executor. For example, it was Myles Standish who oversaw the creation of inventory of Hopkins's estate, a duty ordinarily performed by the executor. See Blackstone, *Commentaries on the Laws*, 1:509.

12. Bowman, *Mayflower Descendant*, 3:154.

13. Bowman, 2:228–229.

14. See Bowman, 2:12–14.

15. By this time, Hopkins's eldest daughter, Constance, who sailed on the *Mayflower*, was married and on her own.

16. George Bowman, ed., *The Mayflower Descendant*, vol. 4 (Boston: Massachusetts Society of Mayflower Descendants, 1902), 114–117.

17. Gervase Markham, *The English Housewife 1615*, ed. Michael R. Best (Montreal: McGill-Queen's University Press, 1986), 167.

18. Bowman, *Mayflower Descendant*, 4:117.

19. See Bowman, 2:12–14.

20. The business deal is yet another indication of the powers that Standish was given as supervisor under Hopkins's last will and testament, for it was typically only the executor who had the power to collect and transact business trades with the assets of an estate. Blackstone, *Commentaries on the Laws*, 1:510–513.

21. Bowman, *Mayflower Descendant*, 4:117.

22. Bowman, 4:114; Johnson, *Here Shall I Die*, 158–159.

23. Johnson, *Here Shall I Die*, 159. There is nothing documented in colonial records or other primary sources that indicates what caused Ruth's death. Disease frequently took the lives of English colonists, however, and would be a likely culprit. In 1650, for example, disease caused a significant uptick in mortality rates. See Morton, *New England's Memorial*, 161. Ruth Hopkins might have died in this contagion.

24. Bowman, *Mayflower Descendant*, 4:114.
25. Nathaniel Shurtleff, ed., *Records of the Colony of New Plymouth in New England*, vol. 3 (Boston: William White, 1855), 14.
26. Nathaniel Shurtleff, ed., *Records of the Colony of New Plymouth*, vol. 7, *Judicial Acts 1636–1692* (Boston: William White, 1857), 80.
27. Bowman, *Mayflower Descendant*, 4:114–115, 118–119.
28. Bowman, 4:118–119. By 1659, Giles Hopkins was living even farther out on Cape Cod, in Eastham. Nevertheless, he assisted with the disposal of Elizabeth Hopkins's estate.
29. Shurtleff, *Records of the Colony*, 1:75; Bowman, *Mayflower Descendant*, 2:14-17.
30. See Bowman, *Mayflower Descendant*, 2:14–17.
31. Philbrick, *Mayflower*, xvi.
32. See Bowman, *Mayflower Descendant*, 2:12–14.
33. Bowman, 2:14–17.

Epilogue: Hopkins's Legacy: "Friend of Indians"

1. "Notable Descendants," General Society of Mayflower Descendants, accessed June 10, 2018, https://www.themayflowersociety.org/the-pilgrims/notable-descendants. In 2014 President Obama posthumously awarded Cushing the Medal of Honor for his conduct during the battle, where he was wounded three time before dying during the climax of Pickett's infantry assault.
2. Rich Hall, "Famous Kin of Stephen Hopkins," FamousKin, accessed June 10, 2018, https://famouskin.com/famous-kin-menu.php?name=24679+stephen+hopkins; "Stephen Hopkins (1581–1644)/List of Famous Descendants," Familypedia, accessed June 20, 2018, http://familypedia.wikia.com/wiki/Stephen_Hopkins_(1581-1644)/List_of_Famous_Descendants.
3. Amos Otis, *Genealogical Notes of Barnstable Families*, vol. 1 (Barnstable, MA: F. B. & F. P. Goss, 1888), 463.
4. Margaret Ellen Newell, *Brethren by Nature: New England Indians, Colonists, and the Origins of American Slavery* (Ithaca, NY: Cornell University Press, 2015), 55.
5. Otis, *Genealogical Notes*, 463.
6. Charles W. Upham, *Salem Witchcraft, with an Account of Salem Village*, vol. 1 (Boston: Wiggin and Lunt, 1867), 102–103; also see Hubbard, *A General History*, 164, 642. Davenport was killed in 1665 as he lay in his bed by a bolt of lightning that shot through an open window.
7. George W. Ellis, John E. Morris, *King Philip's War* (New York: Grafton Press, 2001), 151; Upham, *Salem Witchcraft*, 1:124–126.
8. Otis, *Genealogical Notes*, 463.
9. Shurtleff, *Records of the Colony*, 1:163.
10. Shurtleff, 2:4.
11. Shurtleff, 2:36.
12. The case might have unintentionally prefigured the Fugitive Slave Clause of the United States Constitution: "No person held to service or labour in one state, under the laws thereof, escaping into another, shall, in consequence of any law or regulation therein, be discharged from

such service or labour, but shall be delivered up on claim of the party to whom such service or labour may be due." US Const., art IV, § 2, cl. 3. Up until 1772 there were no generally accepted standards for how different sovereign jurisdictions handled escaped slaves. The English court decision in *Somerset v. Stewart* provided guidance when it held that a fugitive slave from Virginia was a free person upon reaching England, where slavery was prohibited, and could not be returned to his previous owners. See Steven Lubet, *Fugitive Justice: Runaways, Rescuers, and Slavery on Trial* (Cambridge, MA: Belknap Press, 2010), 17–18.

13. The following year, in the summer of 1643, Plymouth and the Bay Colony and the settlements in Connecticut would combine themselves into a loose confederation whose purpose was primarily a military alliance. J. A. Doyle, *English Colonies in America: The Puritan Colonies* vol. 2 (New York: Henry Holt, 1889), 233–234. One of the provisions of the accord specifically called for the return of any fugitive from one colony to another. Jon L. Wakelyn, *America's Founding Charters*, vol. 1 (Westport, CT: Greenwood Press, 2006), 273–276. But in 1642 Bradford and his assistants had no formal obligation to appease the Bay Colony by sending the boy back to what he'd likely described as a cruel servitude.

14. Shurtleff, *Records of the Colony*, 2:38.

15. In April 1646 Hatch married the granddaughter of William Palmer. Otis, *Genealogical Notes*, 464. William Palmer and Stephen Hopkins lived as children together in the same village in rural England. When Palmer and his son arrived at Plymouth in November 1621 they lived for several years, possibly through 1627, in Hopkins's house. See Johnson, *Here Shall I Die*, 118.

16. Charles F. Swift, *Cape Cod: The Right Arm of Massachusetts* (Yarmouth, MA: Register Publishing Company, 1897), 76.

17. Randall S. Peffer, *Logs of the Dead Pirates Society: A Schooner Adventure Around Buzzards Bay* (Dobbs Ferry, NY: Sheridan House, 2000), 77; Swift, *Cape Cod*, 125.

18. Swift, *Cape Cod*, 125; H. Roger King, *Cape Cod and Plymouth Colony in the Seventeenth Century* (Lanham, MD: University Press of America, 1994), 185. Not only did Hatch have familiar relations with the native people, he also developed an openness toward his fellow Englishmen, for within a few years many Quakers, who were especially persecuted by the Puritans from the Bay Colony, began to seek refuge in Succanessett, where Hatch welcomed them.

19. Shurtleff, *Records of the Colony*, 3:6; Bushnell, "Treatment of Indians," in Vaughan, *New England Encounters*, 65.

20. Shurtleff, *Records of the Colony*, 3:138.

21. Shurtleff, 5:39; Bushnell, "Treatment of Indians," in Vaughan, *New England Encounters*, 65.

22. Fraser, *Mayflower*, 155–156.

23. Vaughan, "Indian-European Encounters," in Vaughan, *New England Encounters*, 12.

24. Vaughan, 12; Drake, *King Philip's War*, 4; Philbrick, *Mayflower*, 345.

25. Vaughan, "Indian-European Encounters," in Vaughan, *New England Encounters*, 12.

26. Lynn Hudson Parsons, "'A Perpetual Harrow upon My Feelings': John Quincy Adams and the American Indian," in Vaughan, *New England Encounters*, 328, 350.

27. Parsons, "'Perpetual Harrow,'" in Vaughan, *New England Encounters*, 326.
28. Parsons, 325, 343.
29. Shurtleff, *Records of the Colony*, 5:207.
30. Shurtleff, 5:210; Bushnell, "Treatment of Indians," in Vaughan, *New England Encounters*, 75.
31. Bushnell, "Treatment of Indians," in Vaughan, *New England Encounters*, 75–76.
32. Philbrick, *Mayflower*, 345.
33. Bushnell, "Treatment of Indians," in Vaughan, *New England Encounters*, 75–76.
34. Philbrick, *Mayflower*, 332, 345.
35. Philbrick, 253.
36. Nathaniel Shurtleff, ed., *Records of the Colony of New Plymouth in New England*, vol. 6 (Boston: William White, 1856), 14–15.
37. Bushnell, "Treatment of Indians," in Vaughan, *New England Encounters*, 65.
38. Shurtleff, *Records of the Colony*, 6:14–15.

INDEX

Page numbers in italics indicate illustrations